AMERICAN PROMETHEUS

Carnegie's Captain, Bill Jones

To Jim,

 Sharon shared with me
your interest in history + the 2nd
Industrial Revolution. My great grandfather
was a Titan at that beginning. Yesterday
at the Pumphouse in Homestead, I
had a packed house to hear my
family's story. Hope you enjoy.

 Best,

 Tom Gage

Tom Gage

Humboldt State University Press

HSU Library
1 Harpst Street
Arcata, California 95521-8299

hsupress@humboldt.edu

Cover design by Lina Carro
Interior design and layout by Lina Carro
Editing by Carolyn Mueller & Lina Carro
Consulting provided by Mikaylah Rivas

[Cover image: Bessemer Converter]
courtesy of *Rivers of Steel National Heritage Area*, Homestead PA

ISBN 10:1-947112-01-5
ISBN 13:978-1-947112-01-8

TABLE OF CONTENTS

I dedicate this book to Farris Noor Serio, Orion Rutledge Al-Jarrah, and Julian Thomas Al-Jarrah, who share the heritage of Steve Jobs, another Merlin reminiscent of our American Prometheus who changed cityscapes around the world.

ACKNOWLEDGEMENTS

There are many who made this family memoir possible, in addition to those voices through whom I cast the life of Jones. These include my three daughters, Ondine, Shelley, and Tyche, who persistently encouraged me and often provided me with sound editing and moral courage. As Shirley Brice Heath of Stanford claims, in the age of telecommunications, we learn from youth (before the industrial revolution, we learned from our grandparents and parents and since the onset of the automobile age, from our peers).

This project was sparked during an evening at home in Fortuna when my wife, Anita, and I entertained Jim Galvin, now with the Writer's Workshop at the University of Iowa, and his wife, Jorie Graham, the 1996 Pulitzer poet, now at Harvard University. Our discussion led to their encouraging charge to get it done.

Many have read early drafts and provided guidance in editing, correcting, and providing new leads: Dick McPherson, Terry McLaughlin, and comrade of forty- five years Anthony Turpin. Janet Crane especially provided a succinctness, grace of prose, and substantial research, a stellar editor.

Many supportive persons at Humboldt State University helped me in assembling what I needed: Cyril Oberlander, Dean of the Library; Kathleen L. Corridan, Julia Graham, and Sherry Gordon, of the Library's Interlibrary Loan office and especially Lina Carro; Riley Quarles, Andrew C. Jones, Sean McFarland, Robert Gray, and Kris Newsom of the Courseware Development Center; Steve Newman, Director of Media; and Dave Shaw of Veterans Upward Bound. Recent assistance was provided by Justin Oakes of the Christiana Apple Store, Delaware. Carolyn Mueller provided editorial assistance for this version, and Lina Carro whose guidance with page design and layout has been of such value.

Investigation can take one far afield but there are hometown resources, two of whom here in Humboldt, who occasioned primary revelations that provided me with what my parents' generation never knew: Don Wattenbarger, who alerted me to the Cradle of Civilization's current usage; and, Scott Leonard who found Jones' plan to deliver it to Youngstown.

Professor David Demarest, English department at Carnegie Mellon University, hosted me on several occasions and led me to key figures who provided with much historical information that complemented what I knew from my family. William Gaughan, especially, shared his experience as a third-generation steel worker and local historian; he taught me a curriculum of steelmaking. Other helpful resources were Randy Harris of the Steel Industry Heritage Project, Homestead, PA; Professor Mark Brown of Grinnell College; Dr. Robert J. Plowman, National Archives; former student, Dr. Scott Leonard, Professor in English, Youngstown State University; and Dr. Philip Scranton, the Melvin Kranzberg Professor of History of Technology at the Georgia Institute of Technology and director of the Center for the History of Business, Technology, and Society at the Hagley Museum and Library in Wilmington, Delaware.

Philip Scranton's essay "Tom Gage's Captain Jones: an Appreciation," appearing in the Winter 1997/98 issue of *Pittsburgh History*, significantly influenced my finishing this project. He provided me with the *Whipple Notes*, material not previously published from which I fashioned dialogue in chapters 3 and 4. Likewise, much of the dialogue for chapter 5 was taken directly from Nathan D. Shappee's dissertation, *A History of Johnstown and the Great Flood of*

1889: A Study of Disaster and Rehabilitation. Much of the text in chapter 6 was from my father's unpublished memoir, "To My Kith and Kin." Thanks also to those who have given me permissions to reproduce images.

But above all, thanks to Anita, who has patiently endured my sequestration in my office to complete this debt to my mother, Alice Frances Farmer-Gage.

Alice Farmer Gage, the author's mother, in the year 1925.

PRELUDE

American Prometheus is a detective story focused on my great-grandfather, Captain Bill Jones, the details of whose death and loss of fortune have been a mystery for more than one hundred years. To penetrate the opacity of time, I have relied upon Voltaire's method of retrospective prophecy, embodied in his story "Zadig" (Huxley 1997).

Zadig, an Abassid philosopher, is strolling down a pathway to the river Tigress near ancient Baghdad. Approaching him, a panting eunuch asks, "Have you seen the Queen's dog, Zadig?

"It's not a dog, it's a bitch," corrects the scholar.

"That's quite right, my man," responds the eunuch out of breath.

"It's a spaniel," Zadig continues, "which has recently delivered a litter of puppies and paces on a game right foreleg,"

"Right again!" says the eunuch, "Which way did she go?"

"I don't know, I didn't see her."

Stunned and speechless, the eunuch rocks back on his heels just as a third, the King's Officer of the Horse, arrives.

"Where is the King's horse?" asks the officer.

"A fine stallion, standing five-feet tall, with a three-and-a-half foot tail, shod in eleven-penny silver and bridled in solid gold?" responds Zadig.

"Exactly, which way did it go?"

"I don't know, I didn't see it," proclaims the retrospective prophet.

Immediately, the two arrest Zadig and throw him into prison. The judges sentence him to die within the fortnight. Fortunately for Zadig, within a week the two animals of the royal family are found astray in the city. The judges feel it just that he should try to clear his good name, so long as he pays four hundred pieces of gold for cost of retrial.

Zadig proclaims his innocence by explaining the methodology of retrospective prophecy. He had observed tracks of a small dog with the right front paw impressing less deeply in the soft turf. He further had noted that faint parallel lines framed the paw prints, indicating a short dog with long ears. Within the paw prints, another pair of interrupted lines grazed the dust, suggesting pendent dugs of a bitch. Knowing of the popularity of canines in the kingdom, Zadig inferred that a limping spaniel, which had recently delivered a litter, had preceded him along the path.

Furthermore, Zadig had observed that where he had walked, dust had recently been brushed clean from the boles of palm trees on both sides of the seven-foot- wide path. The evenness of the hoofprints suggested an outstanding pacer, proportioned according to Pythagorean lineaments. He concluded that these effects indicated the passage of a trotting horse, approximately five feet tall with a three-and-a-half foot tail. Zadig, a schooled alchemist, noted that its hoofs had struck small pebbles in the roadway, depositing a metallurgical alloy. Apparently, the horse had cornered sharply, colliding against an embankment, and its bridle dashed against stone leaving another alloy, this time of gold.

The judges reasoned Zadig innocent, but his kind of logic, though not a crime, was certainly dangerous to social order. Keeping Zadig's pieces of gold, the judges reinstated his death sentence.

Just as Zadig inferred causes from effects, I have reached conclusions about Captain Bill Jones's death on the basis of an examination of family oral history; the written lore of others about the Captain Bill; my grandparents' and Andrew Carnegie's correspondences; many inherited artifacts laden with history; and records in archives in Pittsburgh, London, and Washington, D.C. Discrepancies exist between the official story and my family's recollections of what happened during the month of Captain Jones's death. This led me to investigate the steel industry's private archives buried deep in a Pennsylvania mountain, hollowed out in the 1950s as a sanctuary for CEOs of USX for the anticipated war. I also visited a number of libraries, including the Library of Congress in Washington, D.C., and interviewed historians in England and the eastern seaboard of the United States. What follows will describe what happened to Captain Bill Jones who, with "more patents to his credit than any other single individual in the history of steelmaking," "was killed," to use Carnegie's words, and why his family lost all of those patents in less than a month after his death (Wall 1970, 532).

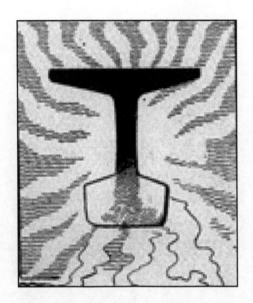

Forging a steel railroad track   The strength and quality of **ingots**, (above) molded to forge steel for America's Industrial Revolution, were ensured solely due to the homogeneity that the invention of the Jones Hot Metal Mixer provided.

(Carnegie Brothers & Co., Limited, 1890.)

William R. "Bill" Jones worked with Alexander Holley, William Kelly, John Fritz, Robert Hunt, James Howard Bridge, Andrew Carnegie, and Charles Schwab. (Rivers of Steel NHA Museum, Homestead PA)

PREFACE

Although nearly every study of nineteenth-century iron and steel references the contributions of my great-grandfather, Captain William R. "Bill" Jones, it is always in the context of someone else's life or in the histories of Johnstown, Braddock, or the Carnegie Brothers Company. Jones worked with Alexander Holley, William Kelly, John Fritz, Robert Hunt, James Howard Bridge, Andrew Carnegie, and Charles Schwab —all now with better documented contributions to the growth and consolidation of the American steel industry. His role and theirs were inextricably intertwined; he had correspondence with most of them and their stories are incomplete without inclusion of his role in their lives. Although his entire life story has not been told, he was such a colorful figure that he appears in three well-known novels: *The Valley of Decision: A Novel of Steel* (1937); *Out of This Furnace: A Novel of Immigrant Labor in America* (1941); and *In Sunlight, in a Beautiful Garden* (2001). Some claim that Jones is the basis for mythic Joe Magarac, dramatized by Nobel Laureate Eugene O'Neill. The prime minister of Great Britain, who won the First World War, and the emperor of Germany, who lost it, retold stories of Captain Jones, even though neither had ever met him (*Gazette Times* [Pittsburgh, PA] Oct. 25, 1923). And as recently as 2002, an historian described him as a "folk hero who shaped the elements of hell" (Krass 2002, 269).

Most family stories never find their way into history books, and I suspect that one reason my great-grandfather's story has never been told is because in some ways it resembles the stories of many other nineteenth-century factory men. He started out an ordinary workman and he died a horrible premature death that many would have preferred forgotten. Industrial accidents in the iron and steel mills were not uncommon events. But my great-grandfather was also one of the most extraordinary men of his time: his family knew it and so did all the men who ever worked with him. He was accorded enormous recognition and respect by congressmen, leading philosophers such as Matthew Arnold and Herbert Spencer, wealthy industrialists such as Karl Wittgenstein of Austria, and the British prime minister and the German emperor. Even if only a few of the things my family said were true, Captain Bill Jones's story has begged to be told—to put the life of Andrew Carnegie, the conditions behind the infamous Homestead Strike, and the fate of the American steelworker into a more honest perspective. In Pittsburgh three full generations after he died, I met men who had been told by their fathers and grandfathers that they had worked with Bill Jones. To them Bill Jones was an American hero; he was also a great inventor and engineer.

In 1905, my grandfather, Daniel D. "D. D." Gage, began a biography of fifty thousand words (Whipple n.d.). This manuscript was last cited by John Steinbeck in 1937, the year I was born (Gage 2012, Chapter 1). The enigmas behind the missing biography drove me to spend nearly two decades researching the life of Captain Bill Jones in order to unearth answers about the struggle between an inventor and capital.

Writing this book presented me with a dilemma: should I compose a biography or a personal essay. According to convention, never the twain shall meet. A personal essay shares a felt sense of what one has lived through, one's private experience. Writing history requires adopting a distanced stance for encapsulating the subject's life by condensing in words the happenings of time and space. I chose to write a family memoir of an American hero.

author Tom Gage, great-grandson of Captain Bill Jones

INTRODUCTION

When in 1889 my great-grandfather Captain Bill Jones died unexpectedly at the age of fifty, ten thousand mill workers, factory managers, and city folk walked in the largest funeral procession the Allegheny region of Pennsylvania had ever seen. His employer, Andrew Carnegie, cried openly when he heard the news. When Carnegie himself died, some thirty years later, the only adornment in his bedchamber was a portrait of the Captain, on which Carnegie could gaze from his bed. Ironically, perhaps providentially, Carnegie during his final hours fixated upon that single picture and mumbled to his secretary about the 325 million dollars that he had given away (Hendrick 1932, 383).

Three generations of my family have been obsessed with Bill Jones's life and death. By all accounts he was a giant of a man, someone who stood out in every group of which he was a part. Unschooled after the third grade, he inherited his father's considerable library of some 150 volumes and was extremely well-read. His was a house in which books played a major role, and from a young age he was able to recount long passages from classical writers ranging from Plutarch and Shakespeare to contemporary Americans like Ralph Waldo Emerson and George Lippard. It was also a house known for its conviviality. Bill loved people, and visitors rich and learned, as well as poor and local, gravitated to the welcoming warmth of his home both from next door and from all over the world.

Jones was legendary for being subject to fits of rage and acts of inordinate kindness. He regularly invoked the most colorful of ribald language and could quote from memory long poems of Longfellow and the soliloquies of Shakespeare. He was imaginative and an innovator, yet he was practical to the core. He was solidly against national labor unions, but favored company unions and involved himself tirelessly in the affairs of labor and the safety and well-being of his workers. He influenced all who came within his orbit and no one forgot him—neither the rich and powerful nor the poor and weak. He stood up to the former and was mercifully generous to and considerate of the latter. His labor philosophy and notions of company responsibility were far ahead of his time in the United States: the eight hour day, without a reduction in wages, and ethnically diverse teams are among his innovations. He was, in every respect, an authentic original, his own man: an American hero.

While Jones was superintendent at the Edgar Thomson Steel Mill (ET) in Braddock, Pennsylvania, from 1875 until his death, the Jones family lived comfortably. The house was staffed with five servants, in part because his wife was not well; Harriet Jones had long suffered from the intermittent symptoms of multiple sclerosis and other ailments. When Bill Jones died, Harriet had been a bedridden invalid for most of the prior ten years. His daughter, Cora, was a sheltered, indulged Victorian lass of twenty-two, prevented by her mother's strong disapproval from marrying her sweetheart, the singer Daniel D. "D. D." Gage. Harriet had hoped for a more promising match for her accomplished and winsome daughter. Thus, a significant portion of Cora's time was spent thwarting her mother and finding secretive ways to meet with D. D. Will, the Jones's eldest living child and four years older than Cora, had studied some piano, completed high school in Braddock, and later worked in the mills. He was considered a ruffian and practical joker who liked to party and didn't amount to much, according to the rest of the family. He was not reliable. If Bill Jones had held hopes for his son, they were not realized. Also in the house was Harriet's mother, Mary, now an old woman, who had for many years cared for the children and served as the anchor of the household in her ailing daughter's stead.

Thus it was that, when Jones was whisked to the Homeopathic Hospital in Pittsburgh with serious burns all over his body and a possible concussion following a freak explosion at Edgar Thomson Steel Works, his family was ill-prepared to defend him and advocate for him medically or in any other way. There was no strong family member who insisted on staying close to Bill at the hospital to monitor his condition, consult with his physicians, and deal with the world. It also seems unlikely that any member of the family truly knew the financial situation Jones had left nor what legal papers he possessed at home and at his office. The Jones family in their shock and grief were extremely vulnerable to unscrupulous business interests and hastily-made transactions.

Bill's younger brother, John Lewis Jones, had been entering the furnace shed at ET when the explosion that injured Jones occurred, and John had carried his badly burned brother first to receive medical attention at the company office, then to the flagged-down train at Braddock Station, and he accompanied Bill to Pittsburgh. When John had left Bill, who had been sedated for pain for the night, word was that he would recover, that he had his eyesight and that he was conscious, but that amputation of a hand and possibly one or both of his legs might be necessary.

But there the record begins to fade. For the first two days, Jones had been expected to recover, albeit with serious permanent disabilities. Cora and her friend D. D. had visited the hospital on the day following the accident. Bill had been conscious and talking, emphasizing that his eyes were okay and expressing concern for the family. His sister, Mary Bowman; Andrew Carnegie, his boss; and Henry Clay Frick, the general manager of Carnegie Brothers also saw Jones on Friday. The family described him to Harriet as glistening from the chamomile oil and phenol, antiseptics and disinfectants applied to the burns. Reporters for the region's newspapers, present at the hospital, all published statements that Jones would live, that it was his arms and legs that had primarily been affected, with his torso largely unburned. Another burn victim, Quinn, was not expected to survive.

On Saturday Jones was visited by family members and by Henry Clay Frick and Andrew Carnegie. Visitors found him swathed in bandages. Word was that Andrew Carnegie had sent for his personal physician, Dr. Carmondy, who was at the time in California, to come to Pittsburgh to treat Jones, although his arrival would take several days. Carnegie himself left for New York on Saturday, sending condolences to the Jones family.

When family members received word that Bill had died late on Saturday night, complete shock and grief overwhelmed them all, for his death truly had been unexpected. Over the days that followed, Carnegie Company men came to the Jones house. Cora was taken for a walk (a second version has it that she went to the piano room) while business was conducted indoors with Jones's frail widow. By the end of October, most of Jones's many and valuable patents had come into the Carnegie Company's possession. It was only many years later—after Harriet, too, had died in 1896, and the Carnegie Steel Company became involved in lawsuits over the Jones Hot Metal Mixer patent—that the family began to go over events and attempt to piece together what had happened in the years prior to and just after the

Captain's death. Indeed, we have been doing it ever since, with a growing belief that not only an injustice, but quite possibly a crime, had been committed. The search for truth began with my grandfather, D. D. Gage, who married Jones's daughter, his longtime sweetheart, Cora, nearly eight years after Jones's death. D. D. worked on a biography of Bill Jones in the early 1900s. He did this on the advice of his cousin Henry T. Gage, the former governor of California, who surmised that presenting Andrew Carnegie with a researched life story might force the wealthy old man to face up to his responsibility to Jones's heirs. The family made a trip to New York to confront Carnegie with the facts but D. D. did not give Carnegie the manuscript. Two copies of D. D.'s detailed account —it came to 114 pages—had been made, but they both have been permanently lost.

After thirteen years of marriage, my parents divorced before I reached my second birthday. I never knew my father and saw him for the first time when I was twenty. I saw him only a few times after that. One of the interests we had in common was Captain Bill, and he dominated our conversations. Dad celebrated Jones's brawling over a good cause, his enthusiasm for sports, and his drinking camaraderie. He vicariously relived Bill Jones's celebrated Civil War career by walking the battle site at Chancellorsville and arguing at parties about the incompetence of the Union's commanding generals. He would go positively wild telling about sitting in Carnegie's lap when he was a child during the family trip to New York. Dad looked at the Carnegie-Jones relationship as his claim to knowing famous people.

My mother got caught up in the Jones mythology because she and my father lived with D. D. and Cora in Los Angeles for the first two years they were married, from 1926 to 1928. My mother and Cora established a deep bond, and Cora poured out a lot to Mom, including Bill Jones's creation of the eight-hour workday, the lost fortune, and Jones's mysterious death. As a five-year old, one of my earliest memories is of speaking on the telephone with my grandmother, Cora. She asked, "Tommy, do you like baseball? Your great-grandfather started baseball in Pittsburgh." I was listening, but unable to speak. "Can you hear me?" she continued. "He built a diamond right inside the Edgar Thomson Steel Works." I looked up at my mother, who was standing near me making facial gestures. "Say something," she whispered. My grandmother continued. "The Steel Works is where he started the eight-hour workday." But I felt embarrassed and quite confused about diamonds and said nothing, although I have remembered the conversation as clearly through all the intervening years as if it had taken place only yesterday.

Cora herself had grown up listening to stories about the historic events that her parents and grandparents had experienced in the six years before her birth—the flight from Chattanooga and the outbreak of hostilities between North and South that ignited

Cora Jones at midlife

the Civil War; Bill's valorous service for the Union in the Civil War; and Harriet's and her parents' difficult adjustment to life in Johnstown, far from the urbane world that they had previously known. She related all the incidents about her romance with D. D. and the experiences she and D. D. had trying to get money from Carnegie. Like her father, Cora loved parties, and she and D. D. entertained a lot, much of it quite lavish. Cora was a very generous person; my mother couldn't understand how Cora could give such expensive gifts to people, including her gardeners, who didn't understand their value. My mother

William "Bill" Gaughan, 3rd generation steel worker recognized in western Pennsylvania as an authority on the local industry. (Wm. J. Gaughan Collection, Hillman Library, U of Pittsburgh)

viewed Cora's marriage to D. D. as almost ideal. The only flaws she saw in Cora were an unreasonable jealousy and that perhaps she drank too much.

After the deaths of my Uncle Dan, my father, my older brother, and my mother, I had accumulated a mountain of papers, books, and memorabilia related to Bill Jones. I had been given strong exhortations by both Uncle Dan and my mother to discover how Bill Jones's patents had passed from his family into the possession of Andrew Carnegie and finish what D. D. Gage had started—to validate my family and to restore Bill Jones's name and contributions to history by writing it all down. I had resisted the burden, because for many years that's exactly what it felt like.

But in 1995, after I had attended an English conference in Pittsburgh the year before and used the time to make contacts and visit places connected to family history, I traveled East to begin research for this book. To prepare, I had been reading many of the best-known books on steel and Andrew Carnegie. In Homestead, I met and interviewed a third-generation steel worker, William "Bill" Gaughan , recognized in western Pennsylvania as an authority on the local industry and as a collector of memorabilia of steel's glorious past. We had breakfast with William "Bill" Gaughan at Michael's, the traditional breakfast haunt just blocks from the now-vacant Homestead lot. The mill had been bulldozed in the 1980s.

"Jones was hands-on, all over. He really had it—technical smarts. He was a problem-solver and innovator." Bill Gaughan elaborated on how Jones had labored at every position in a steel works at some time during his forty years working iron and steel.

"There's a guy I worked with," Gaughan remarked, nodding at a man just entering the restaurant. "How're yah doing, Eddie? Good to see yah. We did many years together at U.S. Steel. This is a friend, Tom Gage from California. D'yah ever hear of Captain Bill Jones over at ET?"

Eddie and his two friends looked at me. "Oh, yeah," they uttered in unison.

"This is his great-grandson. He's doing research on the old great-grandpa."

"Oh," said the laconic Eddie, the lines in his face grooved from years of wrestling glowing metal. The men looked at one another, saying nothing; they seemed pleased to meet me. Eddie's Macintosh was spotless but a size too big, testifying to a time when it clung to a beefier body. He shared with Gaughan that carriage of authority, of being a steel man.

Gaughan had already validated for me Captain's Bill's technical genius. That morning he helped me map out how to piece my story together. He mentioned biographers of men who had worked with Jones, like Jeanne McHugh, Robert Hessen, Joseph Frazier Wall, David Demarest, and Kenneth Warren, some of them authors with whom my Uncle Dan and my dad had corresponded. But the most exciting thing that occurred sitting in the booth opposite Bill Gaughan was that I heard living testimonies that echoed all that I had internalized over the years from Mother, Dad, and Uncle Dan. I felt a long lost sense of community, linked to a family I knew of only through the stories of others. Then the four listened as I told a little about Cora, D. D., and their sons, Uncle Dan and my dad, in California. "Do any of you know of a biography of Captain Jones, written by Daniel D. Gage, my grandfather?"

None of them did. I explained that it was lost, and that I hoped to find it.

"The letterbox is all business correspondence," Gaughan explained. "In the old days, letters were written backed with carbons. At year's end the carbons were assembled and filed alphabetically as company correspondence for that year. These were records of business dealings, but I only have the one for 1877. You might find a lot in Frick's Clayton Archive here in town, if they'd let you in. Only Kenneth Warren has ever gained access to Frick's ma-

The late Professor David Demarest of Carnegie Mellon University and author of **The River Ran Red***, standing in front of a torpedo car, a modern version of Jones's Cradle of Civilization.* (2004)

terial, as far as I know."

Back in my room in Homestead, I could not get out of my mind the meeting with Uncle Dan following his first stroke. That rainy day in Sacramento, he had me search for a file of papers containing original documents and copies, nested between two key sources for this story, James Howard Bridge's *The Inside History of the Carnegie Steel Company* and Joseph Frazier Wall's *Andrew Carnegie*, the most authoritative study of the man. Uncle Dan told me that the Captain had filed patent letters to secure ownership of his inventions; with these he'd have his autonomy and a secure future.

Entrance to the fortress-like
Annandale Archives.
(Annandale Archives, Boyers PA)

Uncle Dan had sat in his leather-bound Morris chair pondering a duplicate copy of Bill Jones's 1874 will and remarked how the Captain had worried about his Plan. "Tom, when he wrote this, he had only the Civil War sword and his gold watch from Cambria; he hadn't even reached Pittsburgh." But he would patent more inventions for iron and steel in the next fourteen years than any other individual as a protection for himself and his family if anything happened . . . Is it credible that the man who had the most patents for iron and steel never updated that 1874 will?" Dan held the copy that the family attorney, a man named Yost, filed in 1889 at the Temple in downtown Pittsburgh.

I spent several days at the Annandale Archives, literally a fortress built in a hillside near Boyers, Pennsylvania, where the records of the various Carnegie companies and USX were stored. At the time, few researchers had been granted access to them. The documents in the fifty-four boxes that were delivered to me mapped what began as the Keystone Bridge Company and the Carnegie, Kloman, and Company through Carnegie Brothers and Company, then conflating into Carnegie Steel Company with Frick as the chair as of January 1, 1892— all the way into the twentieth century when U.S. Steel became USX. There I found abundant business correspondence between Carnegie and Bill Jones. Most of it dealt with labor, Jones's technology, travel, matters of philanthropy and culture. Many letters were heated, with Jones's language fiery when it came to wages and steady work.

The following week I spent two days going through Carnegie's personal records at the Library of Congress. Most disappointing and—the longer I thought about it—shocking, was that I found only one item of correspondence between Carnegie and Jones from late September 1885 on, a single terse little note from the usually-effusive Carnegie, dated April 1, 1887.

"You see Furnace F's performance has impressed the highest authority in Britain, Sir Lowthian Bell."

For the four controversial and key years from late September 1885 through Jones's accident on September 27, 1889, there was only one document in Carnegie's private collections to capture the entire written exchange between perhaps the two most important figures in American steel. Someone must have cherry-picked this correspondence and left only a cryptic snippet dated April Fool's Day for posterity. But who? And why? After my return from Washington, D.C., I wrote to Joseph Frazier Wall, Carnegie's biographer, about the curious absence of letters from 1885 until Jones's death. Written on October 5, 1995 in a very shaky hand, Wall remembered his correspondence with Uncle Dan years earlier:

> Where the letters between Jones and Carnegie [between 1885-1889] has me as mystified as you. . . .I too wondered why there was almost no correspondence between Capt. Bill and AC in the Carnegie papers. Carnegie was very meticulous in keeping his correspondence, so either they did not write each other and kept their communication largely limited to conversations when AC visited Pittsburgh as Jones was the one person AC was always eager to see when he came to the Mills, or else—and this seems somewhat unlikely, AC deliberately destroyed Jones's letters lest they might be used against him and the company in the event of any suit over patents.

Over the telephone Peter Krass, whose biography, *Carnegie*, was published in 2002, told me the same thing that Wall and Paul Roberts, editor of *Pittsburgh History*, told me: all three were surprised at the missing letters.

All my life I had heard about the Captain's Plan from Uncle Dan. My mother called it his Scheme. It was Jones's strategy for patenting in his own name inventions that would be without strings binding him to a particular firm or individual. Jones had watched the financial insecurities of inventors and mechanically gifted men like William Kelly and Alexander Holley. Both had counseled Jones to secure patents on all his designs and ideas. My uncle, Dan Gage, repeated what he had learned from his mother about the many visits Holley and Jones had over the years. "Holley warned Jones not to end up like him. Holley scolded him for not filing letters on every one of his inventions, even though he had a fist full. Patents are the kinds of documents you need substantiate historical fact" (McHugh 1980, 377).

I found records indicating that in the year 1876-7, soon after ET had started production, Jones filed several letters with the U.S. Patent Office. Holley credited Jones with a number of discoveries in an article he wrote for *Engineering* in 1878—devising cotter-links, hot-curing apparatuses—valuable both for economy and for preventing damage to rails when straightening and a process of steam-compressing ingots. Jones must have known that all of these early inventions were likely to be short-lived but to have filed gave him power over Carnegie.

To strengthen his Plan, Captain Bill needed to invent and file a patent letter for something that would endure, that would guarantee that Shakespeare's "envious and calumniating time" (*Troilus and Cressida*) would not devalue his accomplishment. Although he filed another flurry of patents in 1886-7, it was not until the Jones Hot Metal Mixer and Direct Process patents that Jones achieved his goal. Yet, amazingly, not one item of correspondence relating to these phenomenal inventions exists for the period of four years leading up to Jones's death. The mixer had been in place at ET by early 1888, more than a year and half before Jones died.

Jones had watched Andrew Carnegie deal badly with Andrew Kloman, Tom Scott, William Shinn, and Tom Carnegie through the conditions he put on partnerships in the com-

21

panies he controlled. While Carnegie was building his own fortune, he cashed out his partners and inventors on terms disadvantageous to them, which motivated Jones to become self-sufficient.

The last time I saw my uncle alive, he had a surge of good health and was even somewhat limber. "Uncle Dan, tell me again why the Iron Clad Agreement was so crucial to what happened." Adopting as professorial a stance as possible given his condition, Uncle Dan gave me perhaps his last lecture on business administration: "Andrew Carnegie had amassed the world's greatest steel conglomerate by convincing his board to delay reaping monetary rewards. He convinced each partner to suspend personal comfort from earnings and instead to reinvest annual gains to further expansion. He followed the Captain's recommendations to install the newest and most efficient technology. When Carnegie's brother Tom died, the board of directors faced a problem: any member's death could drain needed liquidity for maintaining or building new technology. But families of a deceased principal partner might want cash. Carnegie was lucky with Tom's wife; he could stretch out payments over time with future earnings rather than drain present available capital. Lucy Carnegie had resented how Carnegie had cheated her father, William Coleman, but she settled with Andrew after Tom's death and moved her brood to a scenic island off the coast of Georgia and retired there. Her son, Billy Carnegie, lived in Santa Barbara. He was quite bitter over the memories (Gage "Kith", 5). You can get away with doing things conveniently to relatives that you can't do with business associates who want money. The board agreed that they had to write out the Iron Clad Agreement to guarantee pay-out over time and ejection of a partner with pay-out of owned stock at book value. Carnegie offered the Captain partnership, but Grandfather worried about the Iron Clad policy."

Then Dan reached for a carbon copy of a letter inserted in a book next to his chair. "When I wrote Joseph Frazier Wall after his biography was published, I confirmed what Wall wrote, that the Captain did not want to distance himself from the workers for fear they could no longer trust him once he was management. But more pointedly, the Captain did not trust the man. The Captain felt safer with the possession of title to the patents in his own hands."

Throughout the 1880s Jones was in great demand by other companies as the greatest mill superintendent of the time, and he did look at other jobs. He was determined to draw a high salary, and he certainly was worth it, another protection against getting involved in a partnership.

In a letter of November 9, 1880, Jones wrote to Carnegie:

> Three different parties have been sounding me to ascertain if I could be induced to take charge of other works. . . .Yesterday I had poked at me an offer of $15,000 per annum. I sent word through a friend that I would not enter into any agreement or contract with any company as long as I was in the employ of this company. . . .This does not seem to have appeased the zeal of the other party, who announced that if 15,000 would not, 20 or $25,000 would . . ."

Carnegie thereafter paid Jones $25,000 per year, which gave him a comfortable living.

By the 1930s, when Stewart H. Holbrook wrote *Iron Brew*, the public marveled at the money Carnegie had made and at his very public philanthropy, visible in towns and churches all of the country in the form of libraries. No one remembered his breaking of the U.S. labor

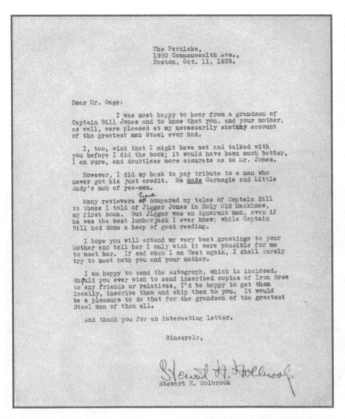

The Parklake,
1980 Commonwealth Ave.,
Boston, Oct. 11, 1939.

Dear Mr. Gage:

I was most happy to hear from a grandson of Captain Bill Jones and to know that you, and your mother, as well, were pleased at my necessarily sketchy account of the greatest man Steel ever had.

I, too, wish that I might have met and talked with you before I did the book; it would have been much better, I am sure, and doubtless more accurate as to Mr. Jones.

However, I did my best to pay tribute to a man who never got his just credit. He made Carnegie and Little Andy's mob of yes-men.

Many reviewers of compared my tales of Captain Bill to those I told of Jigger Jones in Holy Old Mackinaw, my first book. But Jigger was an ignorant man, even if he was the best lumberjack I ever knew; while Captain Bill had done a heap of good reading.

I hope you will extend my very best greetings to your Mother and tell her I only wish it were possible for me to meet her. If and when I am West again, I shall surely try to meet both you and your mother.

I am happy to send the autograph, which is inclosed. Should you ever wish to send inscribed copies of Iron Brew to any friends or relatives, I'd be happy to get them locally, inscribe them and ship them to you. It would be a pleasure to do that for the grandson of the greatest Steel man of them all.

And thank you for an interesting letter.

Sincerely,

Stewart H. Holbrook

*Letter to author's father, Bill Gage, from Stewart H. Holbrook who wrote **Iron Brew** in the 1930's.*

movement or his ruthless treatment of partners and competitors. Bill Jones, who had been far better known than Carnegie during the last ten years of his life, was now a footnote to steel history. Carnegie was the name people remembered. My dad, like my Uncle Dan, always wrote to authors after books came out. But it was too late to change the emphasis. Typical of the response from authors is a letter Bill Gage, my father, received from Stewart Holbrook about Bill Jones's achievement. "He [Jones] made Carnegie and Little Andy's mob of yes-men." Peter Krass told me that articles in the early issues of the journal *Iron Age* often cited Jones for the phenomenal success behind ET, and Carnegie's name was rarely mentioned.

It was the Jones Hot Metal Mixer that changed everything. In the last two years of his life Bill Jones had done it—created an invention that became essential to all steelmaking. It saved labor; it improved the quality and consistency of steel. It saved fuel. Only a man with intimate knowledge of steelmaking could have designed such an ingenious device, one that is still used today: an invention worth millions of dollars, even 120 years ago. So, even with Jones's unexpected death, the steel world knew who had invented it, knew its worth. And from my reading, correspondence, and conversations I now know that Carnegie knew exactly the value of the Jones Hot Metal Mixer: it was worth a fortune.

But to substantiate such hyperbole and ground it with family lore, I needed to pick up the trail in Pennsylvania to bring fragments of information deposited in archives and court records into one cohesive story.

At this point in the drama of steel there steps upon the stage perhaps the most interesting figure of all who have played a part in it— Captain William R. Jones. It was Bill Jones who took the invention of Kelly and Bessemer into his strong hands and developed it into one of the wonders of the world. It was his work that gave the Carnegie Company its first uplift from among a mob of competitors. It was his amazing record that first startled England and left it far in the rear (Casson 1907, 20).

Harriet Lloyd Jones   Captain Bill Jones

Cora Jones   D.D Gage

Mimi Yost & Cora Jones

Alice Frances Farmer Gage

Alice & Bill Gage, parents

Uncle Dan and Andy Gage

(L to R) *The Gages: Bill II; author's father, Bill; John, and author, Tom Gage*

Governor Henry Gage

Andrew Carnegie (1878)
Project Gutenberg [PD], via Wikimedia Commons

Henry Clay Frick
Bain News Service [PD], via Wikimedia Commons

Daniel Morrell

Charles Schwab
creator of US Steel & Cora's piano teacher

John Potter
Superintendent at Homestead 1892 Riot and Cora & D.D. Gage's landlord

Alexander Holley
Principal negotiator of all steel patents in US and Cora's Godfather

Cast of Characters

Civil War Years

General Humphries, commander at Fredericksburg & Chancellorsville
Casper Easley, copperhead planted in Jones's company
Henry Curry, regimental comrade & eventual colleague at Carnegie Steel
Gen. Burnside, cautious at Antietam & reckless at Fredericksburg
Gen. Hooker, failure at Chancellorsville
Harriet Lloyd Jones, southern belle marries Yankee
The Rev. Wm. Lloyd, failed Paris Ironworks, prominent Tenn. Preacher

Johnstown Cambria Iron & Steel in Johnstown

Theophillus Heyer, fellow veteran & comrade at Cambria Iron Works
Daniel Morrell, owner of Cambria Iron Works
George Fritz, mentor & Cambria superintendent
Robert Hunt, Cambria chemist & future superintendent of Troy Steel
William Kelley, inventor & cartel representative for steel patent in US
William Bessemer, UK & US patent holder of steel
Tom Johnson, flood hero & socialist Ohio politician

Braddock

Andrew Carnegie, hired Jones to build ET, the World's Forge
Tom Carnegie, firm chair & Jones's friend
Henry Clay Frick, coal monopolist, firm partner
Charles Schwab, Jones protégé, future president of US Steel
John Potter, Jones protégé, victimized by Homestead Strike
Thomas Gilchrist Thomas, inventor who equalizes nation's entry to steel
William Yost, family lawyer in collusion to acquire patents
Joseph Butler, Ohio manufacturer lured Jones to leave Carnegie

Jones/Gage Family and Friends

Captain Bill Jones, inventor, architect of Carnegie's ET, & marshal of labor
Cora Jones, daughter, wife, & mother of author's father
Daniel D. Gage, Cora's husband & author of missing Jones biography
William Richard Gage, author's father & resource
Alice Gage, author's mother & resource
Governor Henry Gage, cousin & counsel in Carnegie litigation
John Steinbeck, family friend who pondered writing this book
Tom Gage, great-grandson & author

Chapter 1 Sections

1. Apprenticeship
2. An Odyssey North
3. Fredericksburg
4. Mud March
5. Copperheads and Rebels
6. Chancellorsville
7. Second Tour of Duty

CHAPTER 1

CIVIL WAR

Section 1: Apprenticeship

Western Pennsylvania in the second half of the nineteenth century was alive with resource exploration, ingenuity, and industry. Its coal, ores, oil, and rivers attracted men with money, entrepreneurs who invested in coal mines, iron furnaces, lumber mills, canals and waterways west, the building of railroads, and bridge construction. Its population was growing apace as migrants from the East Coast and Europe streamed in to fill the new jobs being created. In every mill and other establishment, inventors and investors applied them-selves to new methods of production and new ways to make money. The three went together: capital, invention, and labor.

The Jones family was one of many that had come from a mining area in Wales to find a better life in the United States. Bill Jones was born in 1839 in Luzern, Pennsylvania, in number 314 in a row of company houses to Welsh parents who had immigrated some nine years before and who, in all, had eleven children. Jones lost his mother when he was eight. His father, John, was a pattern maker in iron as well as an itinerant minister of the Calvinist Welsh Nonconformist denomination. Sticking up for a friend in the third or fourth grade caused a fight with the teacher, which ended Bill's formal education when he was ten. His father, however, possessed a sizable library, and Bill, by all accounts, was a voracious reader throughout his life—especially the works of Dickens, Shakespeare, Plutarch, and later, the Americans Horatio Greenough and George Lippard.

Reverend John Jones, Bill Jones' father
₍₁₈₅₀₎

As soon as he left school, young Bill Jones began working in the anthracite mill of David Thomas in Catasauqua, Pennsylvania (Schweikart 1989, 290). In Wales, Thomas had been a friend of Bill's father. Thomas's genius in hot-blast smelting of coal had occasioned the Lehigh Crane Iron Company to bring him from Wales to Pennsylvania, where he introduced to the United States a new fuel, anthracite, for use in smelting iron. He became known as the "Father of the American Anthracite Coal Industry" (ibid., 292). His was the first really efficient blowing machine for blast furnaces, which doubled available air pressure. To fully exploit this innovation, the height of the furnace stack needed to be extended up to fifty-five feet. What Bill Jones learned at age ten was cutting-edge knowledge that prepared him to become an authority on blast furnaces within a decade. At the foundry, Jones labored beside Daniel Jones, no relation, whom he was fated to meet again working iron and steel at Johnstown, Pennsylvania.

Upon the death of John Jones when Bill was fourteen, his already-impoverished stepmother was left with ten children from her deceased husband's former wife. Bill left home. By 1854, the fifteen-year-old reached Philadelphia, where he found work as a machinist at the well-known firm of I. P. Morris, Inc. This job gave Bill, who already possessed a natural ability, a solid practical foundation in machinery and engineering that later served him well. Family stories tell of his aptitude for working iron during this early age of American invention and of his passion for reading.

Jones became fascinated with the ideas of George Lippard. Lippard was primarily a writer of dime gothic and historical novels, who eventually became a social activist, writing essays that dealt with inequities in the distribution of wealth (Lippard 1995, xii). He died at age thirty-one in Philadelphia the year of Jones's arrival, but his socioeconomic ideas were already being widely discussed in the city, and Jones's ideas about wealth, labor, and civic duty seem to owe much to Lippard.

When an economic depression put him out of work in Philadelphia, Jones took on a variety of odd jobs that included rafting on Pennsylvania canals. Then, when shipping freight on the canals began to decline due to the rise of the railroad, his rafting skills were no longer needed, and he moved to the newly opened northern Pennsylvania oil fields at Pit Hole for a period. He even took a job on a farm, perhaps his most unsuccessful venture. Apparently one morning the farmer asked him to stick and hang a pig. The operation entailed a surgical thrust with an ice pick-like knife in the jugular to kill the pig, then hanging the carcass so that its blood would drain—a relatively efficient, non-messy job of butchering. A novice with livestock, Jones slit the pig's throat from ear to ear, causing decapitation when he hoisted the carcass, losing fluids useful in the kitchen and making an enormous mess—a performance that ended his career in animal husbandry.

In 1859, Jones drifted into Johnstown, Pennsylvania, where Cambria Iron Works was well on its way to becoming a major iron-producing enterprise. It was in August 1859 that, only seventy-five miles north of Pittsburgh, the first oil well in nearby Titusville became profitable. Connellsville, in central southern Pennsylvania, was becoming a coal mining and coke-producing center. It was also in 1859 that Pittsburgh was the site of the first blast furnace blow of a load of pig iron, an advance in metallurgy akin to vaulting technology from the bicycle to the combustion engine (Ingham 1991, 27, 237 n10). With all of western Pennsylvania's innovative mining and manufacturing activity, Jones had entered center stage at the dawning of the Second Industrial Revolution.

Jones quickly established himself as a skillful mechanic and engineer, sharing with his new employer what he had learned from David Thomas and I. P. Morris. So competent was Jones that by the end of his first year, Cambria's plant managers, John and George Fritz, sent the twenty-year-old to help construct a new furnace in Chattanooga, Tennessee. The new furnace, run by yet another Fritz brother, William, was located near the northern borders of Tennessee and Alabama, in a part of the South that was ramping up its iron production. William Fritz and Bill Jones built the furnace in eighteen months.

Section 2: Odyssey North

During the year and a half that he worked in Chattanooga building the Port Richmond furnace, Bill Jones witnessed the growing fever of secession. Following Abraham Lincoln's 1861 inauguration as president, Southerners feared that his and the Republican Party's position on a strong central government would radically change Southern states' rights and property rights—which most notably included the issue of slavery. By the time the furnace was finished, it was clear that Jones could not remain in Tennessee, for he was a strong abolitionist.

Among the Southern gentry of Chattanooga, the hard-working, well-read Yankee caught the eye of lovely Harriet Lloyd, the daughter of William Lloyd, a Presbyterian minister. The Reverend William Lloyd had been a former ironworks owner in Paris, France, where Harriet was born. After the 1848 Revolution in France, the Republican government expropriated the Lloyd family patents and property. The Lloyds immigrated to America in the mid-1850s and settled in Tennessee, where, after some premature efforts to start up an iron works—Lloyd was accustomed to the life of the Parisian middle class and avoided laboring at the newly founded iron works — he decided on the ministry. As a minister with abolitionist beliefs, he was openly at odds with many in his congregation, a growing number of whom left his parish.

The lovely Harriet Lloyd

(1869)

On April 14, 1861, two days after General Beauregard fired on Fort Sumter at Charleston, Bill married Harriet. He had convinced the abolitionist Presbyterian and his family to leave for Johnstown in Pennsylvania, and they immediately departed Chattanooga with Harriet's sister, Eileen. Tennessee was a politically divided state; not everyone favored secession. Andrew Johnson was stumping for votes around the state in opposition to joining the Confederacy. But Johnson and Jones's in-laws represented a minority; only two months after Jones and his new family left Tennessee, the majority of the voters approved secession.

On April 17, the five stopped briefly at Harpers Ferry, Virginia, where sixty-seven years earlier, George Washington had established the national armory and arsenal following the Revolutionary War. The year before the Joneses' and Lloyds' arrival, the abolitionist John Brown had tried and failed to capture the Federal Arsenal. Captured by Colonel Robert E. Lee, he was quickly tried for treason against the Commonwealth of Virginia, found guilty by a jury, and hanged. Earlier in the month, the politically divided residents of Harpers Ferry and its environs had sent the purportedly pro-Union civil superintendent of the arsenal, Alfred Barbour, to the Virginia Secession Convention at Richmond. While the convention was meeting, Fort Sumter was fired upon, and many Virginians declared their Confederate leanings, including ex-governor Henry Wise and Alfred Barbour. Returning to Harpers Ferry on the very day the Joneses and Lloyds arrived in town, Barbour received a hero's welcome from residents with Confederate sympathies. Barbour convinced many of his former employees at the arsenal to join him in a take-over of the arsenal as soon as Virginia's secession was announced on April 18. Word of the planned take-over had leaked out, however. Unionists in town warned U.S. Army Lieutenant Roger Jones, who commanded the forty-five man guard at the arsenal that General Kenton Harper, leading a large force of Virginia militia, was planning to commandeer the arsenal's weapons and ammunition for the Confederate cause (Wellman 1960, 21). An innkeeper told Bill Jones and his in-laws how outnumbered the Federal guard would be if Barbour succeeded in asserting his authority over armory employees. Bill and the Reverend Lloyd offered to lend a hand to the Federal troops.

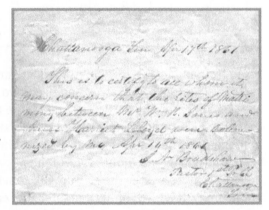

1861 marriage license of Harriet Lloyd and Bill Jones.

Bill quickly sized up the city, since the topography of Harpers Ferry resembled that of Johnstown. Both towns are situated in alluvial lowlands at the confluence of major rivers and surrounded by steep hogback mountains. Lieutenant Jones, commander of the troops guarding the arsenal, was able to successfully foil much of the planned seizure when he and his troops used explosives to destroy some of the buildings and almost seventeen thousand rifles and pistols. Once armed, Jones and Lloyd were among the fifteen volunteers who helped the army torch the armory. Jones and Lloyd then helped fortify the railroad bridge across the Potomac for the retreat of Federal soldiers. Many of the arsenal's weapons were ruined before General Harper and his militia force reached the city from the south. Southern sympathizers working at the arsenal had been able to pour water on some of the gunpowder, which prevented some buildings and the remaining gunpowder from being destroyed.

The explosions had temporarily deafened Lloyd, and the two impromptu activists sought cover, but soon they fled north across the railroad bridge to join Harriet, her sister, and mother. The three women had finished preparations for the remainder of their wagon journey up the north road. Back in Harpers Ferry, secessionist residents and newly arrived militia under General Harper fought the raging fire that had spread after the explosions. They seized whatever remained of gunpowder and weapons, machinery, gun and pistol barrels and locks that were sent south and used to manufacture weapons during the war (Knowles 2001). Only a few Unionists were captured. Lieutenant Roger Jones and most of those troops loyal to the Federal government escaped across the bridge. According to Stackpole, "The capture of all that priceless material was a Godsend to the limited armament potential of the Confederacy and undoubtedly played a major part in advancing its

> *Jones and Lloyd were among the fifteen volunteers who helped the army torch the armory.*

capacity to wage war" (1988, 40).

The family arrived safely in Johnstown on April 24, 1861. They found a home off Market Street, and Bill Jones returned to Cambria Iron Works as a machinist. He followed the war's development by reading the daily newspapers and quickly began a long personal struggle over whether to sign up to fight in the war he had helped start at Harpers Ferry.

The first year of the war had not gone well for the North. Despite superior numbers, the Army of the Potomac suffered from indecisive leadership and a disastrous rout at Manassas just outside Washington, D.C. The only bright spots had been two Union victories at Forts Henry and Donelson in the west in early 1862. Then in April came the victory at Shiloh, but the casualty numbers were the highest ever experienced in warfare, and the press was brutal to Grant, the Union commander. The next month, President Lincoln called for three hundred thousand volunteers to begin a nine-month tour of duty.

Two days after the call-up, Bill Jones decided to enlist, in spite of an additional responsibility, the birth of his daughter Ella earlier that month. When he left for duty, Jones, who was a good shot from years of hunting, took his own musket and as much food as he could carry, since foraging for rations was discouraged in the East, and army fare was infamous.

Section 3: Fredericksburg

When the war began, Cambria Iron Works was the largest iron-producing company in the North. The Federal government discouraged those working iron from volunteering for duty, because iron was essential for the weapons of war and the rails used in troop movement. In contrast, the Confederacy drafted all laborers, including ironworkers, a policy that was perhaps a factor in the South's defeat, since the Union's navy blockade of Southern ports prevented the import of matériel from abroad (Livermore 1957, 92). At Cambria, skilled, experienced workers who filled essential positions in iron production sat out the entire war without being judged slackards. The war acted as a stimulus to innovation and production in iron making, with government contracts contributing to real prosperity in the industry. Jones could have continued to work at Cambria Iron Works and never put himself in danger, but he eventually served two tours of duty, leaving Reverend Lloyd to take care of both families.

Jones was a patriot and would have had it no other way. On July 31, 1862, two weeks after he signed up, Bill Jones became a corporal in A Company, the first of ten companies totaling nearly a thousand soldiers of the 133rd Regiment, Pennsylvania Volunteers, in McClellan's Army of the Potomac. Corporal Jones's company numbered about a hundred men from Johnstown. His angling companion, Filius Heyer, was one of the company's sergeants.

Jones was a patriot and would have had it no other way. On July 31, 1862, two weeks after he signed up, Bill Jones became a corporal in A Company, the first of ten companies totaling nearly a thousand soldiers of the 133rd Regiment, Pennsylvania Volunteers.

The Pennsylvania soldiers respected their immediate superiors, Colonel Allabach, a Pennsylvania veteran of the Mexican-American War, and General Humphreys. However, they despised the incompetence of the generals above Humphreys, men like Burnside, Butterfield, and McClellan, who had commanded Antietam's slaughter.

During August, the four regiments of Allabach's brigade were stationed at Arlington Heights and Washington, D.C., where they were all given smoothbore Springfield muskets, a light shelter tent, and six rounds of ammunition. On August 30 they were moved toward the front at Fort Ward, in Alexandria, Virginia, one of the many forts built to protect Washington, D.C. There Jones's regiment was involved in picket duty and in building entrenchments. From there they were moved to Sharpsburg, where they arrived during the battle, which they could hear but were held in reserve for the morning of September 18.

The previous two days, McClellan's army had engaged Lee's in ferocious fighting along Antietam Creek. General Burnside's troops, which could have made a difference in the outcome, arrived late in the afternoon of September 17 at the bridge over Antietam Creek that came to be known as Burnside's Bridge. Burnside slowly funneled troops through the narrow bridge instead of aggressively scouting and crossing the creek over several easy nearby fords. This failure of leadership and initiative against the exhausted Army of Northern Virginia allowed the Confederates to bring fresh troops from Harpers Ferry and drive Burnside back, squandering a potentially decisive Union victory. On that day alone there were approximately 23,100 casualties from both sides, a figure that exceeds the number of American casualties in all the other nineteenth century American wars combined (Faust 2008). The fact that Antietam-Sharpsburg prevented Lee from moving into Union territory was a politically significant outcome of this engagement and paved the way for Lincoln's emancipation proclamation three months later.

On September 18, Allabach's brigade was positioned for action, but Lee had withdrawn his army. Corporal Jones saw the blinded, the wounded, and the dead atop mule-drawn wagons wending down from Sunken Road and the Bloody Cornfield to cross Burnside's Bridge. His regiment was involved in covering the casualties that morning. In the afternoon his brigade marched to a site on Shepherdstown Road, Sharpsburg, where the Fifth Corps set up camp. General Humphreys drilled the eight thousand soldiers of his Third Division thoroughly over the next six weeks and promised that they would have their moment of courage.

Also in Allabach's brigade was an acquaintance of Jones's, Sergeant Henry M. Curry of the 155th Pennsylvania Regiment, a flag-bearer. He was four years younger than Jones and had enlisted for a three-year tour; he fought the duration of the war, carrying the flag in some of the war's bloodiest battles. His commitment to his superiors seemed to surpass logic and, at times, was almost religious in its conviction. Curry was wounded at Five Forks on April 1, 1865, and discharged by general order three weeks after his regiment on June 22, 1865.

Corporal Jones was far more apt to question authority. He recounted stories after the war about the "daft man" who was Burnside's counsel, Brigadier General Daniel Butterfield, nicknaming him Butterfull and Flutterfield. Always ready with a good story or colorful epithet, Jones's wit endeared him to his fellow soldiers. The twenty-three-year-old machinist was both older than most in his regiment and was also more familiar with the countryside, for he had traveled through it the year before. He spent most of his first tour only a dozen or so miles from Harpers Ferry, in northeastern Virginia at Falmouth, a few miles from George Washington's family home.

General Humphreys, a West Point graduate, had little combat experience before Antietam and Fredericksburg. In time the soldiers under him came to value his discipline, particularly when they realized how effectively he had prepared them for engagements at Fredericksburg, Chancellorsville, and Gettysburg. Humphreys's personal valor, rigor, profanity, and wry humor and Allabach's camaraderie may have served as models for Jones's later management style.

After a string of early battlefield failures and only modest success at Antietam, the methodical but hesitant McClellan was relieved of his high command and replaced by Burnside. McClellan had failed to use all the troops he had available or to act upon intelligence regarding Lee's troop movements.

Burnside's Army marched through mud and fog toward Fredericksburg from Sharpsburg on October 30 and set up permanent camp at Falmouth across the Rappahannock River about a mile northeast of the city. There Jones saw the first aerial surveillance, Union balloons carrying scouts to ascertain the layout of Confederate artillery on Marye's Heights and the size and movements of Lee's force. The two armies were so close that he could hear the sounds of banjos and singing, raucous laughter, and clattering messware from the Confederate camp at Fredericksburg. The two armies had amassed 175,000 men in a small arena straddling the Rappahannock. The Union, with nearly 113,000 men, had a distinct numerical advantage.

Across the river to the west of Fredericksburg stretched an open field, drained by creeks locally referred to as runs. Behind, or west of, the field rose a high ridge, Marye's Heights, crowned with Confederate artillery and troops that guarded river access to the town. Just below the ridge was a half-mile stone wall that protected it: here Robert E. Lee positioned more troops. Two thousand Georgian and South Carolinian sharpshooters, four deep, sighted down from behind the wall.

On the morning of December 13, Bill Jones doused his face in branchwater, slung his suspenders over his shoulders, hefted his forty-pound knapsack, and prepared for battle. He later described a unit of Keystone Zouaves that fought alongside him attired in crimson pantaloons and white spats, similar to Henry Curry's uniform. The German population in Johnstown had recruited volunteers who wore a uniform fashioned after the French North Africa Corps (Reardon 1995, 89).

Union engineers constructed a network of pontoon bridges for the infantry to cross the river and enter Fredericksburg; three were positioned just east of the city, and another three were positioned about a mile and a half to the south. The sharpshooters took their toll on those securing the pontoons. Smoke mingled with fog beyond the river during that bitterly cold December week. The Rebel troops and artilleries, under General Longstreet's command, shelled Federal soldiers crossing the river and as they entered Fredericksburg. The North's objective was to take Marye's Heights, but the four-foot wall protected the shooters, who were using rifles that were accurate at a distance of 250 yards.

Dan Butterfield had an eye for headlines; he had been born in Utica, New York, to a prominent business family and was no more a trained soldier than Jones. Although he had enlisted as a sergeant with the New York militia, within five months he was a brigadier general in the army. General "Butterfull" had sent order after order for the Fifth Corps to take the wall before night.

Bill Jones's division marched across the bridges into town where they were held in reserve for a late afternoon attempt to reach the wall. Charge after charge of blue-clad soldiers left the protection of Fredericksburg to cross the flat plain and the runs, then dash up toward the mossy stone wall. Years later Jones reminisced on his untested comrades' staying power in the face of those seceshes, the Confederates fighting for their right to secede from the Union.

Even troops moving around Fredericksburg were in danger. Streets ran parallel to the river with intersecting streets leading straight out into the open field, up the slope to the wall. When his time came, Jones marched through the snow-littered street, past broken furniture, books, and bottles, when he heard somebody pounding on a piano. Cannons were going off everywhere; men were screaming, and in the middle of it all, there was the sound of jamming piano keys. Entering Princess Anne Street, Jones saw the piano with three legs, tilted against brick stairs where looters had dragged it down past pylons that once had supported a front door. A crazed, drunken soldier was pounding the keys.

After the thirteen earlier assaults that day, the last two of the Union's brigades—Tyler's and Allabach's, from Humphreys's Division, totaling eight thousand men—prepared for the day's final charge from the city. At four o'clock Butterfield ordered them to leave town and move forward. A distance of roughly a quarter mile lay ahead: a swampy stretch approaching Mabel Run just outside town, then high ground with slight ravines through which flowed a now frozen, mud-encrusted creek bed, then open plain for seventy-five yards up to the wall.

Bill Jones's company looked up into the sights of the Rebel rifles and artillery facing back down at them. There was no cover, no shielding. They just ran and died. Cannon fire from Marye's Heights rained down canister and shrapnel on the exposed troops, and shattered the trees and charred buildings of Fredericksburg, which hurtled rubble onto the oncoming troops. Jones's greatest worry was of being blinded, a fear he maintained through the war and for the rest of his life when he faced molten sparks of iron and steel from fire-breathing furnaces.

The regimental chaplain, the Reverend Andrew Jackson Hartsock, survived to record the day's struggle and provided vivid documentation. Jones chucked his overcoat as his comrades dumped their knapsacks and heavy equipment in the few dry areas so their charge would be unfettered by excess weight. As artillery pounded the mire, Humphreys ordered Allabach's Second Brigade to regroup to the left of Telegraph Road ahead of Tyler's First Brigade. Henry Humphreys, the general's son and a youth only a year older than Bill Jones, flanked his father. General Humphreys ordered his officers twelve paces in front of the line, and cavalierly said, "Young gentlemen, I intend to lead this assault, and shall be happy to have the pleasure of your company" (ibid., 92).

Sixteen-year-old Henry Curry carried the colors for the 155th in front of Humphreys's charge, traversing the two hundred yards to the still crouching New Yorkers of an earlier attack, many of whom were hugging the little bit of ground they had gained. They shouted "get down" or tugged the trousers of charging infantrymen, an action that destroyed the forward momentum. Humphreys's wing faltered when his infantry stopped, crouched to fire, then, in disarray, charged again, making little progress against the continuous rifle fire from the wall. Among dead horses and crumpled forms, officers and soldiers hovered behind the rise of the ravine. All of Humphreys's officers were killed, and the general was ultimately alone on the battlefield, rallying his troops.

Jones's 133rd and the other Pennsylvania regiments in Allabach's brigade regrouped where the New York Second Corps held the ground. Humphreys ordered fixed bayonets and called for a second assault. Jones's brigade advanced again, holding a line for nearly one hundred yards, and then the soldiers broke, scrambling over dead and wounded, past downed flags and crushed drums, with the wounded tripping up still others who looked ahead at the impenetrable wall. An officer alongside Jones, a captain, was hit twice in the chest. Jones's momentum carried him beyond the furthest line, on down then up over fences and slippery embankments of the ravine to within fifty, then twenty-five, yards of the wall.

Four flag bearers had been felled, but Henry Curry found shelter behind the ruins of a house. Young Daniel Berkett, whose family lived two blocks from Jones's home in Johnstown, fell with a hole over his left eye. From behind, the downed Second Corps fired over them, mistakenly hitting a few of their own men. In the 133rd, men dove into the mud to take aim at the sharpshooters behind the wall. Others crowded behind the brick building where Curry crouched. The charge, unable to advance further and reduced in numbers, finally disintegrated into a chaotic retreat. Thousands of blue-jacketed forms lay inert, their tattered uniforms blowing in the wind.

> Yes, I was with Bill Jones during the first enlistment. We were together in the second battle of Bull Run, Antietam, and Chancellorsville. At Fredericksburg, the regiment went in with 900 men in the morning, and that afternoon there was 400 and less than 30 answered roll call when we came off the battlefield.
>
> We charged right up in front of a stone wall at Fredericksburg in a leaden hailstorm when the 66th New York made us drop to the ground. We hid together for quite a while before we were given an order to rally. Our company advanced several paces, when we were ordered again to lay [sic] down. And the moment a man lifted his head from the ground in that battle, it was shot full of lead. The field was strewn with the dead and wounded. Over 13,000 [sic] were killed there that day.
>
> ("An old friend.")

Bill Jones and others sought cover wherever possible and were praying for dark, when they heard Humphreys's order to hold. According to Allabach, dozens of men in the 133rd advanced to within twelve paces of the wall (Rable 1995, 72). A comrade's note remembered Jones and the battle that day.

Still later that afternoon, river fog, moiling up toward the wall, met cannon smoke settling down from Marye's Heights. Tyler's First brigade waited, then advanced over the bodies of wounded, dead, and exhausted Union troops pinned to the ground. Jones waited, hoping that Tyler's four regiments could progress beyond his own. Rebel fire subsided until Tyler's line of four thousand men was thirty yards from the wall when it seemed to explode, and Tyler's regiments vanished in the cloud of smoke.

One final attempt that cold December day was made by Getty's division from the south, but it, too, failed to reach the wall. All told, fourteen charges advanced against the wall which proved to be impenetrable. The sun was fading on the horizon behind Fredericksburg, and Jones knew he was pinned down for the night. He spent it lying in the spot

> *He crept down the ravine, passing the dead—three deep in places. He recalled that one could reach town by stepping only on blue.*

where he had been when Tyler's line was stopped. In the blackness, he witnessed a "cosmic blow:" a well-documented aurora borealis marked the heavens over Virginia the night of December 13, 1862. Jones, to help himself forget the cold, matched up the mysterious colors in the heavens to the spectrum of colors of a furnace blast.

He spent all night among corpses frozen together in mud. Occasional shots behind the nearby four-foot wall silenced a wounded Yankee or dropped a stretcher-bearer illuminated by the aurora borealis. Christmas was only two weeks away; he would certainly miss his family in the warmth of his home near Stone Bridge in Johnstown.

An acrimonious debate over who got closest to the wall endured among veterans until the beginning of the twentieth century (Humphreys 1886, 13). Bill Jones had come within twelve paces. Early in the morning of December 14, he gave up his ground to return into the protecting fog, stiff and frozen. He crept down the ravine, passing the dead—three deep in places. Shadowy masked figures carried stretchers past mud-caked flags, dismembered limbs, and what he called jelly of man-mutilation. He recalled that one could reach town by stepping only on blue.

Jones and Henry Curry ran into each other in the early morning darkness of December 14. As the roosters crowed and the first cannon fired in the distance, they stumbled into smoking Fredericksburg. Later in life, these two veterans of Fredericksburg reminisced about how Jones's devil-may-care attitude never wavered in the face of danger, and about how, as they were entering the city on Princess Anne Street in the fog, Jones recognized Colonel Jay Allen of Henry's regiment.

Colonel Speakman of the retreating regiment ordered Corporal Jones to spell the exhausted man in the basement to tail bottles up into the street for the wounded (Maltese 1910, 109). The hole led to the wine cellar. Jones settled in the basement and passed bottles up to soldiers stacking a wagon, but he also filched quite a few for his mates in A Company. He emptied that cellar and climbed out as the liquor wagon went on to Lacy House, the temporary field hospital. Later Jones, carrying the bottles that he had stashed for his company, returned to Camp Humphreys at Falmouth across the river where his regiment bivouacked. That night in camp the Pennsylvanians of A Company in the 133rd celebrated with the finest wine of New York, Baltimore, or Washington, D. C.

The remainder of that day, Burnside had asked for, and Lee granted, a truce to aid the wounded and bury the dead. Fewer than 17 percent of the nearly 1,300 dead were identifiable, so heavy had been the shelling (Rable 1995, 55).

On that day at the same battle Walt Whitman searched among the casualties for his wounded brother and tended to the injured at the hospital, inspiring the words:

> *At my feet more distinctly a soldier, a mere lad, in danger of*
> *bleeding to death, (he is shot in the abdomen,)*
> *I stanch the blood temporarily, (the youngster's face is white as*
> *a lily,)*
> *Then before I depart I sweep my eyes o'er the scene fain to absorb*
> *it all,*
> *Faces, varieties, postures beyond description,*
> *most in obscurity,*
> *some of them dead,*
> *Surgeons operating, attendants holding lights, the smell of ether,*
> *odor of blood,*
> *The crowd, O the crowd of the bloody forms, the yard outside also*
> *fill'd,*
> *Some on the bare ground, some on Planks or stretchers,*
> *some in the death-spasm sweating,*
> *An occasional scream or cry, the doctor's*
> *shouted orders or call,*
> *The glisten of the little steel instruments*
> *catching the glint of the torches,*
> *These I resume as I chant, I see again the*
> *forms, I smell the odor,*
> *Then hear outside the orders given, Fall in, my*
> men, fall in. ("A March in the Ranks Hard-Prest, and the Road Unknown")

Fredericksburg was a disaster for the Union. As for the Pennsylvanians in Humphreys's division, they had proved their mettle.

Section 4: Mud March, 1863

On January 1, 1863, President Lincoln proclaimed the emancipation of the slaves in the rebelling states, thereby establishing as fact what Southerners had feared. In the short run, this act strengthened the Confederates' two major, non-military stratagems to win the war: first, to cultivate and promote Northern defeatism; and, second, to incite the midwestern states to secede following the Confederacy's lead (Gray 1942, 216). The latter objective targeted populations of western Pennsylvania, Ohio, Indiana, and Illinois. Meanwhile, abolitionists from Massachusetts were accusing fellow Northerners, especially those from western Pennsylvania, of being Copperheads, Southern sympathizers. Before war broke out, most in the North—including Lincoln—cared more about the Union and less about the evils of slavery. But many Northerners hated having to abide by Fugitive Slave Laws in a United States that required Northern communities to return runaway slaves. Better, reasoned some abolitionists, that the nation be divided, than to return runaway Negroes to servitude. Such agitation in Johnstown increased the divide between the loyal opposition to Lincoln's governance and outright treason.

The residents of Johnstown fell along a spectrum of political beliefs regarding the war: the Republicans were committed to preserving the splintering country. The pure abolitionists, the radical Republicans, were divided over whether the war was worth the sacrifice. Loyal Democrats were critical of Lincoln's freeing the slaves, and many preferred a negotiated armistice with the South. Some were indifferent to slavery but others feared that emancipation would further strengthen Southern resolve by deepening the divide. Yet another group, the Peace Democrats, was ambivalent about both slavery and secession, while the Copperheads, somewhat related, were violent in disrupting order.

Finally, there were members of the Order of the Golden Circle, the proslavery secessionists, who found many of their members among the Peace Democrats (Gray 1942, 70). A remnant from the Mexican-American War, they resurfaced in nearly every state in 1861. Their original mission had been to extend slave states by colonizing Mexico and the Caribbean islands, to form a metaphorical Southern golden circle of slave states. If successful in conquering all the way to Yucatan, they would have reinstated slavery manumitted in those Mexican territories since the early 1800s and would have asserted privileged liberties of slave owners in the seceding states. But after the outbreak of the war, their mission of conquest was sidelined in order to support the Confederacy. In the Northern states alone the order numbered nearly 350,000 members, with many trained in armed militia. Johnstown, in rural Cambria Country of western

General Burnside planned a movement that would approach Lee's army from the south. It became known as the Mud March.

Pennsylvania, had become a center for the Knights of the Order of the Golden Circle, a militant secret society that exploited tensions among abolitionists and Confederate sympathizers (*Cambria [PA] Tribuen 1863, April 1*). They harassed abolitionist families, like the Lloyds and Joneses, whose sons and husbands were in Federal uniforms at the front. This group of Southern sympathizers often foiled Federal government recruitment and even assassinated pro-Union volunteers (Green December 16, 1862-January 26, 1863).

In late January of 1863, General Burnside tried to redeem himself from the disaster at Fredericksburg by planning a flanking movement that would approach Lee's army at Fredericksburg from the south. It became known as the Mud March. The Army of the Potomac left Falmouth on January 20 after weeks of mild weather, traveling along an unpaved road following the north bank of the Rappahannock River. In the afternoon a drizzle began, followed by a full-blown nor-east rainstorm, with heavy winds, that lasted for two days, causing the route to quickly become a knee-deep quagmire. Supply wagons, artillery, horses, and the entire infantry were soon bogged down in mud. There was such protest among senior officers that Burnside had to abandon his plan and return to Falmouth, where some of the camp was now flooded. The Confederates remained in Fredericksburg, and Lincoln, unhappy with the general, removed Burnside from his command and replaced him with General Joseph Hooker, another veteran from the Mexican-American War.

The tensions from home reached into camp at the front. On January 26, alongside the soldiers of the Pennsylvania 118th, Bill Jones fought in a drunken brawl against soldiers from the Massachusetts 22nd Regiment in pelting rain on terrain that turned to muck from the rain and later freezing temperatures. Men in the 22nd had insulted Pennsylvania soldiers for being disloyal (*Johnstown [PA] Democrat* 1864, 23 February). With emancipation, the issue of slavery had become a principal motive for the war, equal to preserving the Union; but, among some from Massachusetts, abolishing slavery had now become even more important. This brawl was symptomatic of a general malaise affecting much of the North.

Back in Johnstown, Colonel John Bowman, editor of the *Cambria Tribune*, supported Lincoln. But some of his staff, angered by Lincoln's emancipation of Southern slaves, opposed their editor. They feared the Negro Plot, a paranoia-driven rumor, derived from an anonymous pamphlet that advanced a conspiracy theory (Stackpole1988, 14) that freed African Americans would overtake the country and pillage the white world. One such reporter for the *Cambria Tribune* was Caspar Easley, a corporal in the 133rd Regiment who wrote anonymous articles from camp. An overweight hulk with rounded shoulders, Easley was described as having the eyes of a frightened dog. He won most arguments with bombastic rhetoric, evident in his writing. His language intimidated readers who avoided rebuttal for fear of appearing less educated.

Other reporters on the *Cambria Tribune* who shared Easley's feelings and convictions broke from the *Tribune* to organize the *Johnstown Democrat*, which published its first issue on February 24, 1863. The new periodical relied upon Easley to continue his anonymous columns from the front. His identity was revealed when Burnside's successor, General Joseph Hooker, stipulated that colophons, identifying authors, accompany articles, forcing Easley to go public.

In A Company, outspoken critics damned Lincoln for freeing the slaves. They rallied members in B and E companies to fuel discord. In reaction, Jones found an odd ally in the chaplain, the Reverend Andrew Jackson Hartsock. The two despised one another but a common enemy created a temporary truce. Jones said Hartsock preached the gospel like he was fighting bumblebees. Hartsock's style of religion was too close to that of Jones's own father, the Reverend John Jones, which Bill had rejected for Unitarianism. Although Hartsock disliked Jones as well, he recognized an important ally who supported the efforts of the Union League, a pro-Union association. According to his diary, Hartsock would rely on the very devil to battle those "peace sneaks." Although Jones allied with the chaplain to support the Union League, he'd be damned if any preacher would succeed in criticizing him for his use of Shakespearean or Rabelaisian profanity: powerful language effected powerful results.

Section 5: Copperheads and Rebels

Many Union troops were discontented for legitimate reasons. Paymasters each month held up empty hands as soldiers filed for their pay. Those like Jones who had families worried how those at home could endure the terrible winter without money. Only in February did Jones receive $84.00 for his service since his enlistment in July. Those on farms could live off the land, but the families in cities needed currency to exchange for goods.

At fifty-six, Reverend Lloyd was responsible for the families of both his daughters, but he was not well. Uprooted and reestablished for the second time in his life, he found it difficult to organize a viable Presbyterian congregation in a religiously diverse city composed primarily of Lutheran and Catholic German Americans and Baptist Welsh American ironworkers. Consequently, the families struggled.

From home, Harriet Jones supplied her husband weekly with words of love and family matters; sometimes with food; and regularly with news clippings and poems by Ethel Lynn Beers and George Henry Boker, and the "Boston Hymn" that Emerson recited on New Year's Day to commemorate Lincoln's Emancipation Proclamation. Sometimes a loaf of bread got by the provost guard who carefully inspected packages and mail from home before distributing them, and Jones would find a surprise bottle of old rye.

Army mess food and moldy gifts from home were poisoning many in the army. Corporal Jones shared his packages with fellow soldiers he knew from the Cambria Iron Works; he suffered diarrhea when the "mess of eatable" arrived late, with his favorite cigars, his "tobys," soaked in melted butter from a stuffed Shanghai rooster. Cora later recalled her father joking that he needed Harriet's vial of lavender water to open some of these "demoralized" boxes. He often chanced eating home-sent food after weeks of a soldier's fare, cold raw pork and hardtack—stale bread he could not break by leveraging it against his thigh.

> *Army mess food and moldy gifts from home were poisoning many in the army.*

That winter had been particularly bitter for the Union army at Falmouth. Soldiers overwhelmed the local countryside foraging for food and cutting trees for firewood. Although the camp was not far from supplies in Washington, D.C., the distribution of rations and blankets was inadequate. Sergeant Filius Heyer was among the many men who suffered from dysentery, which landed him in a hospital tent among the wounded. When Hooker instituted furloughs to help curb the high desertion rates, the suffering Heyer requested one and soon departed for Johnstown. While resting up at home, he fell in with Robert Hunt, a chemist, who was among Jones's friends. These two men, with others from the Cambria Iron Works, joined the newly formed Union League to confront the pernicious effects of the Copperheads, the vocal antiwar Democrats.

Hunt and Heyer drafted a Union League loyalty oath to the Federal government and solicited signatures from people about town and the countryside. Signers of the resolution pledged to support Lincoln and the integrity of the Union. The league's activities included discussion of the war and addressing rampant rumors of defeat and general demoralization in the North. It fostered awareness of the issues that Lincoln and Congress were debating. It would be difficult to assess the league's effectiveness, but it was an organized rebuttal to rumor, hysteria, and Confederate sympathies.

When Filius Heyer returned from his ten-day furlough he brought a package from Harriet: a box of food and a copy of the first issue of the *Johnstown Democrat*. Heyer and his German American wife, Gertrude, were close friends with the Joneses. Filius worked at Cambria as a roller but his preferred activity was fishing for trout in Stony Creek and the Little Conemaugh. Back at the front, Heyer collected signatures from the regiment in support of the Union League's efforts in Johnstown. Bill Jones and Reverend Hartsock signed the petition. Hartsock jumped upon the opportunity to canvass for the league throughout the regiment.

Caspar Easley responded with ridicule to the Union League members' activities at the front in his column:

"Our Army Correspondence"

. . . The Chaplain [Hartsock] being called on made an apology but managed to express his hatred of "copperheads" in his effort. John Jones, of Company "G," then made a short oration, reminding one forcibly of schoolboy days. Company "A" comes in the ring again in the shape of Wm. R. Jones, and if insane curses and the most depraved language a human being can use is to be considered sense, then Jones talked sensibly. I would respectfully suggest that this gentleman (!) should take lessons in moral behavior. (Duram and Duram 1979)

Most of the soldiers in Jones's A Company supported the Union League. There were those in camp from other companies, however, who listened with great interest to Caspar Easley. In one of Easley's many columns in the *Johnstown Democrat*, he implied that Jones's comrade, the "deserting" Heyer, had seized on the Union League as a means to return to the front with honor:

"Our Army Correspondence"

I see some pretty extensive reports have been published in various "loyal" papers of what purports to have been the vote of this regiment on the subject of 'Union Leagues,' etc. To the very labored report of those who were the principals in that affair, I beg to offer a few objections. In the first place, the meeting was anything but "large and enthusiastic," but little over one hundred being present. In the next place, all present by no means gave their approval of the insane resolutions passed by these embryo politicians. The person

[Theophilus Heyer] principally instrumental in getting up the meeting bears the epitaph deserter, and those acquainted with him set him down as being the possessor of very little sound sense. After the meeting was called to order, a vote was taken on the propriety of elevating the Sergeant Major of the regiment to the position of chairman. The character of this individual [Heyer] can best be described by stating that at various times he purchased apples, tobacco & etc. to sell at exorbitant rates to the privates of the regiment. The ayes and noes having been called, Companies "E" and "B" exercised their rights by voting no. But as they are set down as "copperheads," no attention was paid to their vote—Horton of "A" Company was duly elected secretary . . . . While the committee were absent getting the resolutions out of their pockets, the proceedings began to flag, so a speech by the secretary was suggested. Horton having been elected stood up, and after making great but unappealing efforts to get off something witty, at length subsided. (Hamilton 1921)

Jones answered this article in a letter to the editor of the *Cambria Tribune*, which appeared in the issue dated April 10, 1863, entitled "Sergt Heyer Defended in the Camp"

Col.:

Dear Sir: In the "Johnstown Democrat" of the 23 March, I noticed an article headed "A Caution to Soldiers" and aimed apparently at T. H. Heyer to whom it did a great injustice. The author of the article accuses Sergeant Heyer of having misrepresented the Democracy of Johnstown, and as he seems to speak knowingly, I beg leave to contradict the gentleman, if he be one, of which I doubt.

Sergeant Heyer did not misrepresent the democracy nor make the statements alleged in the "Democrat" and every honorable man in the company will testify to the truth of this denial. As regards the asserted misrepresentations of Sergeant Heyer having influenced your correspondent No! I know it to be an unmitigated falsehood. The letter of your correspondent was written by himself, on his own accord, on reading the first issue of the "Democrat," which was denounced not only by "E" but by every man in this Company. These are facts which I am able to substantiate.

In one place in the article the author spoke of venting his spleen in the following manner. "The fellow [Heyer] is notorious for getting into such positions as will effectively secure him from danger and the possibility of doing any other real service than keeping rations from spoiling."

The Democrat has exposed his ignorance. When Sergeant Heyer was offered the position [as quartermaster] he was averse to accepting it and said to me he intended to decline the appointment. Believing him to be physically unable to perform all the duties required of an infantry soldier and especially those on the march, I expressed myself to him. Indeed I did not then nor do I now doubt that he would have been an inmate of the hospital had he refused the position offered him. Finally, after consulting with Captain Downey, the Sergeant concluded to accept the offer. Now, let me here say that judging from my own experience on the battlefield, a position in the ambulance Corps is not an enviable one; for if anything will try the mettle of the soldier it is the cries and groans of the wounded and dying men. For my part I would rather fight all day then for one hour be engaged in the removal of the wounded.

Sergeant Heyer has by his gentlemanly deportment won the esteem and friendship of his comrades in arms. As regards his bravery I have yet to hear it doubted. But I do not think the author of that article is a brave man. I do not think a brave and honorable man would make such a mean and cowardly attack on one who has sacrificed the comfort of his home and the society of his family to do service for his country.

Now, in conclusion, if the author of the Democrat editorial takes exception to my remarks and thinks the livery of my country protects me, I shall be in Johnstown about the middle of May, and that I hold myself personally responsible for this article.

Camp Humphreys, April 3, 1863

The Union League may well have been a vestige of George Lippard's Brotherhood of the Union that had so interested young Bill Jones during his days in Philadelphia. An organization that flourished in the 1850s and that ultimately had chapters in nineteen states, the Brotherhood of the Union had sought to rectify excesses of greed that corrupted church and law in Philadelphia, and to promote patriotism and labor and election reforms, objectives that found expression later in Jones's labor policies.

All spring the *Democrat* continued to carry editorials attacking Lincoln, emancipation, the recruiting of Negroes to fight against the South, and Congress's newly legislated conscription of soldiers now that volunteerism was drying up (Robertson 1996, 17). Its editors and columnists filled pages with articles reminding readers that the abolitionists a dozen years earlier had opposed the Mexican-American War as an imperial war to expand the Union, and had themselves advocated secession instead of supporting a war they believed was being fought as an opportunity to extend slavery. Editorials reminded readers about the madman abolitionist John Brown, who personally split the skulls of a family of five settlers in Pottawatomie, Kansas, before storming the Federal Armory at Harpers Ferry (Stackpole 1988).

With each passing week the two Johnstown newspapers became increasingly polarized over activity at the front, the *Democrat* becoming more an overt voice of Southern sympathies and the *Cambria Tribune* more and more an expression of abolitionism. Some

Northern newspapers like the *Democrat* provided the Confederacy with a good source of intelligence, a means of spying that the North entirely lacked, a major reason why Hooker required that the authorship of war reportage be revealed—to differentiate opinion from spying.

The following article from the *Johnstown Democrat* seems typical of what Jones and other Johnstown soldiers read from home while at the front:

"Our Army Correspondent"

What a sad tale the widows and orphans will have to tell of their wrongs and all for the sake of the dirty black negro . . . Our country is fast becoming overrun with those vile creatures, and what will be the end if the Republican party gets the sway. But God, who has ordered all things, will bring all to judgment who are trying to keep up a war for the sake of the blacks. If God had wanted the nigger free amongst white men, He would have ordered it so; But He has said they shall be servants of servants—we as the servants of Him and they as the servants of the white man. And why does this party want to set up opposition to Him, who has brought them into existence? He can and He will put matters out in their true light.

Earlier in the winter, Private Elias Miller had deserted from A Company, showing up in Johnstown within a week. In Johnstown, Miller spread horror stories about the terrible march west through thigh-high mud, the harsh discipline of incompetent generals, and the heavy casualties at Fredericksburg, which a sympathetic press had misrepresented as a Union success. Harriet Jones wrote her husband about Miller's stories and mentioned that many men at Cambria, who had previously considered joining up, were now not going to leave jobs and families for such misery and possible death. Recruitment of volunteers from Cambria County and the rest of western Pennsylvania slowed to a trickle. The *Johnstown Democrat* carried columns on "Desertions from the Army":

Throughout the medium of army statistics . . . we are made acquainted with the fact that the muster rolls exhibit desertions to the number of one hundred and thirty thousand men. We cannot believe that this is owing to dictates for military life, but are of opinion that it furnishes the strongest and most convincing evidence of a widely spread dissatisfaction in the management of the war.   (April 8, 1863)

Similar editorials could be found throughout the North, but in areas west of the Alleghenies and north of the Ohio River they incited action. The government assigned troops from the embattled Union Army to put down increasingly hostile city demonstrations. The war's nadir came that winter, with an army in the East that was nearly broken. Food was insufficient. For days Jones wore clothes that were waterlogged from incessant rains. Whenever the sun came out, he boiled them clean. Disarray on the battlefield paralleled disarray among the citizens of the North, as rumors spread that other states might follow the rebellious South and secede. In spite of threats of court-martial, Jones and Easley went at it verbally and with fisticuffs following the Heyer incident. Both soldiers became a grave concern to their officers, including Colonel Allabach, who commanded the entire brigade.

Heavy Union losses, particularly at Fredericksburg, caused wavering, and in many areas, declining public support for the war, as evidenced by significant Democratic gains in the midterm elections of 1862. It was a weakened Lincoln who issued the Emancipation Proclamation on January 1, 1863. When he replaced Burnside with Hooker, Lincoln somewhat assuaged a hostile public, yet many still seethed about emancipation. Casper Easley shared clippings like the following from the *Jonesboro Gazette*:

> The Emancipation Proclamation of the President, the late Act of Congress authorizing the enrollment and organization of Negro regiments and the other impolitic and injudicious proceedings of that fanatical body have wrought much mischief. We . . . the ridiculous Democrats contended that the Proclamation absolved a soldier's obligation to fight and some press openly encouraged desertion (Hennessy 1996, 17).

Initially, all, including Bill Jones, were encouraged that Hooker replaced Burnside, and Hooker's presence resulted in the men rallying together and in heightened morale. "Fighting Joe" Hooker was showy. He was a fellow engineer who had commanded the artillery at the battles of Chattanooga and Missionary Ridge. With the onset of spring and a hunch that Hooker might avenge the useless waste at Fredericksburg, Jones put aside his enmity toward Easley and fell in with his squad for the next engagement.

During Hooker's first two months in command, he worked to improve the conditions, readiness, and morale of the army at Falmouth. He improved sanitation, established bakeries, and generally provided better food. Since desertion affected fully half of his entire army, he instituted furloughs and leaves of absence. (Jones himself never had a day off during his first nine-month tour-of-duty.) By the end of April, Hooker had turned his charges from a sodden rag-tag crowd with terrible morale into a relatively optimistic, disciplined force of one hundred thousand. President Lincoln visited the army in early April to raise spirits. He selected as his chief of staff, Dan "Butterful" Butterfield, who had commanded Jones's Fifth Corps at Fredericksburg. The obsequious Butterfield, after Chancellorsville often referred to as Hooker's Brains, achieved the singular legacy of wartime merit by having composed the evening Taps (Stackpole 1989, 40).

> *Jones was famous for kicking up his heels in a hoedown with fellow Pennsylvanians. He became the star of the Camp Humphreys's Follies.*

The army seemed fit for spring and a showdown with General Lee. For the moment the atmosphere had improved; plum trees blossomed, the land began to dry out between intermittent rain and melting snow, and the men played baseball. "Bill Jones loved his baseball!" His grandson, William Gage, celebrated Jones's enthusiasm for sports, his drinking and fighting, and his rubbing shoulders with the great and grand of his day. "He limbered up his pitching arm and many a time engaged a score of men from the 133rd —they called it stick ball then. You know that Abner Doubleday was in the same corps as [Jones]. Doubleday started the game. They played differently then; when a player got a hit, the man who caught the ball tried to hit him with it as he ran the bases. They used haversacks as bases and the ball was bigger" (personal conversation, August 1959).

Men also brought out fiddles and harmonicas to play, and music drifted among the tents on cold spring evenings. Some soldiers gathered around Chaplain Hartsock and in choral tones sang religious songs by Wyatt. After a nip of whiskey, Jones was famous for kicking up his heels in a hoedown with fellow Pennsylvanians. He became the star of the Camp Humphreys's Follies. This is documented in the etching of Jones among the men of Henry Curry's Company E of the 155th (McKenna1987, 121, 1013487). Other soldiers spent evenings reminiscing with comrades about home.

After Fredericksburg, Jones was put on picket duty, guarding the camp's perimeter from enemy incursions and sometimes dodging sniper shots. On one occasion Robert E. Lee's nephew, bushy-bearded Fitzhugh Lee, attacked the very line that Jones had been on the day before. Lee's horsemen swooped down the pike entering Falmouth itself, causing fourteen casualties and taking prisoners (Duram and Duram1979, 32, 210. During these weeks, locals infuriated Jones; they appeared to be supporters during the day but snipers by night. Some farmers were not so subtle and shouted to him on picket duty that he and all Yankees would rot in hell (Swetnam August 29, 1965, 4).

Sketch by C.F. McKenna, Co. E

"Frequent cotillions and hoe-downs were executed most gracefully in the company streets with Corporal Bob Culp of Company B, the Regimental fiddler, calling the figures. A snapshot sketch of one of these festive occasions, drawn by Regimental artist . . . in which portraits of Sergeant Walter Mc-Cab, Dick Murphy, Bill Jones, and Pat Lynn, well-known comrades, appear as forming the set in hoe-down. Professor Bob Culp is seated "rosining the bow" vigorously."

The Hoe-Down, sketch by C.F. McKenna (Co. E of 155th Regimental Association).

Section 6: Chancellorsville

The Union army still intended to take Fredericksburg. Hooker developed a sound battle plan and objectives that, if executed correctly, would outflank Lee. First, he ordered the First and Sixth Corps to hold Falmouth and, at the right moment, to attack Fredericksburg after crossing the Rappahannock. Hooker ordered the three corps of his main army north and west in a two-day, secret march to beyond the place where the shallower North Branch and Rapidan rivers come together to form the Rappahannock. The Second and Third Corps were to fake a crossing at the closer United States Ford, as a bluff to Lee to conceal Hooker's real intentions. These two corps were then to join the main force farther north and west. The army would arc back southward past Chancellor's farm to attack Lee at Fredericksburg from the west, unimpeded by the elevation of Marye's Heights.

The force left Falmouth on April 27, moving north and west along the north bank of the Rappahannock. Instead of horse-drawn wagons, Hooker used mules to carry supplies to prevent another miring in the mud should it rain. General Meade now had command of the Fifth Corps, which included Humphreys's Division. Corporal Jones marched with what remained of Allabach's Pennsylvania brigade. On April 28 the army crossed the Rappahannock at Kelly's Ford, engaging in only insignificant skirmishing when they reached the banks of the Rapidan. Rebel Jeb Stuart's cavalry carried out hit-and-run attacks that constituted more of an irritation than a threat. Significant, however, was that Stuart's men were able to capture a number of Union laggards; this was how Lee found out about Hooker's plan.

The Confederates had destroyed all the bridges over the Rapidan. When Meade's Fifth Corps reached Ely's Ford on April 29, heavy morning rains had swollen the river, and Union engineers could not plant the pontoon bridge in place until at least 11:30 a.m. Jones, the former canal man and an excellent swimmer, found no obvious place to cross, and impatient with clumsy engineers, broke ranks to test the water himself. He dashed twenty feet into the scrotum-chilling spring runoff, yelling "I'm damned if I'll wait for a bridge." Then, he tripped and fell. His face landed squarely on a submerged rock, splitting his nose. Fellow soldiers reached him and helped him across to the southern side. The rest of the corps followed, having discovered that a bridge was not necessary (Robertson 1996, 185).

A regimental surgeon, who treated Jones's broken nose and slight concussion, recommended that he spend the night in the makeshift infirmary, but Jones would have none of it. Ultimately the field hospital was established at the Chancellor farmhouse. If Jones had been interned there, he might have been taken prisoner along with twenty-one surgeons and their charges when Confederate forces swept through the Union base several days later (Krick 1995, 110). The farmhouse was the site of the eventual rout of Hooker's main force on May 3.

When Corporal Jones awoke on April 30 to a clear sky, his eyes and mind were blurry from the concussion. But he was fit and stubborn enough to march with Allabach's men to Chancellorsville. General Hooker and his retinue arrived soon thereafter to set up headquarters. General Hooker, with ninety thousand soldiers, had covered fifty miles undetected in the rainy weather.

Chancellorsville, not much more than a farmhouse and outbuildings, was midway between the place where Jones and the infantry had crossed the Rapidan to the west and the town of Fredericksburg ten miles to the east. Lee's Army of Northern Virginia, with some fifty thousand troops, was centered on Fredericksburg. His forces were thirty-five thousand fewer than his full army because Longstreet had taken the remainder to forage on the peninsula, but Hooker did not yet know this.

The farmhouse stood near the intersection of three heavily wooded roads, each a raised bed of high ground leading into Fredericksburg—River Road, the Orange Turnpike, and the Plank Road. Hooker's army advanced east along the roads; Jones's infantry under Humphreys and Meade was ordered down River Road toward Fredericksburg. Another division was to advance down the Orange Turnpike, with the Twelth Corps paralleling along the Plank Road.

At times, snipers or small groups of Southern skirmishers hidden in the deep woods drove Allabach's line back off River Road into the woods opposite. Jones later remembered a bullet kicking up mud two feet from his boot and driving him into the brush. But, as the threat of attack faded, companies regrouped and continued the march. Thick forests and dense undergrowth bordered the roads, with only a few open spots in the five miles that they marched. There is, however, a slight ridge which crosses the three roads, and the army reached it, putting troops in a defensible position and with good visibility both front and rear. It had been a deftly designed maneuver. If the Sixth Corps back at Falmouth attacked with perfect timing from across the river, Lee's army would be outflanked and in disarray. Stoneman's 7,500-man Cavalry Corps would attack Lee's rear, and raid and disrupt rail beds between Fredericksburg and Richmond, to completely defeat the Confederates as they retreated back to their capital.

About mid-afternoon and midway to Fredericksburg on May 2, the Union army halted. Some horseback riders passed Jones's brigade, hailing Allabach to cease advancing. Hooker, apparently in a loss of confidence, was inexplicably ordering the march to halt immediately and the troops to return to Chancellorsville. Until the end of his life, Jones shook his head about that moment. Something vanished in the men's spirit; Hooker had switched from offense to defense, and his hesitation gave Jackson and Lee time to act. "To this day, nobody can fathom why Hooker ordered them to stop only about three and half miles from Fredericksburg. Grandfather had another damned Burnside to answer to," my father said during one of our talks about Jones.

Now, instead of the battle line being at Fredericksburg or along the ridge, from an advantageous position, the retreat positioned Federal troops in a labyrinth, which Southern historians and Stephen Crane, in *The Red Badge of Courage*, have immortalized as the Wilderness. In these dense woodlands and mucky terrain, soldiers could lose their bearings and wander aimlessly, as many did. Many also lost their courage and fled the front lines into the maze.

In the late afternoon of May 2, 1863, rumor reached Jones's unit that a brigade on the Orange Turnpike had been under heavy artillery fire all day and that the Twelfth Corps, too, was taking heavy casualties. Digging trenches on the northwest side of Mineral Springs Road, A Company settled in, using their haversacks both as protection and as pillows for sleep. Colonel Allabach's brigade defended the north side of the road. Entrenched soldiers formed a continuous line from the Rappahannock to Chancellorsville. Arcing slightly northwest was another line two miles beyond, a dangling wing left vulnerable to an attack. That evening Corporal Jones dashed back and forth running messages from Humphreys to headquarters, then finally hunkered down on the Mineral Springs Road.

Wounded Confederate and Union soldiers alike burned to death.

In the afternoon, Lee's troops had held off the Union's frontal assault in the very location where Jones's company later bedded down. After the zenith of fiery combat, the two armies continued fighting sporadically into evening, each penetrating the other's lines. Rebel regiments continued to pressure the Federal army down both the Orange Plank Road and the Turnpike. Much later that evening General Stonewall Jackson ventured from behind his lines to assess how to surprise and assault the enemy, thereby compounding the Union defeat by driving his Confederates down to the United States Ford on the Rappahannock. This stratagem would divide Hooker's army, with Meade's Corps pushed back from Hooker at the farmhouse and no way for the Yankees to cross back over to safety. As Jackson ventured through an opening in the woods along Bullock Road, three bullets among a barrage felled the legendary soldier, mortally wounding him within a score of yards from Jones. Jackson's own troops had shot him by mistake. The great general's death was one more contributing factor to the South's ultimate defeat (Krick 1995, 107-142).

Early on May 3, Lee advanced against positions where Jones and the Fifth Corps waited at Bullock Road. An onslaught from the west, the flanking movement planned by Jackson, telescoped that Union line nearly all the way back to Chancellorsville. The Chancellor property was in chaos: wagons were broken and detached; dazed soldiers wandered aimlessly; horses entangled with artillery; the blinded and wounded lay supine upon doors dismantled from the farmhouse, with basins beneath collecting blood; and mules bearing munitions scattered in all directions.

At four in the morning, A Company was ordered to prepare for battle. As the sun rose, Jones retreated for nearly a mile through bramble and bole. Smoke from cannon muted the sun; all morning long, grape, canister, and shot screeched through the air. Cannons roared, as missiles scythed down the trees and shrubs to ragged knee-high hedges. Jones passed dead horses and men and bloody wounded who had waited all night for help. Allabach ordered his brigade to take positions along a line that would attempt to stop the Southern advance. Bill Jones had endured an icy hell at Fredericksburg under the aurora borealis and now experienced a fiery hell at Chancellorsville where the ground literally flamed. The dry leaves on the forest floor had caught fire from the explosion of thousands of shells, and the blaze quickly spread. Wounded Confederate and Union soldiers alike burned to death.

When the fire on the far right waned, Jones, eyes smarting from smoke and still dizzy and bleary-eyed, realized that his comrades were running out of ammunition. Hooker's innovation of replacing wagons that would easily mire in mud with mules for transporting munitions had seemed sound; but in the hellish firefight the sensate beasts panicked. Animals loaded with cartridges spooked and ran in all directions. The first Rebel skirmishers approached shooting before Yankee bayonets could impale them. Then Rebel soldiers in motley uniforms streamed through the smoke and clipped trees, charging and firing, as A Company troops tripped over wounded and dead in a frantic retreat. Henry Curry and Jones stumbled beyond downed trees and clusters of Union and Rebel soldiers fighting hand to hand. Trees exploded from cannon shot. Fire rose up from the ground, and soldiers who had dodged Southern bullets were engulfed in flame. Smoke hovered eight feet above the ground.

A retreating wedge of Federal troops managed to hold the Rebels; the Fifth Corps, of which A Company was a part, provided rear-guard coverage, forming a horseshoe that allowed Union headquarters to evacuate over the United States Ford to sanctuary on the north bank of the Rappahannock. Hooker, who had been injured by a falling pillar, rode in a wagon over the pontoon bridge to safety, still dazed and humiliated (Stackpole 1988, 67).

Lee's army at that stage of the battle was nearly as disorganized as Hooker's. On May 3, General Sedgwick's Sixth Corps had taken Marye's Heights in Fredericksburg, but was forced to retreat on May 4 when he advanced west, because Hooker had abandoned the battle plan. On May 4 and 5, Lee failed to deliver any large-scale assault to finish off the Union army. On May 6, Jones's regiment was the last to retreat north pursued by an army of only forty-five thousand Rebels (Duram and Duram 1979, 98). At Chancellorsville, the Union had just endured a defeat as bad, if not worse, than at Fredericksburg. Northern morale reached an all-time low.

After Chancellorsville, Jones was promoted to sergeant as his nine-month tour of duty was drawing to a close. He wrote Harriet that he would soon be home. He prepared her for a shock, describing his fall in the river and complaining about his split nose and blurred vision. He fumed about

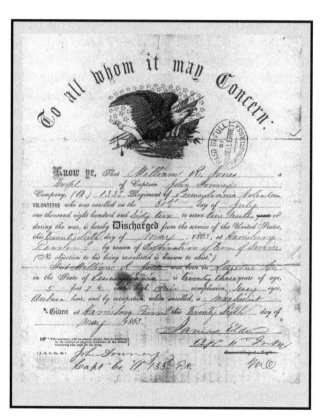

Jones musters out First Tour of Duty, May 26, 1863

54

Washington, D.C., bureaucrats; it had been learned that some fool "General Abhorson" had categorized all those in Henry Curry's 155th Regiment as serving three-year tours of duty. In reality some had signed up for only nine months, as with Jones's 133rd. The camp had gone wild until it was straightened out and those involved were notified of the mistake.

Cora Jones Gage's favorite war story about her father involved the last night of his first tour of duty. Late at night before the day of departure, that whiskey-smuggling, regimental derring-doer, with a few others from A Company, emptied cartridges of powder to mine a stretch of earth to the tent of General Humphreys. Jones over-laid cans and bottles upon the powder trail that led from the parade ground, lit a long fuse and sought cover as the fire-trail crept rapidly toward the General's tent (ibid., 102). All in earshot among the Third Division rallied in the belief that Fitzhugh Lee's cavalry was raiding again. When General Humphreys emerged from his tent, he stormed and threatened to assign the 155th to shoot every one of the sons-of-bitches of A Company in the 133rd (Maltese 1910, 145).

On May 29, Sergeant Bill Jones, and the other members of A Company arrived home to heroes' welcomes in Johnstown. Jones looked forward to immediately getting back to the Cambria Iron Works, where he soon became assistant superintendent to George Fritz. He followed in the newspapers what was unfolding at the front, as Lee pursued the Army of the Potomac north into Pennsylvania. Rumor had it that Lee's major objective was to capture and destroy the Pennsylvania Central Railroad at Pittsburgh. First, his Army of Northern Virginia would invade Altoona, with its vast store of munitions, and then Johnstown, with its iron mills and skilled workforce, on his way to destroy the Pittsburgh railhead. On June 19, the Confederate cavalry invaded McConnellsburg, thirty miles southeast of Johnstown, atop the Allegheny Mountains.

Then, to everyone's surprise, Lee instead met Meade, Humphreys, and Allabach at Gettysburg the following week from July 1- 3. Until Gettysburg, Lee had seemed invincible: thirteen months of war and heavy Union losses at Manassas, Antietam, Fredericksburg, and Chancellorsville. Shiloh had been a bright spot, but at heavy cost. Vicksburg was holding out against Grant's siege. Gettysburg constituted a cumulative *agon*, a death struggle that stopped Lee's invasion of the north. The war in the East had thus far been waged in the area between the Confederate capital at Richmond, Virginia, and Pennsylvania's capital at Harrisburg. During the Battle of Chancellorsville, Hooker's cavalry had raided south to within a few miles of Richmond. Now the Rebels had penetrated the North, approaching Harrisburg.

While Jones was fighting during the Union's most dark and desperate months, the Confederacy was negotiating with European nations for recognition of its sovereignty. Such recognition would make the North's blockade of Confederate ports an act of war against the European powers. The aristocracies of England, France, and Russia had long histories of commerce with the American South and favored the Confederacy, as slave-produced cotton undercut the price of Egyptian. If the Confederacy became an independent nation, it would signify that Europe judged as futile Lincoln's efforts to sustain the Union, a recognition that might end the war. All this changed when Lincoln emancipated the slaves. Since European countries and Mexico had long since abolished slavery, they could not now support the South against the North. After Emancipation, the Confederacy concentrated its diplomacy on instigating secession of other states and triggering discontent and treason to demoralize the North. Jones's agency with the Union League at the front and in Johnstown helped address these threats.

The fortunes of the war began to turn when the South was beaten at Gettysburg—albeit at great human cost. At the same time, Southern armies were surrendering to General Grant at Vicksburg in a second major victory for the Union. Grant had already been successful in a number of lesser battles along the Mississippi—Ft. Henry, Donelson, Shiloh. After Gettysburg and Vicksburg, Generals Humphreys and Meade were promoted; Hooker and Butterfield were demoted. Lincoln finally was recognizing and selecting able generals who would fight and win.

The Cambria Iron Works in 1863 afforded Jones new opportunities. The wartime demand for iron pushed the works to daily double shifts of twelve hours, providing full employment and optimal production. Jones quickly paid off personal debts incurred during his nine-month tour and helped his father-in-law with the household's growing financial demands. The Lloyd's second daughter, Eileen Lewis, had just given birth to a son, and her husband William, working full time, was at last able to establish financial independence.

At the same time, Bill Jones's family was a grave concern to him. While he had been at the front, Harriet had not had an easy time. Her father's church was struggling, and her own physical appearance began to change: her white shoulders and arms lost their tone. Unknown to the family for many years, she was experiencing the first symptoms of multiple sclerosis, a malady that would leave her bedridden for the last ten years of her life. Nonetheless, Jones continued to marvel at his wife's erudition and form; she, in turn, embraced the ruggedness and natural ability of her Yankee, so scorned by the belles back in Chattanooga. These concerns were temporarily suspended when on June 4, 1864, Harriet gave birth to a healthy baby boy, William Milo Coulter Jones, to be known as Will.

Section 7: Second Tour of Duty

Jones faced a daunting year in 1864. Though the Confederate Army no longer was a danger to Pennsylvania, it still threatened the Federal government in Washington, D.C. Just as ominous was the menacing unrest caused by the antiwar, anti-Union element of the Democratic Party, whose region of strength was western Pennsylvania, Ohio, Illinois, and Indiana. Politically, Lincoln faced serious challengers, not only from General George McClellan, a Democrat and the former commander at the Battle of Antietam, but from inside his own party.

Months had passed, and the war crept on. Lincoln had brought Grant, the victor of Vicksburg, east in March 1864 as general-in-chief of the army. Republican governors and representatives from Connecticut to California worried about Lincoln's Conscription Act of 1863. The president had instituted the draft due to the enormous unfilled quotas of volunteers necessary to fight the war. Many believed this conscription jeopardized the Republican Party's chances in the1864 national elections. In New York City a thousand were killed or wounded in draft riots, with several Negroes lynched. In all states the Order of the Golden Circle effectively disrupted recruiting offices. Yet Union soldiers overwhelmingly supported both the draft and Lincoln. Nonetheless, Lincoln himself feared that McClellan, who was running on a Peace Democrat platform that called for a truce with the South, would win the election (Gray 1942, 179).

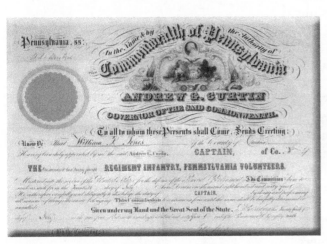

Jones musters out Second Tour of Duty, July 20, 1864

In May, General Burnside, now commander of the Department of the Ohio, arrested a former Democratic congressman, Clement Vallandigham, who had spent his tenure in Washington as the voice of the antiwar Democrats and the noxious Copperheads. After a military trial, Vallandigham was found guilty of seditious statements to obstruct recruiting in Ohio. The verdict ignored the principle of free speech. Lincoln, worrying that Vallandigham might be seen as a Southern martyr, commuted the sentence but dispatched him to the Confederacy (ibid., 146).

Vallandigham escaped to Canada, where he plotted secession for the northwestern states. The Ohio Democrats at their state convention unanimously nominated Vallandigham, rather than McClellan, as their candidate for the presidency. Indeed, it was on Vallandigham's platform that McClellan ran his national campaign.

Ohio Republicans, fearing the Copperheads' increasing strength in the state's Democratic Party, considered nominating Salmon P. Chase, formerly in Lincoln's cabinet, as a

Republican alternative to Lincoln. In Connecticut, the Peace Democrats nominated for governor Colonel Thomas Seymour, who said:

> while we denounce the heresy of secession . . ., the time has now arrived when all true lovers of the Constitution are ready to abandon the "monstrous fallacy" that the Union can be restored by armed hands alone; and we are anxious to inaugurate such action, honorable alike to the contending sections, as will stop the ravages of war, avert universal bankruptcy, and unite all the States upon terms of equality as members of a Confederacy. (Ingham 1991, 237 n10)

The Republicans held their national convention in Baltimore, Maryland, in early June. Dissenting politicians put forth the names of Chase, Frémont, and Butler, but by the time the convention was actually held, Lincoln's renomination was a certainty. His political genius and military successes had held the party together.

In the second week of July 1864, Confederate general Jubal Early surprised a country wearied of war with a dashing raid on the edge of Washington, D. C. On July 9, he soundly defeated General Lew Wallace at the Battle of Monocacy, east of Baltimore and north of Washington, D. C. Despite significant victories in the South by generals Grant and Sherman, Early's penetration into Northern territory jarred Bill Jones into action. At Cambria members of Jones's patriotic Union League had begun to rally the workers. There was talk again of enlisting.

On July 19, President Lincoln issued a call for a half-million volunteers.

When Abraham Lincoln was targeted for assassination, Allan E. Pinkerton foiled the plot and later became Lincoln's security agent.

For the second time in his life, when his president requested volunteers, Jones took only two days to enlist, and, on July 22 an entire company of close to one hundred men followed him for a tour of duty of one hundred days. This time the ceremony was at the U. S. recruiting office in Johnstown; in uniform with the tinkle of epaulettes and martial music, Jones was sworn in with the rank of captain of F Company of Emergency Men, the 194th Regiment of the Pennsylvania Veteran Volunteers (Manakee 1959, 29). His friend and co-worker Filius Heyer was second lieutenant.

The 194th Regiment, which included Jones's company, was first stationed at Mankin's Woods near Baltimore for provost and garrison duty. Baltimore was a hotbed of secessionism. As the November 8 election approached, the city seethed. The upper classes hated the many Union regiments stationed around the city. At balls, debutantes giggled at their own craftiness, smuggling swords and pistols beneath their petticoats past soldiers on provost duty to cutthroats hiding down at the waterfront. Then came the news of Atlanta's fall to General Sherman on September 1, which contributed greatly to Lincoln's re-election. Even in the divided city of Baltimore, and appearances to the contrary, Lincoln actually increased Baltimore's Republican vote in 1864.

On September 1, the 194th moved to Camp Carroll, a mile southwest of Baltimore, and was assigned to the command of General Wallace. For a month Jones's company performed provost duty in the city, patrolling, escorting, and guarding prisoners on their way through Baltimore and, in reverse, reserves and recruits from the North disembarking for the front.

Being stationed near Baltimore as provost allowed Jones to bring Harriet and the children from Johnstown to Baltimore. For a brief period they enjoyed their new life; Harriet's state of mind and health improved, as she felt more at home in fashionable Baltimore than in sooty Johnstown. But soon she began having spells of weakness and her mood grew increasingly gloomy as three-year old Ella experienced trouble breathing and lost noticeable weight. In contrast, young Will was strong, restless, and energetic. Later in life Harriet admitted that she had hoped to find in Baltimore a social life similar to what she had left in Tennessee, but she quickly realized her mistake when she encountered ridicule as the Yankee's wife. War-weary Baltimore was nothing like antebellum Chattanooga.

In 1861 Maryland's legislature voted fifty-three to thirteen against secession, although in the 1860 presidential election only 2,204 of 92,441 Maryland voters voted to elect Abraham Lincoln as president. Later that year, as the newly elected president was passing through Baltimore en route to Washington, he was targeted for assassination. Allan E. Pinkerton foiled the plot and later became Lincoln's security agent. Should Baltimore be taken militarily by the South, Washington, D.C., would be isolated from the North. Baltimore's pivotal position was a constant worry to Lincoln for the duration of the war.

Jones despised the frivolity of Baltimore's wealthy, men who dodged combat by paying poor lads to take bullets for them while remaining in Baltimore to play agents provocateurs. On October 10, Jones was transferred from the 194th to be captain of an Independent Company of the Pennsylvania 97th Regiment; members were men from the Pennsylvania 193rd and 194th regiments, whose one hundred day enlistments had expired. He burned to see action rather than police the city and repeatedly badgered General Wallace for a transfer to the Expeditionary Forces for the assault on Fort Fisher in North Carolina. But, speaking for Wallace, Colonel John Wooly rejected Jones's request: ". . . the best interest of the service is for Captain Jones to remain in his command" (Jones, "Biographical Sketch", LC, 45722). The majority of Jones's original company was mustered out on November 6.

After Early's victory at Monocacy Junction, near Frederick, Maryland, the divided citizens of Baltimore increasingly expressed their frustrations: Unionists hailed Federal troops as saviors; secessionists continued to disrupt Lincoln's war by cutting telegraph lines, derailing trains, and smuggling weapons to collaborators. Captain Jones spent the remainder of his tour of duty securing Union communications and facilitating transportation on the roads and rails that crossed Maryland to Washington, D.C. Andrew Carnegie, who later hired Jones to run his first mill, had, as an employee of the Pennsylvania Railroad, worked on the routing of some of those rails and wires in the first months of the war, but had then paid another to serve in his stead in the army. Carnegie spent the war years out of harm's way.

On April 9, 1865, word reached Baltimore that Lee had surrendered at Appomattox. The streets were full of Union supporters and despairing backers of secession. Jubilant, Captain Jones wired his boss, George Fritz, at Cambria: "Lee has met his boss at Appomattox" ("An old friend").

Captain Jones succeeded admirably with the Independent Company, drilling them daily, training his infantry into crack troops that were Wallace's pride: Wallace recognized in Jones's company what he referred to as "one of the finest drilled companies in the service." At Monument Square in Baltimore, Jones and his myrmidons competed against other troops of the Union Army, defeating in competitive drill the most illustrious companies of the Army of the Potomac (*Contemporary Biography*, 128). In this competition among the ten companies, Jones' company ranked first, and he was presented with the regimental sword.

Some days later, following an afternoon drilling his Independent Company, Captain Jones, while having dinner late in the evening, was informed by cries from the street that Lincoln had been shot. Little Will was sleeping in a basinet near the dining room table, and Harriet dozed in the adjacent bedroom. The Captain, hearing a dirge from a gathering crowd, left the building to see people he knew in the street, muddy from an evening shower. Lincoln had been wounded and might not live! Staggered, Jones returned to the apartment. He did not tell Harriet immediately. He judged such news was best learned when the body is refreshed after slumber. He found surcease in Shakespeare's *Julius Caesar*, reading Anthony's speech mourning Caesar. But Confederate general Joe Johnston had still not surrendered; after Sherman's victory at Bentonville, Johnston finally surrendered in late April 1865. In less than two months, on June 17, 1865, Jones would be mustered out of service, and the family would return to Johnstown.

Bill Jones had entered the Civil War the week of the firing on Fort Sumter. That week as a civilian he torched the Federal Armory at Harpers Ferry to prevent General Kenton Harper of the Virginia militia from commandeering weapons. He fought in two of the Union's bloodiest and most demoralizing losses at Fredericksburg and Chancellorsville, and he concluded the war policing a city that had been problematic to the Union since Lincoln's winning the presidency in 1860. Captain Bill Jones had redefined himself from a Democrat supporting emancipation and the Union to a lifelong Republican who would rally an ethnically diverse workforce in work, play, and patriotic and civic responsibility. He would, in a very original and personal manner, learn from his military experience and adapt the leadership skills he observed to lead workers and steel makers in a new industry. By the turn of the century, author James Howard Bridge credited both Jones and Henry Curry as among "the men who really founded [Andrew Carnegie's empire], Saved it from early Disaster and won its First Success."

Chapter 2 Sections

CHAPTER 2

JOHNSTOWN

Section 8: Cambria Works

Johnstown is located deep in the Allegheny Front Range of southwestern Pennsylvania. Here the Little Conemaugh and Stony Creek rivers join in the steep gorges at Johnstown to form the Conemaugh, just as further west the Allegheny and Monongahela form the Ohio. Over the millennia these waterways have cut deeply into the surrounding hogback ridges, creating a valley that darkened so early in the day that it caused wiseacres to say that in Johnstown the sun rose at ten and set at three. On into the mid-twentieth century, the mills filled the air above the valley with smelting fumes and the rivers below with liquid wastes—sulfides and soot—that washed down to the Mississippi. The valley trapped particles from factories and smoke from houses so that a gray-white smog ascended the valley to mushroom out and create a low-lying overcast that capped, at times, the highest hogbacks. Framed wooden houses with splintered clapboard sidings sat upon stone foundations, separated by stake fences ankle-deep in weeds. Viewed from a distance, the dwellings clustered asymmetrically, appearing to creep up the hogback slopes. Cora Jones Gage always remembered her mother's contempt for the place.

Mary Lloyd, Harriet Lloyd's mother.

(1893)

Johnstown in the 1860s was a good-sized small city of seven to eight thousand inhabitants, most of the men working at the Cambria Iron Works, with the woolen mills employing several hundred. The iron works had flourished filling government orders during the Civil War. Earlier in the century the town had been little more than a few dwellings until the construction of a canal had given the location its first real asset: a means of transportation that linked East with West. Through a complicated series of locks, boats were hoisted over the Alleghenies and then sailed their way down the Ohio to the Mississippi, dropping off thousands of immigrants, who landed on the banks and struck off for the West (Schweikart 1989, 290). The canals operated from 1838 until the beginning of the Civil War, when the Pennsylvania Railroad rendered the canal system obsolete. In the late 1850s Bill Jones had been a raftsman working this section of the system and parts of the Ohio River, so he knew the region well. He fished and hunted in the forests stretching up toward the lake at South Fork and as far away as Loretto, twenty miles to the northeast (Hessen 1975, 5-9).

The Cambria Iron Works had started out as several charcoal-fired forges in the 1840s, one among the many small works scattered throughout the western Pennsylvania countryside. Major investments were then made to convert the furnaces into the more productive coke-fired types, which enabled much higher temperatures. It was John Fritz, with his brother George, whose design and mechanical know-how consolidated the varied components of the ore operations into a complete mill. John Fritz was its superintendent until 1860—in charge of operations. In 1855, Daniel Morrell came from Philadelphia to the Johnstown mill as part-owner and general manager. He had been a highly successful dry goods merchant, and his mandate from the company's Philadelphia investors was to methodically organize and financially stabilize their faltering investment at Cambria (Brown 1989). He more than succeeded at Johnstown: Morrell greatly expanded the plant and its production capabilities and was among the earliest barons who slowly shaped a more hierarchical structure of management and responsibility in factories. Cambria, and therefore Johnstown, grew and prospered, to become one of the most important American iron and steel producing plants of the late nineteenth century.

The iron works had attracted immigrants to work in the mills, primarily from Wales and Germany, in addition to many American-born Welsh and Germans, and they remained the town's dominant ethnic groups throughout the nineteenth century. Many residents spoke two languages, and Johnstown published newspapers in both German and Welsh, as well as English.

While their husbands had been at war, Harriet Jones and Gertrude Heyer spent many hours together. Gertrude had been born in Germany and was as well-read as Harriet, born in France. Harriet preferred speaking French, though it was not her native language, and Gertrude also spoke French fluently. Harriet, who had lived in France for much of her childhood, was considered a bit of a "Frenchified" Southern belle, for she spoke with an accent and had a "continental" air about her, which Bill loved. Her parents, the Lloyds, stood out from the locals. Reverend Lloyd dressed in tweed, and his wife, Mary, in feathered hats, and they had acquired Southern accents during their fourteen years in Tennessee. The three "foreigners" from the South raised eyebrows of many at the mill who, during the war, supported the Union and judged the abolitionist couple by appearances only. Dan Gage much later emphasized how deeply ingrained racism was, even in Johnstown, recalling that Reverend Lloyd had lost a number of his congregation when he asserted, during a Sunday service, his abolitionist convictions that freeing the slaves would not rectify past racial injustice. Reflecting later, Lloyd reasoned that some Negroes might enter heaven and some whites might be shut out (Margaret Gage, personal communication).

When he returned to Johnstown at war's end, Bill, with his wit and raucous ways and his know-how, boundless energy, and strong work ethic, became the assistant to George Fritz. George had taken over when his brother John had moved on to Bethlehem Iron Company in 1860. Bill Jones was clearly a young man on the move.

Less than a year after the family returned to Johnstown, the Jones's four-year-old daughter, Ella, died from a respiratory infection. They buried the child in Grand View Cemetery. Harriet sobbed inconsolably through the night. Years later, Jones would describe his bereaved wife, sipping valerian for her grief and her chronic condition, complaining how wrong the wartime move to the damp seaboard at Baltimore had been and how wasted her own life had become on returning to bleak, smoke-stricken Johnstown.

In 1867, Harriet gave birth to a healthy baby girl, Cora, who became the apple of her father's eye. But Harriet's second and third pregnancies and carrying hefty offspring weakened her, and her health again deteriorated. Family friends and chroniclers have contrasted Bill Jones, the working man's model in the mills, whose quick temper and ribald language made their point and generally got results, with the man at home, where Jones displayed a patience and gentleness with his wife that inspired just as much admiration as did his spiritedness at work (Bridge 1991, 188).

Frequently Jones and the Lloyds brightened Harriet's spirits with a Sunday carriage ride. Sometimes they would travel upstream to Stony Creek River for a swim. For longer outings, they would ascend fourteen miles to the South Fork dam and reservoir, built from 1849 to 1853 to supply water for the Pennsylvania Mainland Canal. Bill had swum in the reservoir during his raftsman days, and the lake was a favorite fishing and boating spot. The Pennsylvania Railroad had bought the abandoned site in 1862; that same year there was a break in the discharge pipes. Because the dam was only half full, there had been some damage along the river in hamlets just below the dam but nothing serious in Johnstown. However, over time, the dam deteriorated because of complete neglect (McCullough 1887, 727).

Section 9: The Tyrant and the Crank

In the mid-1800s any given step in the ironmaking process was relatively independent of the others. The raw ore passed through a series of interdependent but semi-autonomous stations during which amorphous ore was transformed into iron, and was then rolled and cut to produce railroad tracks, which were in high demand after the war as railroads expanded across the continent and into the Northern and Southern states.

Mill work was extremely dangerous, requiring working with heated metals and unpredictable steam-powered machinery in crowded sheds. At any stage mechanical failure, explosions, or carelessness could result in life-changing accidents or even death. Every year there were deaths and permanent disabilities among the workers, causing great hardship and even destitution for the families involved. Mill towns were notorious for their squalid living conditions and lack of sanitary infrastructure, and Johnstown, in the early years, was no exception.

Like bakers of bread, puddlers heated and boiled the ingredients— iron ore, fuel, and shale.

After the war there were forty-eight furnaces at Cambria, making it one of the largest companies in the country. Mill operations ran under the charge of the superintendent and his assistant who were selected for their mechanical expertise as well as their abilities to lead and supervise men. Foremost among the workmen were puddlers, highly skilled craftsmen who worked and essentially managed the individual furnaces in the mill. Like bakers of bread, puddlers heated and boiled the ingredients—iron ore, fuel, and shale—sculpting the mass to remove impurities, then judged when the molten mass was ready for kneading. With long rods, they stirred and shaped sixty or one hundred pound dough-like balls into a consistent malleable mixture of slag and wrought iron. Puddlers earned fees for tonnage produced. As the workers who earned the highest wages and shouldered the most responsibility in the mill, they carried a good deal of authority. They also worked with a great deal of independence. Each puddler had one or two assistants who alternately tapped the liquefied ore and coke from the furnace and drained it into the sow, a trough that branched from this umbilical groove into twelve or thirty parallel molds in which the iron cooled as pig ingots or pig iron. Poorly puddled iron could crust open under pressure, resulting in loss of time, lower wages, and maybe injury. If the crew had "wrought" the iron artfully, it would compress into a strong solid mass.

Each team in the iron production process independently charged fees directly to the mill. The head of the team would divide his payment among those he supervised. Since the puddler earned the most from each iron heat, he set the pace, aiming at tapping six heats per furnace during the twelve- or sometimes fourteen-hour shifts. In the later years of Morrell's tenure at Cambria, sliding scale fees based on tonnage were changed to hourly wages. This change was a major and irreversible modification in labor and management relationships: it badly and permanently eroded workers', but especially puddlers', power, as well as their economic well-being, although they still collected their monthly checks dressed in their Sunday best black suits, starched white shirts, and ties.

At the station beyond the puddlers, the iron was reheated and then passed through a set of rollers, like clothes in a wringer washer, while workers with cranes grasped the hot slab and guided it above through a third roller. The metal bars were then reheated and bonded together. These bars were now ready for any of many distinctly grooved rollers that shaped various iron products.

At Cambria in 1857, John Fritz had designed the country's first three-high rolls, an invention that produced more and higher-quality rails (ibid., 262), and after the Civil War, the Cambria mill specialized in rails. Jones was hired in 1859, and the two worked together for only a short period before Jones was sent to Tennessee. In 1860 John Fritz left Cambria to become general manager and superintendent at Bethlehem, where he had a distinguished career, particularly in Bessemer rail production and battleship armor.

Years later, Cora told her sons that a puddler named James O'Neill was a source of constant annoyance to Jones during his years at Cambria. In August of 1863, O'Neill became piqued at Captain Bill for getting his friend, the veteran Filius Heyer, a job at the furnaces. The Irish had gained control of the puddling craft, reflecting the tendency for particular ethnic groups to dominate specific work specialties. Jones, however, convinced Fritz of the advantage of an integrated team at all workstations. He observed that men from Croatia and other Eastern European countries, cumulatively known as Hungarians or Hunkies, were entering the workforce and believed that he could integrate and bond together diverse nationalities via sportive competition that would carry over into work (Jones 1881, 37). He organized the men into baseball teams and other leagues outside of work; there were also trips to the horse races. These policies, which Jones practiced throughout his managerial career and passed on to protégés such as John Potter and Charles Schwab, were among his great and lasting contributions to management-labor relations.

Puddlers like James O'Neill attacked both the new basis for wages and new technology that cut time and labor, complaining that such inventions took money out of workers' pockets (Fitch 1989, 90-107). This was completely true, because the iron industry was changing in a very basic way, with money and power transferring from skilled workers to the managers of workers and to investors, the managers of money. Work was also being restructured into a more hierarchical system, with those making the product forming the very wide bottom of the pyramid and a very few executives and financiers at the top, making policy. Good middle managers, with their understanding of machinery, the ironmaking process, and labor were extremely hard to come by. Captain Bill, Robert Hunt, and the Fritz brothers were just such men, and during these transition years in the industry they were the key to its success, a fact that has been consistently overlooked by writings on this period.

The rapid development of new technologies and the evolving understanding of metallurgy required constant investment in costly, short-lived equipment. The requirement for constant infusions of money and technology made inventors and capitalists essential to each mill's success as well as that of the industry. John Fritz's three-high rolls eventually became the industry standard in the United States. The more complex machinery also required workers with mechanical abilities to adjust and maintain them. The average worker's responsibility became narrower and narrower—one step in a long, seamless process.

During the Civil War there had been great demand for iron but a short supply of skilled workers, conditions that enabled workers to make good money. After the war, labor was cheap with so many veterans looking for work, and employers set mill wage scales as low as possible. Workers were entirely dependent on the mill and usually in debt to it, which kept them there in a type of debt servitude. There were few other options for employment or purchase of basic goods in the region, the woolen mills being a notable exception.

Many individuals in the iron industry, both in the United States and Europe, were experimenting as they produced wrought iron—searching for a stronger, more consistent product, hotter and larger furnaces, and for a way to make steel in larger quantities. In the late 1840s, William Kelly had established an iron business with his brother in the isolated area of Eddyville, Kentucky. The local iron ore was high in impurities, which produced a low-quality iron. Kelly had earlier received some training in science and mechanics at the Western University of Pennsylvania in Pittsburgh, and this background may have led him to experiment with processes designed to produce a higher quality iron. He found that blowing cold air into the molten ore caused oxygen to combine with the carbon impurities, which blew them off and yielded a higher quality metal. Kelly called his new process air boiling. He doused cold air from the clay-lined pipe down into a boiling cauldron of iron. Red, lava-like clods splashed out of the vessel. Kelly was fearless and attacked them with a mallet, swatting each brick-sized loaf as it landed on the ground to see if it crumbled like a cookie, which at first most did. With enough "air boiling the brew to nature," the clods became more malleable, flattening like fresh bread dough. This indicated quality iron, and probably some steel. One of his 1857 demonstrations in the yard turned into a tornado of sparks that set three wooden buildings ablaze, an event that came to be known as Kelly's Fireworks. Because of great variation in ore quality and furnace temperatures, Kelly's experiments were highly inconsistent, and, in at least a few instances, produced low-quality steel. Throughout the 1850s he incurred substantial debt by continuing his experimentation while at the same time trying to run an iron-producing operation. He borrowed heavily from his father and father-in-law to stay in business. Kelly's air boiling, however, became well-known in American ironmaking circles.

In 1856, Daniel Morrell, curious about Kelly's experiments and their potential, invited him to conduct experiments in the Cambria yard and partially financed him, intermittently, for nearly five years. Morrell assigned a young worker named James Geer to assist him. Kelly was after a quality of metal stronger than iron and less likely to shatter like stale bread. That was the problem with puddled or worked iron; it was brittle, and it had limited strength. Nearly everybody at the Cambria works—and among American ironworkers generally—regarded Kelly as the Irish Crank.

Kelly was well-known to the Jones family, and stories about the eccentric, taciturn inventor have been passed down the generations. He was a small man who had a pet rooster, which he referred to as a dog with feathers. Kelly spoke in short bursts of speech, as if he had too much on his mind and not enough time to funnel thought into coherent sentences. Cora recalled Kelly saying "Morrell's a Quaker, who don't know a tinker's damn about working metal. There's three reasons to know your steel: First, Kelly air-boiled iron is the foundation of the future, and second, this pneumatic steel will be for mankind what copper was to the Egyptian." Cora joked about Kelly losing a reason, because he'd announce three reasons for any point and get through only two.

Kelly had a small rotary converter built in Europe, and in 1861 he apparently conducted a successful experiment at Cambria. Kelly ultimately used the patents from his inventions as collateral on loans from his father, with whom he did not have a good relationship. When his father died, he left his entire estate—including the patents—to Kelly's sisters, who shared most of the neighbors' disparaging opinion that their brother, the inventor and poor businessman, was crazy. According to Uncle Dan, it was William Kelly who first urged Jones to patent anything and everything he ever invented. And it was Kelly who initially impressed on Captain Bill the importance of developing a stratagem that would give him personal financial independence and make him invaluable in the iron/steel business.

A dozen years after Kelley had first processed air-boiled steel, sometime in the 1850s, an Englishman named Henry Bessemer designed an efficient converter in which he blew cold air through the molten iron ore, a process that produced steel with results similar to Kelly's, and which he patented in England. Bessemer had traveled to Paris to promote his invention in weaponry, a cigar-shaped missile propelled from cast iron cannons. Commander Claude Minié, an officer of Napoleon III, helped Bessemer test-fire his weapon at Vincennes. Minié feared that when launching Bessemer's missiles the stress of the explosion would jeopardize the iron cannons. That concern motivated Bessemer to develop his process for producing gross steel, a far stronger material than iron, possibly by plagiarizing Kelly's invention (McHugh 1980, 79). Englishmen had been present at Kelly's 1846 trials, and there were accusations that Bessemer stole Kelly's discovery.

When Bessemer's representatives tried to file patents in the U.S., Kelly learned about it, filed a patent claim, and documented that he was using the process many years earlier than Bessemer. Kelly's process—the air boiling—was awarded priority by the U.S. Patent Office, but Bessemer's converter, in which the process was stabilized, was also patented. After competing for years under various incorporations, in 1866 the two inventors' representatives merged their patents into one company, the Pneumatic Steel Association, and decided to use Bessemer's name. Kelly, who had ceased to be an active participant in steel production, grew increasingly isolated and resented the use of Bessemer's name for a process that he had discovered first.

Bessemer's technology was clearly superior to Kelly's, but despite the new process and converter, there were still problems with impurities in the product they produced. Ore from different locations contained many different elements, such as sulphur, phosphorus, and silicon that were impurities that weakened the product. Iron in furnaces could not be fired enough to be rid of these impurities. Even steel produced in Bessemer's sphinx retained oxygen at the end of a blow. Robert Mushet, a young Scotsman, solved the problem by adding manganese, a measured carbon compound from Germany called spielgeisen, back into the molten ore. The spielgeisen combined with the impurities, which worked to wring out the last traces, strengthened the ore, and allowed it to harden. In the end, the three inventors, in three separate experiments, had found a way to produce a consistent quality product. Mushet was barely recognized for his contribution. Bessemer, with the financial help of associates, built a steelworks at Sheffield that was able to produce steel far more cheaply than England's other mills; eventually his competitors were forced to buy his patent, from which he received considerable royalties. His name was then and now associated with the pneumatic conversion process. Kelly, alone among these inventors, renewed his patent for the pneumatic process for seven years in 1870 and continued to receive royalties. None of these inventors, however, became wealthy, as would the capitalists who amassed fortunes from use of their inventions.

Daniel Morrell first witnessed the production of steel while on a trip to the Wyandotte Works in Michigan in 1864. When he returned to Cambria, Morrell wanted to produce gross steel, not crucible steel. The production of crucible steel, used primarily to make swords and knives, had changed little since the time of Aristotle. The pneumatic method enabled the production of large volumes of gross steel used for railroad tracks, for bridge girders, for structural steel, for buildings, and for modern armor. John and George Fritz and Bill Jones designed for Morrell the new furnaces for producing steel and iron, among the very earliest in the United States.

Morrell's goal was to increase productivity and to cut costs, of which labor was a significant expense. He looked for ways to reduce wages independent of the prevailing price of rails, to enable purchase of new, state-of-the art machinery. As general manager, Morrell clashed with George Fritz, who, like Jones, was somewhat sympathetic to labor. George had lost parts of his right hand working iron some years before. He carried out orders grimly as Morrell sought to increase profits by paying wages based on hours rather than on tonnage from "heats out of the furnaces" (Brown 1989, 87).

Morrell believed Fritz should not allow his assistant to take his crew off to the horse races or break out a ball and bat for a game when they finished a job, practices he considered frivolous. However, he could not dispute Jones's popularity with the workers, nor the productivity Jones achieved with his men. Jones disapproved of Morrell's policy of first making workers accept low wages and then charging them high fees for essentials like housing and groceries (Harris 1883-84, 599-600).

By the early 1870s Morrell ran the most productive, profitable iron works in the United States. He

Daniel Morrell was among the earliest barons who shaped a hierarchical structure of management in factories.

(Mathew Brady [Public domain], via Wikimedia Commons, 1865-1880)

> *Jones organized the men into baseball teams and other leagues outside of work; there were also trips to the horse races.*

drafted commandments that he would read out loud standing before an assembled work force. Bill Jones was there the day Morrell broadcasted: "Any employee helping himself to an arm's full of wood violates the fourteenth commandment and, if apprehended, would have the cost of an entire cord deducted from his pay." If one objected to unreasonable punishment, that person could be fired. Anyone fired had to vacate his company house, which Morrell personally inspected, citing damages to company property. Morrell's fifteenth commandment stated the company could deduct nearly every cent the man was due for wages if he damaged company property. Uncle Dan many years later recalled how Cora had threatened her misbehaving sons with punishment for violating Morrell's sixth commandment, pertaining to insubordination (Townsend 1874, 6 April). Versions of Morrell's commandments became standard Gage family dictums and codes.

Morrell was highly successful in keeping the unions that were increasingly representing mill workers in other establishments out of the Cambria Iron Works, and Cambria remained a nonunion operation longer than any other mill in the country. Morrell's famous ninth commandment unequivocally curtailed a workers' independence by stating: "Any assembly of laborers discussing unionization or of belonging to a secret society would be fired." An ex-worker could be blacklisted from all iron works in the country. Such policies deterred resistance to the growing centralization of management and to the linkage of wages to the price of steel.

Although wages were low in Johnstown, the city had a hospital where Cambria Iron Works employees were treated for free. There were public schools and a library. Company-owned frame houses were solidly built, but Cambria, the only choice in town, charged high rents and high prices for goods sold at the company-owned store. In addition to his control of the mill, Daniel Morrell virtually ran Johnstown until his death: he was president of the waterworks, two of the local banks, and the gas company.

In the iron and steel industry at the time, there had been an unspoken agreement between owners and workers that wages would fluctuate depending on market conditions (Krass 2002, 213). But in Johnstown, Morrell's policies worked to erode this harmony and focused almost exclusively on productivity and profits. When he had been a machinist, Jones had provided a balance between these two competing interests. He tinkered with designs for apparatuses to cool rollers and fashioned more efficient nozzles for steam, technologies that both cut costs and improved the safety and comfort of workers. He knew that his efforts earned profits and could provide workers with great benefits.

In the early 1870s, Captain Bill hired John Potter, only fourteen years old, young enough to be his son. Indeed, Potter became like a son to him. When Jones had had his fill of the likes of O'Neill and Morrell, the two often found their way to California Tom's bar, Johnstown's favorite watering hole. Towel in hand, Tom served up for Jones and his protégé a schooner of beer and a shot of whiskey on the marble bar —a puddler's cocktail, today's boilermaker. Jones also hired William W. McCleary, one year younger than Potter, who was to become his right-hand man. Both Potter and McCleary followed Jones to Braddock a few years later.

Inventors in the Gilded Age generally did not fare well financially. On one hand an inventor might improve technology for greater productivity, but such changes usually channeled profits into the owners' pockets with little or no financial benefit for labor or the inventor himself. Fritz; Jones; Alexander Holley, Cora's godfather; and Potter, her future landlord in Los Angeles, were inventors—their inventions often solved practical day-to-day problems in mill work, but they also permitted great advances in industry. Potter invented the forty-eight-inch slab mill that reduced work and earned profits to which only the company was entitled, because he had failed to patent his invention. Much later, when the Gage and Potter families lived in the same house in Los Angeles, Uncle Dan was weaned on conversations with John Potter about royalties and rewards, mill management, patents, and profits (Gage 1961, 1-9).

Jones, as assistant to George Fritz, eventually earned enough at Cambria for the family to live comfortably again, with several servants to help with the household. For years Harriet grieved Ella's passing, experienced fainting spells, and complained of heart murmurs. The doctor prescribed laudanum, a drug that improved her spirits but is addictive. Six-year-old Will was as big as some twelve-year-olds and rambunctious as his father had been. Young Cora was a protected, spoiled child, but bright and precocious. Mary Lloyd looked after her ailing daughter, Harriet, and Will and Cora were reared as much by their grandmother as their mother, because Harriet was often too ill to tend to the children and the duties of running a large household. Mary also helped Eileen, whose husband, William Lewis, worked with the troublesome James O'Neill at the iron furnaces.

Two events were soon to change the direction of Jones's career, his introduction to Alexander Holley and Morrell's failure to appreciate his genius.

Section 10: Holley's College of Steel

John Fritz's 1857 invention of the three-high rail mill had partially mechanized the production of iron rails, dramatically increasing Cambria's productivity and reducing the amount of labor needed in rolling rails. Two years later, rails produced at Cambria and Bethlehem stretched west across the continent to meet rails coming east at Promontory Point. The track linking the coasts was made entirely of iron. George Fritz, in the 1860s, had turned Cambria into a blooming mill, one in which ingots are reduced to slats and other shapes. But primarily, Cambria produced rails.

Puddlers like James O'Neill had wrestled and squeezed steaming slag and iron, working out pockets of carbon and kneading the wrought material into large ingots, which were then rolled to produce firm iron rails. Many of these rails, however, contained pocketed flaws. An iron track lasted only about nine months until its tensile strength gave out—collapsing, snaking, and twisting under the pressure of passing railroad cars. Iron rails were a dangerous hazard if not regularly replaced. With the adaptation of steel for rails, bonded molecules ensured greater endurance and safety, lasting years of heavy-duty transit rather than months.

Daniel Morrell had visited most of the other iron and steel plants in the country by 1869; he was eager to expand and improve the Cambria mill to produce the more durable, valuable metal for railroad tracks. Initially Morrell shipped in steel ingots from the Pennsylvania Steel Works in Harrisburg for blooming and finishing rails. The core of the Cambria plant had to be reconstructed so the mill could produce steel. Reheating ingots of steel, which are then pressed and cut into steel rails, required more sturdy rollers and more soundly built beds than similar machinery for iron. Jones repaired and improved upon many of the boxes and frames supporting the expensive rollers. With each new improvement, the role of workers was modified.

Until 1890 nearly every institution of higher education in the United States, with the exception of military institutes, educated only preachers and teachers. If one wanted to learn about engineering, one labored at a works. Soon after the war, Cambria became the unofficial college of steel in the United States; the "dean" at Cambria, as well as at the ten other mills that produced steel, was Alexander Holley, the primary mover behind the conversion of America's iron industry into one of steel and the foremost authority on Kelly-Bessemer mills, brought to Cambria to design and install state-of-the-art Bessemer equipment in 1869. He became a mentor to Bill Jones, as well as to Robert Hunt, Daniel Jones, and a number of other talented, ambitious young men working there. In later years, they were all to become either superintendents or managers at the country's largest mills—and remained lifelong friends.

Alexander Holley was the son of a former governor of Connecticut, who had wanted his son to study the classics at Yale. The young Holley chose instead a more practical education in science at Brown University (McHugh 1980, 63). Holley was a dashing, hard-drinking engineer who welcomed nearly all to his counsel. He was a prolific writer; he had written poetry, novels, and many articles on engineering. As a journalist, he published in the *Atlantic Monthly* and in every major scientific and engineering periodical of the time and wrote many definitions in the lexicon of steel for *Webster's Dictionary*.

During the 1850s and 1860s, Holley had worked on and written about European factories and technology. He was a skilled draftsman. He evaluated the ways in which the change from wood to metal had affected locomotives, trains, and ships used in modern travel. The financial backers of the *Monitor*, the Union ironclad in the Civil War, sent Holley to Sheffield, England, to meet Henry Bessemer. When in England, Holley secured the American rights to Bessemer's patents; he became the sole representative for a steel pool, which would, over time, include the eleven American steel manufacturers. He helped design and build nearly every Bessemer plant in the United States, beginning with the Rensselaer Iron Works at Troy, New York in February 1865, where John Griswold was the principal partner. Holley went on to the Pennsylvania Steel Company in Harrisburg in April 1868; and the Cleveland Rolling Mill Company in Newburg, Ohio in 1868; and Carnegie's Braddock plant in 1873. And in 1869, Morrell engaged Holley to plan and design Cambria's new converter house and Bessemer ovens, the grim sphinxes, huge, yawning, open-ended football shapes, tilting vertical to spew flames of rainbow colors. Several years later, finally the day came when the Pennsylvania Railroad flatcars pulled up adjacent to the yard. They contained the first Bessemer converter for Holley's students. Hunt, Jones, Heyer, William Lewis—Jones's brother-in-law— and Fritz watched Holley unveil the grim sphinx that led to Cambria's first steel blow on July 10, 1871.

Bill Jones had become good friends with Robert Hunt, who had been Holley's lead assistant in the building of the Bessemer plants at Troy and Wyandotte and came to Cambria in 1860. Hunt was trained as a pharmacist, and his father, a physician, had died young, leaving his adolescent son to manage the family drug store. Hunt had been active in the Union League until late in the war, when he volunteered for a tour of duty, returning to Johnstown in 1866. He had taken a course in analytical chemistry at the Philadelphia Laboratory, and his knowledge of chemistry was invaluable working with the Bessemer process for he completely understood the importance of Mushet's contribution and of chemistry overall in the production of high quality steel. "Hunt was to Jones what Mushet was to Bessemer," Uncle Dan later summed up. At Cambria, Hunt established the first chemical lab at an iron and steel mill in the United States. He also ran the department that, under Holley's guidance, installed the works' first Bessemer converter (ibid., 214-5). Hunt had wit and finesse; he teased Morrell, a Quaker, claiming he was so parsimonious that at dinner he and his wife would share an egg. Hunt went on to a distinguished career in Troy, NY, working with John Griswold, and later formed his own company, which did testing and analysis out of Chicago.

When at Cambria, Holley spent many evenings with the Jones family before returning to the Eagle Hotel, where he usually lodged in Johnstown. Harriet Jones and Mary Bucknell Lloyd adored the aristocratic visitor to the smog-bound mountain mill town. When he visited for dinner, he shared news of Paris and related how Napoleon III had transformed the French capital. Cora later recounted how Holley's visits enlivened the Joneses' cottage, sparking her father to recite poetry, accompanied by the tinkling of glasses and gut-deep laughter. When Harriet had given birth to Cora in 1867, Jones asked Holley to be her godfather. Holley and his wife Mary had children who were about the same ages as the Joneses' and were to endure similar tragedies. Mary had given birth prematurely to Alexander Junior, giving Gertrude and Lucy a younger brother. Holley, drinking heavily, brooded over his infant son's lingering illness, a depression that Jones well understood since Ella's fateful infancy. One evening a wire was delivered from Morrell's office bringing the news that the boy had succumbed to a fever. Within fourteen months of his son's death, Holley's baby daughter also died.

Holley's biographer, Jeanne McHugh, describes him as a man who, "began what was to become a habit, when confronted with a difficult problem, of packing his bag and journeying around the country to visit his friends. ... Fritz or Hunt or Jones ... might look up from his work at any time to see Holley coming through the gate. The friends would sit down and talk, sometimes for hours until the problem was solved or the worry concerning it eased" (ibid., 230 n20). In this way the men who managed the steelworks of the Bessemer Association stayed good friends and colleagues in a rapidly-changing business. In one of Captain Bill's papers, delivered a decade later, Jones elaborated on the effect of Holley's drawing forth from the ranks of labor those with stellar promise.

> Now as to the cause of the great output of American steel works. On the introduction of the Bessemer process in America, quite a number of young men, who believed that the process would revolutionize the metallurgical world, became anxious to identify themselves with its development. ... At all these works there were ambitious young men closely studying and carefully watching all possible points of development . . . . . Next to the strong but pleasant rivalry of the young men who have assumed control of the works, and who have worked hard and faithfully to excel, the development of American practice is due to the esprit de corps of the workmen. (1881, 370-3)

In post-Civil War America, a new pragmatism was emerging. It surfaced in areas like Harvard's new curriculum, particularly in science, under the geologist Louis Agassiz; in the engineering community of Alexander Holley and Henry Howe; and in the legal adjudication of an Oliver Wendell Holmes, Junior (Menand 2001, 52-7). It was reflected in the Federal government's establishment of the land grant colleges, which developed curriculum in agriculture and mechanical arts in every state. To a great extent pragmatism discounted pure knowledge and abstract theory. Holley wrote at length about the contrast between academics who advanced truths and knowledge for their own sake and those who used books and understanding to solve problems. In an address to his alma mater in 1876, he may have been thinking back to Cambria with Jones, Hunt, and Fritz as the ideal fusion of the two extreme stances of know-how and know-that—practice and theory (McHugh 1980, 267-70). Holley, Hunt, Jones, George Fritz, and the young John Potter held sessions many an evening after work over pretzels and ale at California Tom's. Jones's work ethic embodied this pragmatism. The paradox to Jones as an inventor was that his new technologies, especially in a time of rapid technological change, could soon become obsolete and worthless. Jones would later institute the scrap-heap tradition in Braddock as one manifestation of this paradox.

Section 11: Inventions and Wages

Before the Kelly/Bessemer/Mushet discovery, there had been only two ways to produce steel, the crucible and the cementation method. The ancient crucible principle imitated smelting gold. Firing ore in a long vertical cylinder in a bath of flame yielded a limited amount of quality metal. The equally ancient cementation process involved a bath of iron charged by refracted heat. Cementation produced more steel than the crucible but the product was inferior and the process could take days, even weeks, to complete and required "a forest" of wood. The pneumatic method revolutionized the industry, producing gross steel in a matter of minutes, rather than the days necessary for the cementation process, and it produced quality steel.

During the period of Jones's increasing influence at Cambria, every change in blasting iron or in converting iron to steel entailed economic and social consequences. Bill Jones rose as a leader among his peers and maintained a loyal following. Though Fritz had promoted him to assistant superintendent, the Captain continued to work with the laborers, like William Lewis, the veteran Filus Heyer, the young John Potter, and the intractable James O'Neill.

Bill Jones managed the cranes in Cambria's casting house, in the blooming mill, and in the new converting house. He guided balanced rigs that carried steaming iron to spill red brew into the grim sphinx's mouth. He watched air-blasts shoot through the liquid mass, adding oxygen to the fused iron. As the air blast shot through the bubbling liquid mass, it first emitted a red flame from the mouth of the converter. Then, as oxygen fueled the liquid, a white flame with sizzling sparks rose upward toward the protective hood. In fifteen minutes the color changed to a soft blue. At this point, the cold air was turned off, the Bessemer rocked back, and the steel was ready to be poured into molds to form ingots.

In the 1866 election, Jones actively campaigned for Morrell to put him in Washington, D.C., and while in Congress from 1867-71, Morrell fought for high tariffs on iron and steel to protect American production. Puddlers, following the lead of molders elsewhere in the country, wanted to organize to protect their craft and to negotiate wages, but when Morrell returned from two terms in Congress in 1871, a worker who even asked about wage rates was subject to firing (Brown 1989, 174). In 1871 the miners at Cambria had negotiated sliding scale wages, based on the prevailing rail prices. By then the status of the puddling craft was being eclipsed by the new skills required for steel making. The shift from iron to steel brought with it a demotion of the furnace workers. Rollers then became the highest paid workmen. As the puddlers' pay base shifted from tonnage to hourly wages, which invariably were lower, a new friction between labor and management arose. Puddlers had been among the first to form a union, the Sons of Vulcan, which became a national organization in 1862. It was not until the economic slump in the 1870s, however, that unions really achieved large memberships in the mills. Management at Cambria was particularly successful at keeping unions from exercising much influence.

Since working for Crane Company at Catasauqua in his early teens, Jones had found that most problems at work were unique to the local site. At Morris in Philadelphia, at Port Richmond in Chattanooga, and at Cambria, he solidified his belief that on-site analysis should always supersede dictates from a distance, whether by union officers in Chicago or absentee financiers in New York. How could a New York financier know where to install ventilation to help blast furnace workers during hot summer weather or know what was reasonable compensation for injury or death so survivors could live comfortably? To find solutions to production snags, Jones needed the expertise of all of his employees familiar with the issues and unburdened by outside loyalties. He might put an Irish Catholic to work alongside an Anglican Englishman or a Lutheran German because the job needed the man most suited for it. Those who worked for him knew they must all get along.

As he explicitly stated on two public occasions, Jones himself categorically rejected any organization that excluded membership on grounds of nationality or race, as several of the organizing groups did (1881, 370). However, influenced by George Lippard, he did favor a fair deal for workers and their right to assemble. A mill worker should be able to join with others and negotiate with a superintendent and management as a company union. In these early years of factory production, management was usually a former fellow worker like George Fritz, not someone unfamiliar with, even removed from, workplace demands and workers' tasks and risks. Wages were worked out on a local basis. Jones did not support national unions, but, in time, developments in the steel industry changed how Jones evaluated unionization. His record over the years is not entirely consistent, but he always believed that anyone should have the opportunity to better their lot through hard work, education, and self-reliance—ideals he had formulated and refined by reading Lippard and Emerson and also through his discussions with Alexander Holley.

After the economic downturn in the early 1870s, threats of strikes were widespread, and several reached the stage of lockouts and shutdowns. The puddlers borrowed the miners' sliding scale strategy and hoped for equal success. However, the depression of the 1870s caused the price of rails to plummet. One puddler's opinion in the *National Labor Tribune* captures the intensity of the moment:

> Our despots will hardly allow us to think our own thoughts. We must vote for them to be our rulers in Congress, in the legislature, in the Borough Council; we must be ready to spill our blood, and lose our lives and limbs in defense of the property and their interests; we must petition Congress to increase the tariff, and to enact such laws as will benefit them and swell their enormous profits, while they in turn will not allow us the privilege of holding an organization which is chartered by the government, and which is the right of every, and as we have seen of late, the only safeguard, of an American citizen, against the overreaching, grasping, and avaricious capitalists, in their dealings with the tramped down workingmen. (Brown 1989, 176-7)

In 1873, pressured by Morrell to enforce the ninth commandant against unions, Fritz, in failing health, had to capitulate to his boss's demands to lockout workers and hire scabs, which enraged Jones. In frustration, Filius Heyer left the Cambria works at the height of the 1873 labor dispute, leaving steel forever and returning to his efforts as provost marshal of veteran affairs (Duram and Duram 1979, 108).

One night during the spring of 1873, the roofs of the newly completed rail mill caught fire and left the yards littered with wreckage. George Fritz asked all to work without pay and soon rails were being tailed off once again. But the strain from anxiety and labor tensions took their toll on Fritz. During a terribly hot day in August, he suffered a heart attack and died (McHugh 1980, 242).

With George's death, the most likely candidate for the position of superintendent was Bill Jones. But Jones had open disregard for Morrell's commandments, and Morrell was well aware of the Captain's independent streak and considered Jones's practices too frivolous. As a result, Morrell hired the Captain's boyhood chum, Daniel Jones, who had also worked at Catasauqua, to assume Fritz's responsibilities. Consequently, Captain Bill submitted his resignation. According to Robert Hunt, Daniel Jones

John Potter *invented the forty-eight-inch slab mill that reduced work and earned profits to which only the company was entitled because he had failed to patent his invention.*

(Public Domain)

approached the Captain and offered to turn down Morrell's promotion; he acknowledged Bill Jones as the better choice for superintendent. But the Captain shrugged off the offer. Rebuilding from the fire was still underway, so Bill Jones, in memory of Fritz and out of loyalty to Daniel Jones, offered to temporarily withdraw his resignation in order to complete the erection of the iron roof over the burned-out rolling mill. Morrell refused to rehire him.

John Potter, who had started at the works as a gofer when Jones hired him, remembered well the day Daniel Jones asked him to pass the hat among colleagues at Cambria to purchase a gold watch and chain as a going away gift for Captain Bill. Potter contributed one dollar; W. W. McCleary, fifty cents; and Robert Hunt, five dollars. The account book, which somehow survived the 1889 Johnstown Flood and is in the Flood Museum there today, recorded 210 donations totaling $176.00 to purchase the watch.

On August 19, 1873, the works celebrated Captain Bill's contributions to Cambria, at which Daniel Jones presented him with the watch. Along with his Civil War sword, Bill Jones treasured this watch, which came from donations of those ranging from unskilled labor to managers, as well as a few local ringers that he had hired for their baseball skills.

After leaving Cambria, Captain Bill wrote his will in 1874, which to this day is the only will ever found, a curiosity to which I shall return.

I, William R. Jones of the County of Allegheny and the State of Pennsylvania, being of sound mind, memory and understanding do make and publish this my last will and Testament, hereby revoking and making void all former wills by me at anytime therefore made-

First, To my son William Coulter Jones, I give and bequeath the gold watch and watch chain presented to me at Johnstown, Pennsylvania, August 13th, 1873, by my friends and fellow workmen of that place, Also my sword, which was presented to me at Baltimore, Maryland, by the members of Company "F" 194 Regiment, Pennsylvania Volunteers Second, I give, advise and bequeath unto my wife Harriet Jones her heirs and assigns forever, all the rest and residue of my property, real, personal and mixed of what nature or kind so ever, and whensoever the same shall be at the time of my death. And lastly, I do constitute and appoint my wife Harriet Jones sole executrix of this my last will and testament.

In Witness Whereof I William R. Jones, the Testament to this my will, written on one sheet of paper, set my hand and seal this 18th day of May AD One thousand eight hundred and seventy-four.

Wm. R. Jones

Signed sealed published and declared by the above named William R. Jones, as and for his last will and Testament in the presence of us, who have hereunto sub signed our names at his request as witnesses thereto, in the presence of the said Testator and of each other.

William H Lewis

Eileen W. Lewis

Morrell had cut wages at Cambria by 21 percent in 1873 and began bartering store goods for wages (Brown 1989, 176-7). After the wage cut at Cambria, three hundred workers joined the Miners National Association. When rail prices went up in February 1874, Morrell saw an opportunity to stop the unions once and for all. He rewarded the workers with salaries twice what he paid puddlers. When angry workers accused Morrell of trying to break organizing, Morrell closed down the Cambria Iron Works. Refusing arbitration, Morrell offered reinstatement only to those workers who signed his anti-union pledge. He claimed he had received threatening letters, and he armed over a hundred of what the Captain called "no-accounts" from around town as policemen to rid the city of troublemakers. Working conditions throughout Cambria's mines and mill were horrible. Disgusted, the Captain and his friends in middle management endured for a time, though Hunt quit. With new technology, Cambria was turning into a grim plantation, nearly wage slavery for the unskilled workers.

Concerning the Cambria's coal miners' strike, Uncle Dan said that his father's book recorded what happened when the strikers used an old hall in town to distribute food during the lockout and to dole out money through the union relief fund to hard-up workers. On the Fourth of July over a thousand paraded from Fronheiser Hall down Clinton to the Stone Bridge, with banners declaring "Freedom for Wage Slaves," "Union League," and "High Tariffs, High Salaries." The marchers, some playing musical instruments, announced to the town the forthcoming labor battle. Some in the crowd threw rocks at the sign carriers. The Johnstown community was divided, and this played a role in the outcome. Morrell was in a strong position, because in Johnstown there were few other sources of employment. Due to all the recent technological changes, he no longer negotiated with puddlers, rollers, and heaters as separate subcontractors but with all as employees locked in top-down management. Throughout the industry, the new policy of paying each worker hourly wages put middle managers like Fritz, Hunt, and Jones in the awkward position of having to choose between the owners and workers; crossing the owner or being soft on labor meant the end of a promising career and, in some cases, employment, as one could easily be blacklisted.

Section 12: New York City

After Cora was born in 1867, the year her grandfather, the Reverend Lloyd, passed away, the Jones family purchased a new home so that Mary Bucknell Lloyd could move in and assist her daughter. On November 5, 1871, Harriet gave birth to her last child, Charles, who lived for only three weeks. Following the birth, Harriet suffered serious postpartum depression and lacked sufficient strength for even seemingly effortless tasks like pouring tea. She experienced spells that left her bedridden, her legs losing muscle tone and her energy flagging.

But in the spring of 1874, Harriet again experienced a resurgence of health.

After resigning from Cambria, Captain Bill convinced Harriet that he needed to go to New York to explore job opportunities. He did not want to tolerate again the likes of Burnside, Hooker, or Morrell, whose management he disdained. He wanted to talk with Holley—Lackawanna Works had just fired its first heat in July, and a new plant in St. Louis was under construction. The steel industry was growing apace.

It had been nearly two decades since Captain Jones had left cosmopolitan Philadelphia. In that time, New York had emerged as the center of publishing and commerce. Supported by steel, the downtown buildings reached skyward five and six stories. In Greek mythology Prometheus the Titan defied the gods in order to provide humankind with fire. Now that fire would smelt ore into steel that soon would punch into the heavens, dwarfing church steeples and mosque minarets to eventually exceed the height of the pyramids. Elevated trains formed caverns at the city center under which gathered thousands of the poor in rags and derelict war veterans, some blind, others ambling on crutches. European immigrants wearing motley dress, farmer breeches that swept up from behind for squatting and rainbow colored shirts, survived in squalor, and crime was commonplace. The war had shifted the locus of power from Washington, D.C., to New York where the rich and poor were polarized. The ethnically diverse North was immersed in class warfare. The landed Dutch and British, the capitalists behind the North's industrial culture, lorded it over the Irish and other immigrant groups, who were mostly Roman Catholic.

Jaywalkers dodged horse-drawn vehicles, giving rise to the sobriquet for the Brooklyn baseball team, the Dodgers.

Since 1873 when the brokerage house of Jay Cooke & Co. had closed its doors, great economic depression prevailed. New York mayor Boss Tweed had been subdued after a reign of corruption and scandal, which some said milked the city of more than one hundred million dollars in the post-war years. Corruption was rampant, even in President Grant's cabinet. New York streets were full of pedestrians and traffic—horse cars, victorias, and omnibuses warmed inside by smoking potbelly stoves. Jaywalkers dodged these lumbering horse-drawn vehicles, giving rise to the sobriquet for the Brooklyn baseball team, the Dodgers. Five cents took Captain Bill downtown to Joralemon Street in Brooklyn, where Holley lived with his wife and their two surviving children, Gertrude and Lucy.

On Bill's arrival, Holley grabbed hat and coat, and the two struck off for oysters and beer downtown, even though Holley was currently tempering his drinking at his wife's insistence. Holley's barouche passed Forty-third Street and Fifth Avenue where stood the lavish home of Boss Tweed, who at the time was locked in the Ludlow Street jail. Settling in at the Astor bar, Holley ordered the non-alcoholic Old Jacob Thompson's Sarsaparilla that Cora remembered serving him at their home in Johnstown, while Captain Bill ordered up his puddler's cocktail. The two discussed global affairs— Germany's invading France, Garibaldi's fate in Italy, the slaughter of those at the Commune in Paris, and Emperor Franz Joseph's promise of liberalization in Austria. They talked of traveling together to Europe to investigate how English steel production was advancing. And Jones, of course, brought up his own situation.

Bill Jones, always the reader, was amazed at the number and availability of newspapers: the *Graphic*, the *New York Herald*, the *New York Times*, the *New York Evening Post*, the *Mail*, the *Sun*, and the *World*. Not since Philadelphia had he the luxury of such a range of periodicals. For years he had been limited to the *Cambria Tribune* and the *Johnstown Democrat*, and occasionally a copy of the conservative *New York Herald* would find its way to Johnstown.

Jones and Holley shared a love for the same literature. Holley's favorite poem was "Thanatopsis" by William Cullen Bryant, whose editorship of the *New York Evening Post* was approaching a half-century. Captain Bill read both poetry and prose by Walt Whitman. The two agreed with Whitman's appraisal of society in *Democratic Vistas*:

> . . . We live in an atmosphere of hypocrisy throughout . . . The depravity of the business classes of our country are not less than has been supposed, but infinitely greater. The official services of America, national, state, and municipal, in all their branches and departments, the judiciary, are saturated in corruption, bribery, falsehood, mal-administration; and the judiciary is tainted. The great cities reek with respectable as much as non-respectable robbery and scoundralism. In fashionable life, flippancy, tepid amours, weak infidelism small aims, or no aims at all, only to kill time. In business . . . the sole object is, by any means, pecuniary gain . . . The best class we show is but a mob of fashionably dress'd speculators and vulgarians. True indeed, behind this fantastic farce, enacted on the visible stage of society, solid things and stupendous labors are to be discover'd, existing crudely and going on in the background, to advance and tell themselves in time. Yet the truths are none the less terrible . . .

During Jones's very first days in the city, Holley took him to a many-storied building to ride an elevator, called a perpendicular railway, for the first time. They also visited John Augustus Roebling and his son, who had designed the Brooklyn Bridge, constructed seven years earlier. Holley and Captain Bill attended the theater. Jones loved reading Shakespeare aloud, and Holley enjoyed hearing him recite Shakespeare by heart (Holbrook1939, 211), but he rarely had the opportunity to see a production. Over dinner one night, Holley called Jones's attention to a lesser-known play by Shakespeare, *Troilus and Cressida*, and read parts of it to him, lines that expressed well how fickle "envious and calumniating time" had eroded Holley's position to steer steel production in the United States. Jones subsequently memorized the long passage and recited it to Cora during crises:

> Time hath, my lord, a wallet at his back,
> Wherein he puts alms for oblivion,
> A great-siz'd monster of ingratitude's:
> Those scraps are good deeds past; which are devour'd
> As fast as they are made, forgot as soon
> As done: perseverance, dear my Lord,
> Keeps honour bright: to have done, is to hang
> Quite out of fashion, like a rusty mail
> In monumental mockery. Take the instant way;
> For honour travels in a strait so narrow
> Where one but goes abreast: keep, then, the path;
> For emulation hath a thousand sons
> That one by one pursue: if you give way,
> Or hedge aside from the direct forthright,
> Like to an enter'd tide they all rush by
> And leave you hindmost;
> Or, like a gallant horse fall'n in first rank,
> Lie there for pavement to the abject rear,
> O'errun and trampled on: then what they do in present,
> Though less than yours in past, must o'er top yours;
> For time is like a fashionable host,
> That slightly shakes his parting guest by the hand,
> And with his arms outstretch'd, as he would fly,
> Grasps in the comer: welcome ever smiles,
> And farewell goes out sighing. O! let not virtue seek
> Remuneration for the thing it was;
> For beauty, wit,
> High birth, vigor of bone, desert in service,
> Love, friendship charity, are subjects all
> To envious and calumniating time.
> One touch of nature makes the whole world kin,
> That all with one consent praise new-born gawds,
> Though they are made and moulded of things past,
> And give to dust that is a little gilt
> More laud than gilt o'or-dusted.
> The present eye praises the present object.

Jones well appreciated how appropriately Shakespeare portrayed the fact that time renders obsolete the truth of engineering and science, but he preferred stark pragmatic truths to lofty idealism that had no effect on events.

Jones was now thirty-five, and he learned from his mentor that many of Holley's statutes and contracts, particularly the Bessemer agreements, were running out, as new technology was being developed. The open hearth method of producing steel, which was slower and less dangerous, could eclipse the Bessemer, rendering Holley's licenses and his inventions, such as the Holley Vessel Bottom for Bessemer converters, less valuable (McHugh 1980, 303). Indeed, "the present eye praises the present object." When he returned home to Johnstown, Jones told his wife that Holley looked much older than his fifty-two years.

> *Carnegie learned Morse code, so well that he could listen to the dots and dashes and interpret the code fluently.*

Holley's most promising project involved Andrew Carnegie, an increasingly prosperous Pittsburgh businessman. Carnegie had been successful in a range of businesses, including railroads, the telegraph, and the selling of bonds. Carnegie's father, a weaver, brought the family to the United States when Andrew was twelve and his younger brother, Tom, was four. Andrew was only four years older than Jones, and they shared many of the same beliefs and experiences. Carnegie, like Jones, had a gifted mind but little education. He was taken under tutelage by executives of the Pennsylvania Railroad when still very young, and he quickly grasped how important were transportation and communication to the future of the country. In his teens Carnegie learned Morse code, so well, in fact, that he could listen to the dots and dashes and interpret the code fluently, a feat few in Pittsburgh mastered. Throughout his career, he used Morse code to contact his lieutenants in a language secretly encoded for only those corresponding. In 1858 the twenty-eight year-old Carnegie had used his widowed mother's house as collateral for business deals. The war and several prescient investments had enabled him to be free of physical work by the time he was thirty-four.

The younger Carnegie brother, Tom, preceded Andrew in the iron business with his ownership of the Lucy furnaces, named after his wife. Tom's father-in-law, William Coleman, had surveyed what became the site for the Edgar Thomson Steel Works. It was a stretch of land lying parallel to the Monongahela River and extending up into forested hills, where, in the previous century, General Braddock had been killed (Gage 1998, 149-167). The plant was situated adjacent to the tracks of the Pennsylvania Railroad running to Pittsburgh and to New York City on the north side, the tracks of the Baltimore and Ohio railroads dividing the works, and, along the river, the Pennsylvania and Lake Erie Railway.

After Tom Carnegie's success in the iron business, Andrew Carnegie wanted to produce steel. When Jones visited Holley in Brooklyn, Carnegie had been corresponding and working with Holley, who was already building the foundation of a new works at Braddock's Field, eight miles east of Pittsburgh. Holley was in charge of the design, and an engineer named Phineas Barnes was superintendent of the early construction.

Carnegie was already a millionaire when Holley first suggested that the Captain and Carnegie meet. Bill Jones soon after traveled to Pittsburgh, where he was hired as a mechanic and began work on what would become the Edgar Thomson Works (ET) with Holley and Phineas Barnes. When Barnes's contract expired, Holley quickly recommended Jones as superintendent (Wall 1970, 314). Bowing to Holley's recommendation, Carnegie ordered William Shinn, general manager of the new works, to hire Jones.

Captain Bill tentatively accepted the position. He thoroughly understood iron making, but steel conversion had been the particular province of his friend Robert Hunt, who managed Cambria's Bessemer unit. Coincidentally, he had just learned that Hunt had resigned from Cambria. In a gesture similar to Daniel Jones's generous offer to relinquish his new post to Jones, Captain Bill wired Hunt suggesting that Hunt take the job that Carnegie was offering him, as Hunt was the best steel man to launch Carnegie's project. Later in life, Hunt remembered the episode vividly as "strikingly typical of the man [Jones], and an excellent example of his whole-hearted and unselfish friendship" (1911).

> I telegraphed the Captain that I was out and was leaving for Troy, N. Y., to interview John A. Griswold & Co. in relation to a position. After reaching that city I received a telegram from him saying, 'Do nothing until you receive letter from me.' The letter came, and in it he said: 'When I received your message telling of your leaving, I at once went to Mr. Shinn and showed him the dispatch and said to him, 'Captain Hunt is the man you want; he has been making steel. I have not; give him the charge of the works, and, if you have something else for me to do all right; if not, all right.' Now, old man, come, and no nonsense about it. Don't think of me, for if Shinn won't give me anything I know John Fritz will. Come!' Is it possible for me or for any one to pay in words proper tribute to friendship such as that? But there is little occasion for anyone to tell the people of Johnstown of the noble qualities of William R. Jones. (ibid., 742)

But Robert Hunt demurred and settled at the first mill Holley had designed in the United States at Troy, New York. He was made superintendent and general manager.

Section 13: Original Pittsburgh Pirate

Captain Bill accepted the position of superintendent of the Edgar Thomson Works on the condition that Carnegie give him control of the mill's labor management. Arguing that well-paid, well-rested men worked more diligently and efficiently with less absenteeism and fewer accidents, he immediately insisted upon high wages and established ethnically diverse teams. In contrast with the Homestead Mill, where the Irish controlled the converting works and the Welsh, the rail mill, with unskilled jobs left to Eastern Europeans, this minimized ethnic tension and unrest.

Jones and the Carnegies, especially Tom, his wife Lucy, and her father William Coleman, shared ideas and became friends. Tom had been working for some time with Andrew Kloman, the acknowledged master of iron production around Pittsburgh, and Jones recognized his considerable expertise in iron working; Andrew, on the other hand, knew relatively little about iron or steel. Tom and his wife frequently enjoyed dinner at the Joneses', and the Joneses when in Pittsburgh spent time with them. Both Carnegies and Jones embraced radical credos to help forge a better world. Members of the Carnegie family in Scotland had been Chartists, discontented wool workers, active in attempting to reform Parliament—demanding equality of representation, voting by ballot, universal suffrage, and a lessening of the influence of hereditary privilege in government. Also in Carnegie's background was a strong Calvinist belief in pre-determination: the rich are rich according to God's plan, and the poor are poor because they are essentially flawed. John Geoffrey Jones, Captain Bill's father, also believed and preached an unforgiving Protestantism, but his son utterly rejected Calvinism, absorbing instead Jefferson's and Lippard's ideas from the French and American revolutions regarding the perfectibility of humankind and society.

Carnegie shared many of Harriet's values and should have abhorred much about Captain Bill: he drank and he gambled; he ridiculed religious pomposity; his profanity and his temper were legendary, and, most frustrating, Jones refused to acknowledge Carnegie's authority. When Carnegie's nettling exceeded Jones's limits, he let Carnegie know what he thought of him to his face. As early as January 1876 when Jones resigned for inadequate salary, Holley had to arbitrate between the two headstrong men (McHugh 1980, 309-10). Carnegie appeared to be open to the unorthodox so long as profits accrued; he would cope with Jones's irreverence, his lack of respect, and his seemingly capricious tendency to stop work to play baseball.

Carnegie and Captain Jones began an association characterized by both rich dialogues and heated exchanges. They often joked with each other about facial scars each purportedly incurred during the Civil War. Carnegie's story, told in his autobiography and repeated by numerous biographers, has been shown to be apocryphal, while Jones's scar was received when he plunged into the Rapidan River in spring flood without dislodging his hat. This illustrates a basic difference between the two men: Jones served two tours of duty in the war, risking his life on numerous occasions. Carnegie paid another to do his military service, while he sold bonds far from harm's way. There was another essential difference. Carnegie's early work experience had been brief, and he was fortunate to associate with wealthy and powerful men. Jones, on the other hand, had already experienced a vast and seasoned work life in the trenches.

Carnegie was given to hyperbole and self-promotion, while Jones dedicated himself to hard work and took seriously the charge of his workers. Bill Jones's philosophy was based on what would make things work best, on what would get the job done. He was, more than anything, the ultimate pragmatist, who often did the work himself and waded right in with the men he managed on any given project. Carnegie micromanaged everything by controlling people, but he did it from a distance, behind the scenes. In many ways it is remarkable that their association lasted for all of fifteen years.

Indeed, Carnegie at the outset wanted some proof that Jones's ideas would increase profits; he challenged his new superintendent to demonstrate how his soft-on-labor policy would benefit the new company. Jones's next move quickly proved to the Scot the soundness of allowing Jones's authority to extend to dealing with labor as well as managing the new mill. As we have seen, Cambria was not a happy environment in 1873 and 1874. Bill Jones had an idea that would answer Carnegie's challenge and prove that a fair deal for labor meant profits. As superintendent of the new Carnegie works, Jones went to Bessemer Station. He purchased a ticket for Johnstown and arrived with the first snow, meeting Filius Heyer at the station. After a warm welcome, Jones met that night at his father-in-law's old church with thirty-five of his former comrades from the 133rd and the 194th regiments, as well as with John Potter and W. W. McCleary. These were men whose positions at the mill ranged from office workers to working the furnaces to ministering to the grim sphinx.

That night in Fronheiser Hall the men pledged to Jones that they would quit Cambria and join Carnegie's new plant in Braddock. Furthermore, each promised that he would recruit men from other departments who were likewise fed up with Morrell.

> Bill Jones was a popular leader at Johnstown, and most of the departmental heads of Cambria felt that he had been given a raw deal. . . . Inside of two weeks pretty nearly every top-grade man at the Cambria Works had moved, bag and baggage, wife and children into Braddock. . . . Captain Jones was happy to have his old gang with him on the new job [Edgar Thomson Works]. So was Andy Carnegie. He [Jones] had raided a competitor of all its best men, and every one of them had had long training in making what the Braddock plant was designed for—Bessemer steel. (Holbrook 1939, 209)

Some pirate! My dad loved to tell this story of "the original Pittsburgh Pirate." Within four days, Morrell lost much of his entire production team, schooled by John and George Fritz and Alexander Holley, the finest iron and steel workers in the country. Andrew Carnegie opened the most up-to-date mill with that very work force. In one bold action, Captain Bill showed how he could successfully manage labor his way (Krass 2002, 173). Throughout the country, at every Holley-built Bessemer mill, crews guffawed over Morrell's loss to the new plant in Braddock's Field.

The three-river area centered on Pittsburgh enticed Captain Bill, who was weary of provincialism, and he soon found a house for his family near the acreage laid out for the new mill in Braddock. Harriet cheered up with the move, anticipating that Pittsburgh would be much better for rearing her daughter and son than isolated Johnstown. But Pitts-

> *The men pledged to Jones that they would quit Cambria and join Carnegie's new plant.*

burgh, known as Slag Town, was not Philadelphia nor Baltimore and certainly was not Chattanooga. In 1874, one hundred and seventy thousand people lived in Pittsburgh, and an influx of Eastern Europeans and the northward migration of African Americans from the South continued the city's rapid growth. The new ethnically diverse population provided the necessary labor for the region's growing iron and steel plants. Nearby small towns like Braddock and Allegheny were growing rapidly, and they too, attracted a diverse labor force with a variety of ethnic and religious affiliations. The immigrants brought with them a folk culture of artisans that spawned the arts, theatre, and musical festivals (Casson 1907). City hall in Pittsburgh became a battleground between the old Anglo monoculture and the new diversity.

Bill Jones became known as the Czar of Braddock. Though Cora loved the moniker, this title for the fun-loving and colorful Captain upset his wife and her mother. His raucous swagger and cocky manner were what the townspeople celebrated in Jones, a style that typified a class and culture remote from the once-fashionable Lloyds of Paris and Chattanooga. Cora's Presbyterian grandmother, active in the church revival movement, did not approve of her son-in-law's fun-loving manner nor his business policy of requiring the works to operating on Sundays and said the blaspheming man would burn in a hell hotter than Holley's sphinx. Even so, the strict but tireless and dutiful Mary Bucknell Lloyd took over and efficiently managed the home for her increasingly weakened daughter.

The developing tension at home was relieved by Jones's more fulfilling business associations at ET (Jones 1881, 270; and Jones to McCandless). Cora later said that, upon moving to Braddock, her father became increasingly absorbed in work, which took him away from family life; he also spent more time at Spielgelmeyer's tobacco store; the Irish saloon; Braddock's Field's primarily Italian fire department; and the racetracks at Collins and Friendship Parks in East Liberty, some four miles away.

Jones and Holley often talked about design, function, and form, and the ideas of the philosopher-sculptor Horatio Greenough. In the 1850s, Bill Jones had learned from Greenough how form should follow function when he worked at I. P. Morris in Philadelphia:

> If we compare the form of a newly invented machine with the perfected type of the same instrument, we observe, as we trace it through the phases of improvement, how weight is shaken off where strength is less needed, how functions are made to approach without impeding each other, how straight becomes curved, and the curve is straightened, till the straggling and cumbersome machine becomes the compact, effective, and beautiful engine. (Greenough 1947)

For Jones, a home, like a factory, should be built around its purpose—comfort for houses and efficiency of production for the factory. He appreciated the organic eclecticism of Victorian architecture. The prominent, asymmetrical exterior of a home reveals the owner's individualism. A steel plant had to be Gothic, with the exterior reflecting its inner function—converting ore into steel, steel into rails. Jones and Holley placed the Bessemer core farthest from the town, in case of fire from explosions, accidents, or carelessness. For several years, there were no blast furnaces, and iron was transported by rail from the Lucy on the Allegheny River to the Bessemers in Braddock, on the Monongahela River. The location of the two five-ton grim sphinxes formed the heart around which every other building or shed was aligned. At Cambria the blast furnaces had been at the heart of operations; this made sense when iron had been the final product, but when Bessemers were added, they had to be placed in the space available.

The country's economic depression continued through 1875. Carnegie wisely invested heavily in his new plant for the inevitable bull market to follow. He shrewdly named his works the Edgar Thomson or ET. Thomson, the president of the Pennsylvania Railroad, represented a major consumer of rails and also a powerful political voice that influenced Congress in passing protective tariffs for a nation's budding iron and steel industries. Readily available nearby coal beds and limestone deposits would make possible Carnegie's desire to control all components and stages in steel production.

Keen on establishing good working conditions and benefits for ET's workers, Jones gradually replaced aspects of Morrell's exploitive type of company town with a variety of policies and innovations aimed at worker comfort, self-respect, and self-reliance, not worker dependence and debt servitude, policies years later adopted by Carnegie and United States Steel, when they were headed by Jones's protégé Charles Schwab (Bridge 1991, 80). He instituted a series of incentives like loan programs for employees to draw from to build their own homes (Casson 1907, 31). He personally attended to the ventilation of the shops, altering the walls of the mill to install windows, which allowed better air circulation during Pittsburgh's humid summer months. He provided snacks for breaks during work (Krass 2002, 179). He gave bonuses for achievements. To Captain Bill is also due the system of rewards for exceptional service that afterwards characterized the administration of all the Carnegie properties, such as trying to keep works going so that workers remained on payrolls, and the company maintaining that it had the interest of the workers and their welfare at heart (Bridge1991, 39-4). He had seen a worker "squashed to jelly" (Jones to Carnegie, 1877, March 28) when a crane collapsed dropping a ladle on the man and argued: "We encouraged [the men] to insure themselves in a well-known company, and in certain cases we at first assisted them. But I am not in favor of coddling the American workingman. Let him learn to be prudent like other men. If we can train the workman to be self-reliant, it will be better for the manufacturer and for his people" (Harris 1883-4, 599).

During the building period, Jones teamed mill workers against those at the converter or the furnaces in baseball games to heighten competition in their activities at work. He wrote Manager Shinn: "Our men are like a spirited race horse; it is hard to hold them in. All hands conceived the idea of letting out a little last night." He interrupted work in the early afternoon for a series of innings to heighten the workers' pitch. When workers finished a boiler shed ahead of schedule, he took the crew to the races (McHugh 1980, 251).

One day after ET was well underway, Carnegie invited Daniel Morrell to come to

Pittsburgh for lunch, then the two spent the afternoon surveying the works at Braddock. Carnegie took satisfaction in introducing the ex-congressman to his many former employees at their stations, now manning the most advanced machinery in the world. Finally, after sufficiently rubbing Morrell's nose in Jones's piracy, Carnegie and Morrell approached the Captain. They greeted one another cordially, then Morrell turned to Carnegie and said, "I hired the wrong Jones" (Wall 1970, 316).

Joseph Frazier Wall wrote that Captain Jones was "Holley's greatest contribution to the Edgar Thomson Works . . . the initial and continuing success of the steel mill at Braddock can be attributed to the talents of William Jones." In a letter Wall sent to my uncle, he added: "I spent so long a time in writing the book [*Andrew Carnegie*] and, perforce, living with Carnegie that I began to feel that his associates were mine. Captain Jones. There was no man in Carnegie's long saga that I admired as much as I did him. Compared to almost all of the others he was of heroic stature" (1972, February 16).

Captain Jones, a tested veteran of a terrible war, commanded by inept generals, endured sixteen years at Cambria, where he was passed over because of ideology (McHugh, 1980, pp. 2556-7). He now had the opportunity to orchestrate the newest machinery with the most experienced workers in what soon was called the Mecca of Steel, the Forge of the Universe—masterminded by a man, Andrew Carnegie, who Captain Bill described as being born with two sets of teeth and bored for more (ibid., 315).

THE EDGAR THOMSON STEEL WORKS AND BLAST FURNACES.

The Edgar Thomson Steel Works and Blast Furnaces in 1890.
(Carnegie Brothers & Co., Limited, 1890.)

Chapter 3 Sections

14. Enlightened Labor Policies
15. Jones, Superintendent
16. The Lesson of Shinn
17. Charlie Schwab
18. Student becomes Teacher
19. Cora's Adolescence
20. New Faces
21. Bill Jones' Service to Community
22. Death of the 8-hour Day
23. Bad Weather

CHAPTER 3

DEVISING A PLAN

Section 14: Enlightened Labor Policies

With his pirated workers from Cambria, Captain Bill Jones had proved his value to Carnegie. The Scot was traveling with Holley in England for much of 1874, initially to acquire further funding to complete ET. During this period while the mill was being built, Captain Bill became acquainted with the cast of characters with whom he spent the rest of his life.

ET's beginnings go back a decade earlier, to the 1860s, when Thomas Miller, a Carnegie friend from their teenage years, who, with his wife, had traveled with Andrew to Europe, had asked Carnegie to help settle a business problem (Bridge 1991, 15). Miller and Henry Phipps, another childhood friend of Carnegie, had organized an iron works with Andrew Kloman. Kloman was a brilliant pioneer in the iron industry but was also a cranky and difficult person. Miller asked Carnegie to mediate a disagreement among the parties, because at the time Carnegie was not in the iron or steel business. Andrew Carnegie sided with Kloman and Phipps, and negotiated to replace Miller with his own younger brother, Tom Carnegie, who acquired Miller's shares in the company (ibid., 13). They formed Kloman, Phipps, and Carnegie Company, the Carnegie being Tom. Much of ET's early history was first written down by James Howard Bridge, who became a literary assistant and secretary to Andrew Carnegie in 1884. In his book, Bridge is quite critical of Carnegie, giving much of the credit for ET's success to Carnegie's partners and associates, such as Jones and Holley. He doesn't minimize Carnegie's abilities at making money, but he details some of the brutally unfair treatment of his associates. Bridge sizes up the betrayal of friend Tom Miller and, later, Kloman as Andrew shucking the oyster, the iron interests, with Miller and Kloman getting empty shells and Andrew, the meat. Bridge, ghost writer of Carnegie's *Triumphant Democracy*, had been slighted, humiliated, by Carnegie which undoubtedly accounts for much of book's tone: "[William] Shinn bossed the show; [David] McCandless lent it dignity and standing; [Henry] Phipps took in the pennies at the gate and kept the pay-roll down; Tom Carnegie kept everybody in a good humor, with Dave Steward as his understudy; and Andrew Carnegie? Oh, Andy looked after the advertising and drove the band wagon" (1991, 111).

And in the dedication, Bridge cites as the founders of Carnegie Steel only "those who saved it from early disaster and won its initial successes: Andrew Kloman, David McCandless, William Coleman, Thomas Morrison Carnegie, William R. Jones, William P. Shinn, David A. Stewart, and Henry M. Curry" (ibid, Opening page). Conspicuously missing among these named founders is Andrew Carnegie, whom he might have compared to "a fashionable host,/That slightly shakes his parting guest by the hand,/ And with arms outstretch'd,, as he would fly,/ Grasps in the comer: welcome ever smiles, and /Farewell goes out sighing" (Shakespeare, *Troilus and Cressida*).

ET was the first enterprise that Andrew Carnegie built from the ground up and in which he invested a significant amount of his own money. When the company was capitalized, Carnegie put in $250,000, which was 36 percent of the total; William Coleman put in $100,000, which was 13 percent. Seven other individuals capitalized at $50,000 each. Within three years Andrew owned the controlling interest in the company, and his brother,

Tom, another 16 percent. Carnegie had no official title, although he held more shares than any other individual. He would soon obtain a majority share in ET, then later Carnegie Bros and the mergers with Homestead and Duquesne, in nearly every case through less than upright means.

> *Carnegie took over Coleman's shares of the company.*

Bill Jones liked Tom Carnegie, who was a heavy drinker and ultimately died of complications from alcoholism. Tom, without his wife, spent many evenings dining with the Joneses, sipping port with the Captain; Tom downed thrice the Captain's volume. Several nights Tom slept it off in the downstairs guest room just below Cora's bedroom. Tom's and the Captain's families were lasting friends for over three generations, a point made by my grandfather to Carnegie's biographer, Joseph Frazier Wall (1972, March 11).

Tom's father-in-law, William Coleman, was among the few in ET's early cast of characters who knew anything about how to produce iron and saw the potential of Bessemer steel when he visited the mills at Troy and Harrisburg. Bridge credited the sixty-five-year-old Coleman as the principal, but forgotten, founder of the Carnegie Bessemer steel business (1991, 72). Coleman had followed in the press the discoveries of Heinrich Schliemann, a fellow entrepreneur-turned-archaeologist, who was excavating Troy to ground myth in history. Coleman had himself scrounged for arrowheads around the area just outside Pittsburgh where the French and Indians had killed General Braddock and defeated the British army (Fischer 1994, 34). Coleman suggested to Tom that the area would be the perfect site for an iron and steel factory and, ultimately, he bought the land and became the senior partner of the original company, which was known as Carnegie, McCandless, and Company.

In April 1876, Coleman encountered financial difficulties and approached Andrew Carnegie for cash. Carnegie made moves to take over Coleman's shares of the company to form a closed corporation and divide up the interests among Shinn, Tom Carnegie, and himself, along with Harry Phipps (Wall 1970, 353). Carnegie and Coleman quarreled when Coleman did not want to sell (Bridge 1991, 117). Eventually, pinched for cash, Coleman begrudgingly settled for $100,000 at his 6 percent interest (Wall 1970, 329), a transaction highly advantageous to Carnegie.

William Shinn was first secretary-treasurer of the board, general manager, and a vice-president of the Allegheny Railroad. A friend of Holley's, the tall, lean Shinn had been an accountant and had performed brilliantly when employed at the Pennsylvania Railroad, but he knew little of iron and nothing of steel. He bowed to nearly every one of Jones's wishes, for he well knew that only Jones among all those in higher management understood how to make both iron and steel. Shinn's method of voucher accounting, long used by the railroad, led to considerable efficiencies that somewhat cramped Jones's style, though Captain Bill understood the inherent value of profits (Bridge 1991, 81). Due to his influence at the railroad, Shinn was able to secure favorable transportation rates for Carnegie's firm. Nonetheless, the Pennsylvania Railroad's monopoly in Pittsburgh remained the thorn in

Carnegie's otherwise smooth-rolling acquisition of all stages of the steel producing and marketing process.

When Jones came to ET in the mid-1870s, reminders of the economic depression were everywhere. Because ET was among the few businesses hiring in Pittsburgh, scores of men beseeched the Captain, the new superintendent, for jobs whenever he left for home or took the train west from Bessemer Station, only two hundred yards north of the works. My uncle and father passed on the family recollection of how pained Bill Jones had been at the sight of veterans, among whom were former comrades, crowding the station, some one-legged and disheveled, approaching passengers from the east who were stretching their legs before the final eight-mile trip to Pittsburgh.

Early in 1875 Captain Bill presented his objectives for ET to David McCandless, the banker who was the president of the board.

> Now I will give you my views as to the proper way of conducting these works.
>
> 1st. We must be careful of what class of men we collect. We must steer clear of the West where men are accustomed to infernal high wages. We must steer clear as far as we can of Englishmen who are great sticklers for high wages, small production and strikes. My experience has shown that Germans and Irish, Swedes and what I denominate "Buckwheats"—young American country boys, judiciously mixed, make the most effective and tractable force you can find. Scotsmen do very well, are honest and faithful. Welsh can be used in limited number. But mark me, Englishmen have been the worst class of men I have had anything to do with; and this is the opinion of Mr. Holley, George and John Fritz.
>
> 2nd. It should be the aim of the firm to keep the works running steadily. This is one of the secrets of Cambria low wages. The workmen, taking year in and year out, do better at Cambria than elsewhere. On steady work you can calculate on low wages.
>
> 3rd. The company should endeavor to make the cost of living as low as possible. This is one bad feature at present but it can be easily remedied.
>
> These are the salient points. The men should be made to feel that the company are [sic] interested in their welfare. Make the works a pleasant place for them. I have always found it best to treat men well, and I find that my men are anxious to retain my good will by working steadily and honestly, and instead of dodging are anxious to show me what a good day's work they have done. All haughty and disdainful treatment of men has a very decided and bad effect on them.

Now I have voluntarily given you my views. I have felt this to be a necessity on my part; for I am afraid that unless the policy I have marked out is followed we need not expect the great success that is obtainable. These suggestions are the results of twenty-five years' experience obtained in the most successful iron works in the country:

—Crane and Thomas Iron Works, Port Richmond Iron Works, and the Cambia works.

You are at liberty to show this letter to your father and Mr. Coleman; otherwise regard it as a confidential letter. (1877, February 22)

Captain Bill would have worried at the incongruity of being surrounded, on the one hand, by wealthy entrepreneurs and bookkeepers who knew little of iron and steel and on the other by experienced laborers weaned on making iron, which could result in a stalemate similar to that which he had experienced at Cambria.

ET had been designed as a steel-producing mill, one of the first in the country that was not a converted iron-making facility, and this had certain consequences. The steel converters, the grim sphinxes, were located at the center of the facility. This location devalued the skilled laborers among the rollers and heaters. For its first four-and-a-half years of operation, there were no furnaces at ET and therefore no puddlers. When Jones installed electricity and gas at the works, the Bessemer shifts had to sustain twenty-four hour attendance, seven days a week, for if a sphinx became idle, the interior lining cooled and broke down, stopping the continuous flow of production, and often causing damage to the converter. Consequently, the steelers required other workers in the mill to follow their rhythm. Ironworkers lose their clout in a steel facility. The first Bessemer blow at ET was made on August 22, 1875, and a minor industrial revolution had begun with Bill Jones in charge.

Superintendent Jones was not happy with many aspects of the physical plant that Barnes had overseen in the early construction of ET. For nearly twenty years Captain Bill would be involved in redesigning and bringing the works itself up to his high standards—which he knew would also improve efficiency, cost, and safety. He wrote to Carnegie after about two years as superintendent: "Since these works have been placed under my charge, I have worked almost night and day to bring them to a high standard of excellence, so much so that I would not take Fifteen thousand dollars and go through the same mill. 'The sins of omission and commission' of my predecessor, in faulty construction; and ill-conceived designs, were a huge obstacle to a successful management" (1877, February 22). There were to be many such notes over the years to Carnegie commenting on specific items or mill functions, as Jones changed them to improve the mill operation.

In the early years ET produced no iron. Pig iron was purchased from the Lucy furnace a few miles north on the banks of the Allegheny, where Henry Curry was working for Tom Carnegie. After the war Henry had worked as a broker of iron. Then Tom and William Coleman hired him as superintendent at the Lucy. For five years, the Lucy provided ET with the pig to run Jones's Bessemer converters. At first the iron was hauled by barge and wagon from across the Allegheny River to Pittsburgh, then a small rail line was built in the1870s.

Beginning in 1876, Captain Bill reduced work shifts at ET from twelve to eight hours, with no loss in pay. Three teams with eight-hour shifts, predicated upon Bessemer blows of twenty minutes, formed the twenty-four hour day, running seven days a week. Bessemer workers labored more intensely in a more dangerous setting than did any other employee. These blows required vigilance and endurance that could not be sustained safely for twelve-hour turns. Jones established the eight-hour workday to avoid potentially expensive and crippling accidents, like steel sparks rupturing an eye or incinerating an arm. He consequently increased the number of men employed.

> *Jones established the eight-hour workday to avoid accidents.*

In addition to Captain Bill, emigrants, well-schooled in the philosophies of European anarchists, syndicalists, and communists, were among the most articulate and influential advocates of the eight-hour day. Initially, Carnegie embraced Jones's innovation, one that the unions, though not a strong influence at the plant, opposed, and the eight-hour shift would remain company policy until 1887, with one return to the double shift schedule in 1884 when the price of rails dropped precipitously.

Like the Captain's mother-in-law, the local religious community strongly objected in the press to labor on Sundays: "The ministers of the different denominations of Braddock are taking steps against work on the Sabbath day. The operation of the Edgar Thomson Steel Works, selling of liquors and other employments are to be requested to cease, or the law will enforce against them." Working the men as hard as he worked himself, Captain Bill responded:

> I have notified our bigoted and sanctimonious cusses that in event of their attempting to interfere with these works, I will retaliate by promptly discharging any workman who belongs to their Churches and thereby get rid of the poorest and most worthless portion of our employees. If they don't want to work when I want them, I shall take good care that they don't work when they want to. We bet a dollar they will be glad to drop this agitation. (1879, December 5)

By the end of ET's first two years of production, Jones had already filed no fewer than seven patent letters: in June 1876 he filed a letter for improved washers essential for Bessemer moulds used for forming ingots; on October 16, he filed one for a spiral screw used to tip carriage or suspended ladles so as to fully empty their loads without breaking gear teeth; in December he filed another dealing with ladles, a new means of applying pressure to molten steel just after poured into moulds; on January 23, 1877, he filed a letter for patenting a process to standardize the quality of Bessemer ingots by casting under pressure; on December 12, 1877, he filed two letters on the same day, one for a crane to operate ladles and another for hose couplings for steam pressure; fourteen days later he filed another letter for fastenings for the Bessemer converter; the following August, he filed yet another for a machine for sawing billets and bars. Each patent letter increased his indispensability and solidified his power to manage the mill as he saw fit. Yet, Jones also knew that recent inventions would soon be "Quite out of fashion, like a rusty mail/In monumental mockery" (Shakespeare, *Troilus and Cressida*).

"They didn't carry much importance," Uncle Dan would say many years later, "since Troy or Cambria or anyone could redesign around these inventions and not infringe on claims. [Jones] needed to secure by patent some crucial invention or process that would never be obsolete—we call it autocatalytic, in that the invention self-catalyzes processes in perpetuity. Even the Bessemer, Holley's grim sphinx, would be made partially obsolete by the open hearth method in a few years and [both Holley and Jones] knew it."

ET Superintendent William R. Jones at age 50

Section 15: Jones, Superintendent

Under Jones, sport became an extension of work at ET. Competition among coworkers was not only a source of entertainment on weekends or an activity engaged in on the only holiday of the year, the Fourth of July. For Captain Bill, sports became a pragmatic means of increasing production by knitting together work units and reducing friction on the job. He had plotted an area for a baseball diamond near town and west of the grim sphinxes, where organized teams of workers competed, teams from different departments and, more and more frequently, from other works.

The team rosters crossed ethnic lines, for Jones did what he could to dilute concentrations of members from one ethnic group in particular departments, as had been tradition in the country's iron works. He matched workers not on what tribe they belonged to but on what talent they exhibited. African Americans played baseball at ET even when they were not allowed to integrate with white professional teams. Work and play integrated ET's diverse workforce unlike that of any other iron and steel works of the time. Jones was far ahead of his time in the ethnically aware labor policy that he enumerated to McCandless, an ET practice that six years later in 1881 he reiterated before the British Institute of Iron and Steel in Birmingham, England: "We have representatives from England, Ireland, Scotland, Wales, and all parts of Germany, Swedes, Hungarians, and a few French and Italians, with a small percentage of colored workmen. This mixture of races and languages seems to give the best results and is, I think, far better than a preponderance of one nationality" (Bridge 1991, 110).

After Jones's death, this intentional integration faded and in time the Hungarians handled nearly all unskilled work, with only a very few Anglos performing journeyman work in the trenches with a Hunky (Fitch 1989, 15). Some on the board of Carnegie, like McCandless, took umbrage at Jones's penchant for baseball and his practice of rewarding workers with a trip to the horse races, considering it frivolity; they pressed for greater discipline in the mill. But since Tom and Andrew were delighted with profits, criticism dwindled. C. C. Teeter, whom Captain Bill pirated from Cambria as a clerk, reported for the week ending March 10, 1877, ET had produced 1,062 tons of rails, but three years later, for a comparable week, it produced 2,955 tons (1877, March 3; Jones 1880, November 11; Jones 1880, October 29). There seemed no end to the increases in production that improved equipment and good management could generate.

Jones's leadership and ability to solve problems, the work force's esprit de corps and experience, and Shinn's voucher system of accounting led to increased tonnage every month and profits that appeared to set Carnegie and Company ahead of any competition in the country. But not everyone appreciated Shinn's attention to detail. One laborer castigated him: "There goes that ——bookkeeper. If I use a dozen bricks more than I did last month, he knows it and comes round to ask why!" (Bridge 1991, 85).

Although profits rose steadily, through the years Carnegie badgered those in management, from Shinn and Jones to Frick and Schwab, about costs, even when he was traveling around the world (Wall 1970, 520). With Morse code that he had mastered as a young man during the war, Carnegie always kept apprised of what was occurring in his plants. One message from Sorrento, Italy, read:

> "Pyramids & Mt. Etna & Vesuvius have been our last climbs—Mt. E of course we did only from the base. Tell Capt. Jones there was a proud little stout man who gave a wild hurrah when he saw ET ahead. Was nt it a close race with C I Co. [Cambia Iron Company]?" (Bridge 1991, 102).

The competition among producers became so heated that each sought the other's monthly reports on the number of heats and rails produced. Holley's band of "scholars," most of them mechanics and engineers who had worked with Jones at Cambria, now supervised mills around the country and each was apprised of what the others were accomplishing. Robert Hunt, Jones's Union League compatriot, headed Troy in New York; Robert Forsyth had gone to the North Chicago Works; Jones's former boss, John Fritz, was at Bethlehem; John Fry had replaced Daniel Jones at Cambria; and Daniel Jones was now starting up a works in Colorado.

An indication of Jones's remarkable success, ET's profits steadily grew, even during years when rail prices and wages fell due to overproduction among all steel works in the pool (Casson 1907, 26; Bridge 1991, 102). Yet, as described above, these profits were not channeled into anyone's pockets. Carnegie battled nearly all, some in legal suits and others by humiliation: Phipps, Curry, and even his brother, Tom, his most able president, whose drinking might have been exacerbated by this treatment. Some wanted dividends on their investments, others argued that such profits should be reinvested in machinery to maintain ET's top position in the pool of steel producers. It was these very profits that were to be the major cause of bitter legal battles between Carnegie and Shinn and Henry Clay Frick. No one could force Carnegie, as majority owner, to change his mind, so that few of his early partners shared in any of the incredible wealth that ET ultimately generated. Meanwhile, however, Jones's accomplishments became an inspiration for poetry. Frank Cowan, author of both drama and fiction, wrote:

> Where the cannon of Braddock were wheeled into line.
>   And swept through the forest with shot and with shell-
> But woe to the Britons! In vain they combine
>   The thunder of heaven and the lightening of hell!
> There the turning converter, while roaring with flame,
>   Pours out cascades of comets and showers of stars,
> While the pulpit-boy, goggled, looks into the same—
>   Thinking little of Braddock and nothing of Mars.
>
> Where the guns of the foe were revealed by a flash—
>   A report—and the fall of the killed and the wounded,
> Till the woods were ablaze, and a deafening crash
>   With the wail of the wounded and dying resounded;
> There the ingot aglow is drawn out to a rail,
>   While the coffee-mill crusher booms, rattles and groans,
> And the water-boy hurries along with his pail,

Saying, Braddock be blowed! He's a slouch to Bill Jones.

Captain Bill adopted a curious symbol for a mill's success. To the victor among the rivals belonged an iron broom: a large wrought-iron emblem, hoisted high above a mill's entrance, symbolized the company's sweeping away previous production records. Jones told Carnegie that the tradition began in Johnstown.

"Cambria has suspended a large broom on the apex of their works. Give me a chance & I will bring the broom down here" (1877, January). Within three months, by March 1877, Captain Bill had the broom hoisted over ET's entrance (Jones1877, March 31). The broom remained atop the ET entrance for several years "until the records were beaten so often that the men had no time to remove the broom" (Casson 1907 27).

Captain Bill monitored all departments at ET and visited rival firms as well, including the Pennsylvania Steel Works during March 1877 and the Bethlehem Steel Works in November of the same year. Jones's joviality and confidence are captured in this note to Carnegie:

Dr. Sir:

For the last two months I have vainly endeavored to get actual figures of Con Dept [Converter Department] Cambria Works.

Yesterday I put on my best "bib & tucker" and went up to Cambria, and after some hard work and engineering succeeded in getting their figures from their monthly reports. The results were that I came away from Cambria feeling that I was "a bigger man than old Grant."

In rail and blooming mill practice we beat them as badly as in Con Dept.

Now get returns of all metals used and I will bet you a gold watch or anything else, that Cambria has melted full 200 tons more metal than we did in April.

Very Truly Yours,

W R Jones (1878, May 4)

Jones's pragmatic and competitive ways, viewed as quirky and maverick by most historians, influenced even the parsimonious Carnegie, who was ever trying to cut costs. As soon as a machine became obsolete, Captain Bill would upgrade and dump it in the corner of the mill's lot on the "scrap heap, near the baseball diamond" (Wall 1970, 473). At first Carnegie complained of waste, but Jones's reaction would be to shove a letter of resignation into the little man's palm and go "home for the day" (Holbrook 1939, 209). As Schwab later wrote, "the loss of Bill Jones would mean the collapse of the whole industry" (Whipple n. d., 32). Very quickly, Carnegie embraced Captain Jones's policy. The scrap heap and the baseball diamond were two of Jones's unorthodox but successful solutions for cutting costs and stimulating production.

Though men might be laid off briefly, Jones's policy of steady work for all and the increasing demand for steel expanded the works, so laid-off personnel usually found a new job opening up elsewhere at ET (Holbrook 1939, 211). The twenty-three men who had manned four furnaces at each turn, or the sixty-nine men working three turns per day, were replaced with new appliances that only needed six men, displacing fifty-seven. Similarly at the rail mill, the twenty-one men who had manned machines each turn, a total of sixty-three a day, were replaced by machinery that required only twelve to run it (Fitch 1989, 113).

Eventually eleven plants made up the Bessemer pool in the United States. They continued to over-produce steel rails, causing prices to fall. Yet, as Jones had promised McCandless, there was more steady work for more people at ET than in any iron or steel plant in the country (Wall 1970, 344). In 1885 operations were so uneven that he had to lay off sixteen hundred men but two weeks later reemployed fifteen hundred (ibid., 112-13).

But the Captain, like any manager, did encounter problems. In 1885, the manager of the blast furnaces, Mr. Cremer, was not doing a good job; men were "doing pretty much as they pleased" and production was way off, to the point that it came to Carnegie's attention. Jones found foremen drunk on the job and took responsibility when Cremer was afraid to act. He wrote Carnegie that "If I can't make these works as [a] whole do far better than what has been done this year, I will clear out myself. I am totally disgusted with the way things have been going and things will have to go better or something will bust" (1885, September 16). It was at this time that James Gayley was hired from Ohio to come and run the blast furnaces, and Cremer was let go.

Within two years of assuming control of mill operations at ET, Jones was the model superintendent, owner of several patents which made the Bessemer process more efficient, well-liked and respected by workers, consulted by his peers, and indispensable to the owners. ET had become the standard of excellence in the steel industry (Bridge 1991, 110).

Section 16: The Lesson of Shinn

Every major biographer of Carnegie, from Bridge in 1903 to the present, has discussed at length how Carnegie betrayed those on whom he relied, whether it was for money, expertise, connections, or resources. In later life he may have been seen as a great humanitarian, but he made his fortune through shrewd, often ruthless, business practices, many of them forced on the very men who had helped him the most. By 1877 he had already disposed of Thomas Miller, Andrew Kloman, and William Coleman. The next partner to fall was William Shinn, whom Carnegie earlier had used to oust Coleman. It was a Carnegie practice to have his high-level managers carry out the actual transactions when anything unpleasant was involved, leaving Carnegie above the fray and appearing idealistically farsighted. In truth he ruthlessly swindled partners and withheld dividends and payments until he alone could maximally benefit from them. Only in 1900, when the smartest businessman he ever hired sued him, did Carnegie have his true wealth and modus operandi exposed. It would be his undoing and within months he was out of the steel business.

Despite ET's phenomenal success, Carnegie could not refrain from needling Shinn on costs and Jones on production issues. Krass points out the contrasting responses of Jones and Shinn to their boss's badgering. Shinn was defensive while Jones "took a belligerent, yet pleasantly confident, posture with Carnegie" (Krass 2002, 142). Jones cautioned Carnegie to ease up on the nagging:

> I have invariably noticed that all works that make these special big outputs, weaken very badly afterwards. Tis better to run along well in hand, not overtax machinery and men. When you and our venerable President Mr. McCandless witness the horse race at Louisville, you noticed that they did not rush the horses on the first mile, but aimed at a gait that would give a good four-mile average.
>
> Notice our friend Major Bent of Penna Steel Works last year with all his brag and bluster he had to be content to following rear of the E. T.
>
> North Chicago started off the year with a magnificent spurt. Yet in February, the ET's nose appears in front, we beat North Chicago ably and they worked as many days as we did. And as regards economy in production, we are far ahead of them all. ...
>
> Now in conclusion you let me handle this nag in this race, I think I will keep her on the track, and may keep her nose in front. I think at the end of this year I will have her ahead, and when we stop to rub down, you will find her in excellent condition.
>
> Very Respectfully yours,
>
> W R Jones (1878, March 24)

In a letter dated May 10, 1877, less than two years after ET's beginnings, Carnegie revealed to Shinn a stratagem that foretold what was to be the fate of the letter's recipient: "There are possible Combinations in the future. It isn't likely McCandless, Scott & Stewart will remain with us—I scarcely think they can. I know Harry & Tom have agreed with me that you out of the entire lot would be wanted a future partner & I think we will one day make it a partnership Lucy F Co., U Mills, ET 7. & go it on the basis the largest Concern in the country" (Wall 1970, 354).

Shinn and Jones worked well together, complementing one another. They were physical opposites. "Shinn was a six-footer," according to my grandfather, Daniel Gage, "a skinny, gaunt man whose necktie and collar always seemed a size too large for his chicken neck." For all his dour appearance, Shinn was a teaser, possessing a wry wit and sharp eye that made children laugh. He praised Cora's performance of piano concertos that the nine-year old gamely tried to render with her tiny fingers.

The incongruent two, the barrel-chested, short-statured Jones and the Ichabod-like Shinn, had been responsible for the ET exhibition at the 1876 National Centennial in Philadelphia (*Unwritten History* 1917, 109). They had arranged a display in which fourteen of ET's products dazzled visitors, including a 120-foot rail weighing 2,480 pounds, several twisted rails, a rail bloom, and black ingot weighing 2,700 pounds (Jones 1877-8 Letter-box, items 50 and 58). Cora Jones remembered Shinn from her childhood, my uncle later reported. "Shinn and her father went off to the Philadelphia Centennial Exposition to show off ET's versatility. Shinn brought back for Cora her first banana, wrapped in tinfoil." The cost of a banana was a dime, a monetary peg that my uncle Dan used years later in an article about the banana industry (*Oregon Business Review* 1960).

Shinn had learned from Jones that Carnegie's Lucy furnace, under superintendent Henry Curry, Jones's Civil War comrade, was producing for ET poor quality pig iron at an inflated price. Curry's pig iron lacked sufficient silicon, prompting Jones to look for Bessemer iron elsewhere, slowing down steel output (Jones to Carnegie, 1877, December 11). Shinn and Jones challenged Carnegie, citing that Vulcan Iron in St. Louis was paying a dollar to a dollar fifty less for high quality pig from a nearby furnace (Shinn v. Carnegie, 3OQ). The implication was that the Lucy Works was setting an artificially high price for ET to yield an added profit. At the time Shinn was involved in establishing a company with his brother that would sell shale and limestone low in phosphorus to ET, which suggests that he too may have been involved in duplicitous practices. Carnegie, undoubtedly reacting to both the criticism and the potential competition, quickly moved against Shinn. He accused Shinn of being speculative, a propensity Carnegie practiced privately but publicly scorned in others, particularly when the benefit would not accrue to Carnegie. He wanted Shinn out.

In February 1878 David McCandless, the company's president, died suddenly of heart failure, which set in motion Carnegie's next dismissal. Shinn, for good reason, expected and wanted to be appointed to McCandless's position as president. He wrote this to Carnegie, who was touring in India. Carnegie postponed answering the request, refracting the issue at hand with an allusion to Shinn that "Mrs. McCandless and Helen may be provided for" (Bridge 1991, 122).

"Shinn raged about Carnegie during a visit to the Jones house, complaining that Carnegie was a hypocrite for what he paid the widow McCandless. Shinn warned Jones that Carnegie could not be trusted," Uncle Dan said. He went on to recall that Shinn had proposed to Jones during the late summer of 1878 that Jones join him in visiting the Vulcan Works in St. Louis. In 1876, Holley had completed his last U.S. Bessemer converter beside the Mississippi River. Shinn, Jones, and John Stevenson, in the engineering department at ET, traveled to St. Louis by rail, arriving on September 12 to inspect the works. The board at Vulcan passed a motion to offer Jones and Shinn aggregate salaries. Shinn, as general manager, was offered $15,000 in annual salary with stock amounting to between $100,000 and $125,000 in the Vulcan Iron Works; Jones was offered a salary of $6,000 with stock of $20,000 as plant superintendent (Bridge 1991, 124; Wall 1970, 358). Jones did not want stock in any company for which he worked, as it would stable him. Shinn accepted the Vulcan offer, as did Stevenson. Jones deliberated, for Harriet's condition limited travel from Pittsburgh, but moving to St. Louis would enable her to introduce her son and daughter to the children of her old friends in nearby Tennessee. Nonetheless, Bill Jones remained loyal to Tom Carnegie and stayed at Braddock (Wall 1970, 356-60).

The day after their return to ET, Shinn resigned as manager. He expressed his desire to remain an associate of the company by retaining his shares (Bridge 1991, 122-30). Andrew categorically refused Shinn's request, arguing that the firm had an unwritten policy that on resigning no former officer could own shares. He told Shinn that his shares were worth book value (book value being the cost of the business minus its debt, discounting potential or predicted outcome over time). Shinn was outraged and sued Carnegie.

Carnegie wanted to avoid a public trial, for it would reveal the remarkable profits the steel industry was generating, largely as a result of protective tariffs that limited European competition. Carnegie and Shinn agreed on a three-member team to arbitrate, to which Bill Jones was subpoenaed. The team unanimously settled in favor of Shinn, who received $200,000 for his shares. Carnegie, through the attrition of the original investors, was purging the board of directors to amass more than a majority of shares of the several interlocking companies.

After the trial at the Pittsburgh Temple, a Gothic structure that might have been the inspiration for a Walpole romance, Shinn warned Captain Bill that Carnegie would only approve of the Captain's radical approach to managing workers for as long as Jones's inventive know-how earned profits in the fickle market (Wall 1970, 359-60).

Carnegie had no leverage with Jones because Jones was not a partner; he refused partnership on several occasions. As cited in my uncle's correspondence with Joseph Frazier Wall: "... first, as he told [Carnegie] directly, 'I can do more good for the company if I remain on this side with the men. If I go into a partnership, the men will always think of me as being on the other side.' Carnegie agreed with this line of reasoning. The second reason the Captain kept to himself, but told his family 'I do not trust the man'" (1972, March 11 2).

With patents filed, only Jones could enjoy such independence, an autonomy that so moved one historian to write "It was known inside the company that Bill Jones was the only man living to whom Andrew Carnegie would apologize" (Holbrook 1939, 214). This point Holbrook further reiterated in correspondence with my father (Holbrook to William R. Gage October, 1939, 11). Jones's achievements and mechanical inventions made him indispensable, the one person Carnegie could not fire or humiliate; Carnegie was threatened should Jones desert and he came to detest that.

Deciding not to follow Shinn to St. Louis may have been a missed opportunity. However, for the time being, everyone connected with ET appeared to be a happy family. Tom Carnegie, both witty and able, was made general manager, and he often acted as a foil to Andrew. Jones spent much time with Tom, who revealed as fine a business sense as his older brother and was more knowledgeable. Tom's expertise and conviviality made him a boon companion Jones trusted with his life. He wrote to Andrew Carnegie in 1880, while they were negotiating a new salary for Jones:

> I want you to clearly understand that I wish to be connected with no other concern but the E.T. Your brother T.C. suits me exactly and is a far more sagacious business man that the late Gen. Man. It is a pleasure to me to be associated with him in the management of the Works and I only give utterance to my earnest convictions when I say of him, that he is the cleverest brained business man I ever had connections with. You may well repose confidence in him. (1880, November 5)

The mid-1870s at ET were years of relative harmony with management and labor working together. Good faith was assumed in negotiations. The country's economic depression had, to some degree, influenced this quiet period, which ended by the late 1870s. In the 1880s an over-supply of steel and an influx of Eastern European workers created a radically different situation. From 1881 until 1886 there were 22,336 separate strikes throughout the United States. Workers suffered greatly. Captain Bill's idea was to demonstrate to workers that the company was interested in their welfare, as well as in increasing profits. He convinced Carnegie to provide coal for household consumption at less than cost and to provide better rates for mortgages on homes: his aim was to help but not to hand out, to help without impinging upon a worker's self-reliance.

The relationship between Carnegie and Jones, with Tom Carnegie now in Shinn's former position as general manager and referee, continued, with each goading the other in a manner that resulted in success for ET. Carnegie needed Jones in his stable to assure himself of ultimate power. He offered Jones partnerships on many occasions, an offer which was always refused (*Unwritten History* 1917, 110, n3). Rather than accept a partnership, Jones asked for a larger salary in 1880. Comparing his worth to the salaries of superintendents of other major steel works, Jones and Carnegie agreed on a salary of $25,000 in 1880, the annual salary of the president of the United States at the time (Carnegie to Jones, 1880, November 9).

Captain Bill, after one of Andrew's periodic scoldings, challenged his boss in a letter to shut up or put up by betting Jones on outcomes. He ridiculed Carnegie for mouthing off at the mill and then posturing at competitor works. Carnegie persistently invited many to come to ET to observe how it was done best. These interruptions of those working annoyed all, especially when Carnegie in private badgered and complained. Carnegie had invited the owner of the Cleveland Rolling Mill "to send one of his smart sons here, and that we will show him all our improvements." One team from Cambria spent four days sleuthing at ET, "ferret[ing] out our practice. Columbus made the egg rest on end after all courtiers failed.

Yet how simple it was to the courtiers after seeing how it was done" (Jones to Carnegie, 1880, December 19).

Andrew, who lacked his brother's integrity and congeniality in the workplace, continued to badger heads of departments and workers. Periodically, such antagonisms fired Captain Bill's infamous temper. He continued to submit letters of resignation even after receiving his impressive salary. "He always carried a resignation letter in a pocket," Bridge reported in his book, "which he slapped down before Andrew on many occasions. Carnegie used his brother Tom to appeal to the Captain to accept his apology and withdraw the notice of termination. For Tom's sake, Jones always did back off and Andrew would temper his irritating habits for a while." Carnegie differed from Morrell; he did listen, and he could openly embrace new ideas.

Jones mocked those who succumbed to Carnegie's tyranny. He ironically shared his chagrin as top dog at ET, when he mimicked Carnegie: "Puppy dog number three you have been beaten by puppy dog number two on fuel. Puppy dog number two, you are higher on labor than puppy dog number one" (Bridge 1991, 113).

In 1879, to free ET of the Lucy furnace's expensive and poor quality pig iron, the Captain launched construction of the first of seven furnaces to be built on the ET grounds. Tradition established the naming of furnaces after one's inspiration. The Lucy furnace was named after Tom Carnegie's wife, Lucy Coleman Carnegie. The Isabella was named after Mrs. Herron, sister of another owner. Captain Bill named ET's furnace A, the Cora, after his daughter (*Unwritten History* 1917, 109). Cora remembered all her life how, when twelve years old, she was the Belle of Braddock's Field and fired up her furnace.

Holley came to inspect ET in the autumn of 1879. After dinner, Harriet was wheeled from the table, and the Captain carried her up the winding staircase to her second floor bedroom. Jones returned to hear depressing news from his friend. Managers of some of the firms in the Bessemer pool were reneging on Holley's consultant fees. For years, following his regular tours of European works, Holley had alerted the Americans to the newest European technologies and how Bessemer's designs were being modified there. Holley was worried that open hearth conversion would out-compete the Bessemer process, the kind of information for cartel leaders that foretold Holley's loss of influence.

Holley had lost weight—whiskey drove him so that he could write and travel for the cartel. That fall, Jones saw him in his cups often, but his mind was as hard as steel. A graduate of Brown University, he had infuriated academics at his alma mater, condemning excess philosophizing, arguing for balancing theory with practice. Practice without theory was meaningless activity. Theory without practical application provided teachers with a salary but was of little use for students lacking experience. According to Holley:

> The art must precede the science. The man must feel the necessity, and know the directions of a larger knowledge, and then he will master it through and through. Mark how rapidly the more capable and ambitious of practical men advance in knowledge derivable from books, as compared with the progress of Bookmen, either in books or in practice. Many men have acquired a more

useful knowledge of chemistry, in the spare evenings of a year, than the average graduate has compassed during his whole course.

Under what comparative facilities does the mere recitation-room student, or even the mere analyst of the hundred bottles, study applied chemistry? It is to these a matter of routine duty, without a soul; they are neither stimulated nor directed by a previously created want. (McHugh 1980, 269-70)

Holley's once-successful arrangement of brokering Bessemer's licenses in the United States now limited him and threatened his financial security. His only income came from a few patents, consultant fees, or honoraria for talks at colleges and symposia. His patents were primarily tied to the Bessemer process but were not inventions that were essential to converting iron to steel. Holley, like Jones, needed to develop a process more basic to steel production, a process that would not become obsolete.

Jones was eclipsing Holley as an inventor of steel machinery and processes. Holley had influenced the early growth of steel production: he was a prolific writer and renowned as a speaker on steel. The lord mayor of London had hosted him as the foremost American engineer and crucial to Bessemer production. In his last years and after his death, Holley was perhaps best recognized for distinguishing the subfields of engineering—mechanical from chemical. This academic distinction, however, did not feed his family and in the last year of his life things were difficult in the Holley household. The rise of the open hearth process in steelmaking threatened both Holley's inventions and some of Jones's as well (Holley and Smith 1878, 3, 4, 6, 7).

"Don't forget those lines that Bill Jones learned from Holley," Uncle Dan urged, reflecting on his grandfather's command of Shakespeare's canon.

if you give way,
Or hedge aside from the direct forthright,
Like to an enter'd tide they all rush by
And leave you hindmost;
Or, like a gallant horse fall'n in first rank,
Lie there for pavement to the abject rear,
O'errun and trampled on . . . (*Troilus and Cressida*)

The nags following were now trampling Holley, the horse that led the pack. Holley urged Jones to patent everything he had already invented. Jones reasoned that to go back to earlier achievements was to take time from present projects that augured a constantly changing future. Jones filed two groups of patents, in 1877 and then in 1878. Then, he held back and worked on his greatest achievements (Wall 1970, 532).

Section 17: Charlie Schwab

On his way home from ET on a freezing December day in 1879, the Captain stopped by McDevitt's store to purchase cigars. Spiegelmire, the building owner, had hired a youth to work for McDevitt, a renter in the German American's establishment. Seventeen-year-old Charlie Schwab, big-boned and with teeth that spanned a broad face, had a grin that made people smile and anticipate a bawdy joke. Charlie had timing, the timing that made him a good musician. Jones hired many young men to work at ET, and on that day he was sufficiently impressed with the youth who sold him cigars to offer him a job assisting surveyors in the engineering department; he began with a salary of one dollar a day.

Early in Charlie's employ, a draftsman left the department; the Captain gave Schwab the title of assistant and placed him in the newly emptied office with his own desk. The following year, the Captain surveyed his employees looking for one to fill an opening, a good promotion. He asked his department heads, "Which one of your draftsmen shall we send up to Scotia?"

"Why, any of them will fill the bill, Captain," was the answer.

"But there must be one more capable than the others. Who is he?"

"I don't know. They are all bright hustling youngsters."

"Tell every man to stick on the job until seven o'clock. I'll pick out Scotia's chief for you," Captain Bill said. In 1880 Carnegie Brothers had bought and begun open pit ore mining at Scotia Mines at Benore, Pennsylvania. It was a slow period when rail prices were very low, so all the young men were surprised at their extended day. At a little before seven o'clock, Captain Jones returned to study the scene. Each man but one glanced up at the clock

Charles Michael Schwab *(in 1901) would organize the world's first billion-dollar industry, United States Steel.*
(PD via Wikimedia Commons)

and returned to his work with little effort. At the crack of seven all the draftsmen put down their pencils and rose to retrieve coats and hats, except one, who remained at his desk, apparently unaware of the bustle around him. He diligently computed his figures as Jones walked up to his chair and exclaimed: "Charlie Schwab, you have a job at Scotia."

Schwab oversaw three younger men—all named Bill: there was fun-loving young Will Jones; Bill Richards, the son of an owner of a steel mill in England, who was interning at ET to prepare him to assume in time his father's position at home; and Bill Carnegie, the son of Tom and Lucy Carnegie. All were apprentices, and not one was interested in steel. They drove Charlie crazy with their antics, fighting continually, joking and showing up late, and

Schwab

became

Cora's

piano

teacher.

sabotaging each other's work. One afternoon Will Jones and Richards held down the slight Carnegie and shaved off his mustache. Tom's son then retrieved the mustache and sealed it in an ET envelope marked Carnegie's Mustache in the most elaborate calligraphy for posterity—but the letter mistakenly was sent to humorless Uncle Andrew, who thought that pranks eroded profits.

Charlie often visited the Joneses at home. He was a talented musician, and Jones hired him to teach twelve-year-old Cora and her older brother to play the piano. During the next four or five years Schwab would visit the Jones home twice a week to give Cora and her brother lessons. Cora soon was performing pieces by Brahms and from opera after her parents' lavish dinners. When, after dinner, Cora helped move Harriet upstairs, the mood of the guests below changed for the rest of the evening. Though Schwab was young, his singing and hail-fellow-well-met manner often resulted in an invitation to these gatherings. Later after she had gone to bed, Cora would hear all departing, except Andrew Carnegie's brother, Tom who occasionally spent the night in the guest room.

Charlie's tenure as a piano teacher continued as he quickly moved up at ET. Cora remembered how her brother labored over the ivory keys for weeks to learn a piece called "The Turkish Patrol." One afternoon the Captain entered the living room with his reading spectacles and the butt of a cigar in his teeth, commanding: "Let's end this lesson and you let Charlie play the damned Turkish thing!" That was the end of Will's music lessons. Cora, in all, studied for nearly five years with Schwab, and, thanks to Charlie, became quite accomplished, something my mother recalled when in the 1940s I had to take piano lessons, and likely possessed the talent of Will Jones. (Whipple n.d., 24).

In the early 1880s Captain Jones invited Charlie Schwab to accompany him on a personal reunion at the wall at Fredericksburg, where so many of his comrades had died. It says something about both relationships that Jones took Schwab and not his son, Will, on this pilgrimage. A pair of Morgan horses drew their carriage south through Maryland to Virginia to the battle site. Jones drove the team around Falmouth and out to Camp Humphreys, named after the general who had commanded the Third Division in the Fifth Army Corps, and who was one of the men from whom Jones had learned about leadership. From there they drove to the nearby site of George Washington's childhood home, then over a new bridge spanning the Rappahannock into the town of Fredericksburg and out Telegraph Road up to the wall. They tethered the team and got out, walking across in front of the wall and climbed a fence not there twenty years before in the snow-covered, body-littered field. The ground was muddy as they walked east to a level area within the declivity of the hill.

"Here's where I slept the night of the battle." Just as Jones said it, a farmer's voice shouted, "look out for the bull." The Captain and Charlie rushed to a fence and vaulted over it, as the bull, puffing and snorting, drove into the sturdy barricade. "Damned," said Jones, panting, "This is the second time I've been chased off this here field (*Royal Blue Book*, 24)."

"Schwab was close to Cora; they remained in touch for the rest of their lives. He visited us in Los Angeles around 1926 to pick up D. D. Gage's biography of Captain Bill," my mother said many years later. Schwab was five years' Cora's senior, but she may have been sweet on him. She was shocked by Charlie's sudden marriage in 1883 to his landlord's stepdaughter, Rana Dinkey. Rana, with her brother Alva, helped her mother run the Wagner Boarding House on Braddock Avenue, down the street from Spiegelmire's. Several mill workers rented rooms at Wagner's. Rana was a heavyset young woman and sharp-tongued, but she was also quite caring. Her brother, Alva, was another of the young men Captain Jones hired and groomed for leadership in the industry. Alva Dinkey was a year older than Cora, and Jones hired him as a water boy two months before Schwab had started working at ET. Dinkey shared the Captain's knack for invention, later patenting some key components for steel production, like the Dinkey car. Eventually, Dinkey was promoted to the presidency of Carnegie Steel Company.

Charlie's marriage to Rana was quite a surprise to everyone, especially since he was a Roman Catholic and she a Presbyterian. The Dinkey enterprise hosted the wedding ceremony of this young man, who was rapidly ascending to positions of leadership at ET, and who, in 1886, at only twenty-four, became the superintendent of the Homestead Works (Hessen 1975, 29).

Some called the Captain a Merlin, a wizard with rituals and superstitions. Bill Jones was convinced that if the works were not operating on New Year's Day it augured badly for the coming year. On the first day of 1884, the twenty-two-year- old Charlie was reeling from the flu, and his wife forced him to stay home in bed. About two hours later, she bustled into the room: "Charlie, look outside—Captain Jones has just pulled up in a wagon full of what looks like your office!"

Since Christmas, the board had approved the Captain's proposal to build a massive mill, and he had assigned Schwab to draft the specifications. When Schwab was missing on New Year's Day and Captain Bill learned he had the flu, he simply moved Charlie's office to Charlie's house. Captain Bill carted stool, desk, drafting board, inkstand, and drawings to Charlie's room in the red brick, six-room house, which was provided by the firm (Whipple). Charlie used one of the six rooms for a chemistry laboratory to freshen up his understanding of what he studied at Loretto. That left the bedroom, bathroom, wash room, the kitchen, and the dining room, so the Captain maneuvered the bulky table top into the dining room and planted it squarely atop the dining room table:

"Charlie, always work on New Year's!" he boomed.

Charlie's wife, trailing behind, complained, "But where will we eat?"

"We'll just eat in the kitchen, Rana," retorted Charlie from the bedroom as the Captain, before returning to the wagon for the stool, hoisted the feverish Schwab out of bed and guided him into his own dining room.

What was to become one of the Captain's supreme achievements, the rail mill, was sketched out on the Schwab's dining room table. By the turn of the century, Schwab would organize the world's first billion-dollar industry, United States Steel.

Section 18: Student becomes Teacher

Captain Bill stayed current on professional developments. He belonged to a number of professional associations: the American Institute of Mining Engineers, the American Society of Mechanical Engineers, the Society of Western Pennsylvania, and the Iron and Steel Institute of Great Britain. He traveled to attend and was active in the American Institute of Mining Engineers and was in Troy, New York, for the 1883 meetings. In 1884, he wrote to Andrew Carnegie: "I intend visiting Cin. this week to attend meeting of Mining Engineers and arranged with Mr. Bouscarin to take a trip on Cin. Southern as far as Chattanooga (where I was married in 1861) and will take a look at the rails we furnished them, and see how they are wearing. Expect to be gone one week" (1884, February 17).

He also visited other works. As early as March 1877, he wrote to Carnegie "... I visited Penna Steel Works on my return home. The 'Natives' there were thunderstruck at what we were doing." In some ways Jones continued what Holley had started, attending meetings, visiting works, comparing installations and production, and maintaining friendships and contacts. He clearly loved the competition, the mechanics of the process, and the men involved.

Carnegie wanted Jones to investigate a new process, and he wrote to Jones on February 10, 1880, asking him to travel to Wales with Holley (Wall 1970, 503). Iron ore high in phosphorous converted to brittle, flawed steel, and something in the Bessemer converter's lining impeded the purging of phosphorous. Jones and Carnegie were interested in the claims of an amateur Welsh chemist, Sidney Gilchrist Thomas, who had patented a means of lining the bottoms of Bessemer converters to neutralize an acid/base problem that affected phosphorous in poor-quality ore. The potential of this invention was important for ET, because most of the iron in Pennsylvania had high percentages of phosphorous.

To obtain proper ore for the finicky Bessemers, most U.S. steel producers transported ore from the Lake Superior region, where the ore was low in phosphorus. If Thomas's discovery worked, the Carnegie Company could purchase nearby ore high in phosphorous at a considerable savings. Once Thomas had perfected his method, any U. S. producer could save on transportation, but more ominously, any country with poorer quality ore could produce quality steel. From this date until the First World War, Germany, Austria, France, Italy, and Russia competed with the steel industries of Britain and the U.S. for hegemony in the production of this material that was eventually used for weapons of mass destruction.

Carnegie's request for Jones to accompany him put Holley in a difficult position. Holley's influence with the U.S. pool of Bessemer producers was waning. Could they accuse Holley of complicity with Carnegie by including Jones as a Trojan horse? Concerned about diplomacy, Holley suggested that Carnegie ask permission of the pool to allow Jones to accompany him. Carnegie was insulted by Holley's request, as if his integrity was being questioned. Consequently, Jones cancelled plans to sail with Holley, and instead Cora travelled with her father to England; the two would meet Holley in London. Holley tried to assuage Carnegie in a follow up letter:

I naturally inferred that he [Jones] was to travel and study the steel with me.

As the Besr. Steel Co. insists that the results of my work in every sense shall be common to all the eleven works, I had of course to ask their endorsement of my having Mr. Jones as a professional companion. Your conclusion that Mr. Jones shall not sail with me is a disappointment to me, and it is quite unnecessary in view of anything I have written . . . I regret that I am to be deprived of Mr. Jones' company and judgment. (McHugh 1980, 349)

After several days in London, Captain Bill and his daughter traveled by train to Manchester and then on to Birmingham. There they met Lowthian Bell, Sidney Gilchrist Thomas, and the recently-knighted Lord Bessemer, whom Cora remembered smelled of curry. Cora also remembered that her father had worried about not cutting a fashionable figure. Cora, though, quoted Tennyson when she described her father to Alice Gage, her daughter-in-law, years later, as "Oiled and curled [like an] Assyrian bull/Smelling of musk and insolence."

Jones delivered a paper before the British Iron and Steel Institute, held that year in Birmingham. This association had earlier scorned his fellow Welshman Gilchrist Thomas, whose initial claim for improving the steel process they failed to even consider. The audience for the Captain's paper was composed of the world's leading engineers and scientists. Muttering in the audience caused him to stammer a bit. Some took issue with the eight-hour day, and the body language of others suggested doubt about his statistics. How could ET, built only six years before, surpass production of the great iron and steel works of England? It would take time for Jones's ideas to be digested and taken seriously. When the Captain finished, Lowthian Bell, a regal figure in the industry, uttered words in praise for the Captain's speech: "What he ha[s] accomplished in the production . . . revolutionized the steel industry" (McHugh 1980, 368). *The Chronology of Iron and Steel*, published in 1937, singled out Captain Jones's 1881 address as one of the ten most important developments in steel production in that year (Goodale1931, 135). Jones's apprehension about presenting his unorthodox policies had been unwarranted.

Captain Bill and Holley went their separate ways touring European steel works. Jones and his daughter left England for the continent, where they toured Belgium, Germany, and the Austro-Hungarian capital of Vienna. Holley had more time, taking another route and eventually reaching Russia via Poland. The Captain visited the Krupp Factory in Essen, Germany, the first American to be invited to observe the open hearth process in this German plant. Cora remained at the hotel.

With Meerschaum pipe now clenched in his teeth rather than a toby, the Captain with Cora disembarked from the ship that brought them back to the United States. On arrival, they received word from Mary Bucknell Lloyd that Harriet was experiencing a severe spell and needed the two back in Braddock. Before they could book tickets for the train, they learned that Harriet was recovering, and they spent a week in New York.

Only weeks after settling back into their routines — Cora resuming her music and the Captain catching up on correspondence and complaining about what had been mismanaged while he was away—the shocking news arrived: Holley was dead! After a history of hard drinking followed by periods of abstinence to please his wife, he was only nearing fifty when he died of peritonitis, perhaps resulting from drinking and a career of rugged travel and tough negotiations. The lessons of the master were to persist in guiding Jones to personal decisions that ironically and coincidentally influenced conditions relating to his own demise at nearly the identical age.

Holley was dead!

The Captain immediately prepared to journey to New York City, packing his bags; ordering his secretary, Getty, to purchase a roundtrip ticket; and deputizing Tom Cosgrove, his old side-kick from Johnstown days, to take over. Jones left Bessemer Station for New York with a heavy heart to honor the death of his mentor and Cora's godfather. After some hours on the train, he arrived, and, in a hackney cab, landed at the Hoffman House near Madison Square Gardens. He and Cora had stayed at the nearby Brunswick Hotel, which catered to an international clientele. But on this occasion, Jones preferred to be by himself.

The next day at the funeral, the Captain grieved with those whom Holley deemed the Order of the Bessemer Boys (McHugh 1980, 371). These included such leaders as John Fritz of Bethlehem, John Fry of Chicago, and Robert Hunt of Troy, all of whom had benefited so greatly from the wisdom of the master's teaching at Johnstown. In the case of Jones and Hunt, some even exceeded Holley's achievements, as is the dream of every great teacher.

A month after Holley's passing, the Captain wrote Carnegie with an issue that revealed his own self-interest and that within nearly a decade would constitute the reason for his leaving Braddock and Pittsburgh. He and Holley had occasionally reviewed what they possessed, beyond salaries and commissions, that would fund their lives in old age and secure their families' welfare. Within a month of the funeral, Jones wrote Carnegie, asking him to try to influence some of the other representatives of the Bessemer cartel to provide what they had to date reneged on:

> Mr. Holley made a dying request of myself, as well as others to press the Bessemer Association to purchase his Patent for removable Converters, so as to provide for the maintenance of his family. For his very eminent services in developing the Bessemer process in this Country, I candidly believe it would be the proper thing for the Association to accede to his dying request. Will it be too much in me to ask you to press the matter. (1882, February 28)

Coincidentally, most of the European works had purchased the Holley Patent but many of the eleven U.S. steelmaking works had not (McHugh 1980, 268). Jones's request of Carnegie, advocating for Holley's dying wish, paid off, as the Bessemer Steel Company did pay $50,000 to his widow at the March meeting. The group's decision honored Holley's memory, as it was becoming clear that the open hearth would eventually make obsolete the Bessemer process, an opinion that both Jones and Holley had shared.

From January to November 1882, Holley's posthumous report, "The Siemens Direct Process,"— his analysis of what he had learned at European works during the trip on which the Captain was initially to accompany him — was being finalized (Holley 1882, November 20). These findings, with Jones's own from his independent trip, focused upon a crucial project, the direct process, which would engage Jones for this rest of his life. Direct process is a general term used on many occasions when a step is eliminated along the chain of processes from extracting ore to stacking a steel rail. The ultimate direct process would be a wizard, schooled in alchemy, picking up a fistful of dirt and casting it into a finished rail.

Holley's discussion specifically addressed the better of two direct process methods in the open hearth spectrum of transforming hot iron ore to steel blooms, from which rails derive. Both the Siemens and the Catalan method eliminated steps in cooling and heating, which translated into less time, less fuel, less labor, lower cost, and cheaper rails. It was the germ of this concept that would engage Jones in inventing and filing for two patents in 1888. The Jones Direct Process using the Jones Hot Metal Mixer would be that key innovation for both Bessemer and open hearth, so that should Bessemer be eclipsed, the Jones mixer would be indispensable no matter what steel conversion technology entered the field. In one operation, the Jones Direct Process symbolizes the verticalization of the industry, a far cry from the autonomous entrepreneurs of only a decade earlier producing links in the chain at various locales.

Holley's bust in Washington Square Park, New York City bearing the inscription:
In honor of Alexander Lyman Holley foremost amoung those whose genius and energy established in American and improved throughout the world the manufacture of Bessemer Steel, this memorial is erected by engineers of two hemispheres.

(By Jim Henderson (Own work) [CC0], via Wikimedia Commons)

117

Section 19: Cora's Adolescence

The trip to Europe in 1881 was Cora's Grand Tour. It gave her a sophistication that few in Braddock possessed. When they visited London, the Captain and Cora stayed at Claridge's Hotel in Mayfair and toured the city for three days. The Captain bought Cora a diamond and platinum necklace, a ring that Cora gave to her closest friend Mimi on her marriage to William Yost, a diamond-encrusted broach for Harriet, and an opal bracelet for his mother-in-law. The two visited an art exhibit featuring the works of Edward Burne-Jones. Cora shared her father's taste for pre-Raphaelite artists and writers. She particularly liked the wallpaper designs of William Morris and purchased several patterns to share with her mother for the living room on Kirkpatrick Street. The Captain admired Morris for his writings in political theory.

Cora at age 16

After seeing the Elgin Marbles in the British Museum, they viewed the casts of replicas of famous pieces at the Museum of Manufactures, today known as the Victoria and Albert Museum. Father and daughter walked through the courts and halls filled with replicas of sculpture, including Michelangelo's David, and portions of classical buildings such as Trajan's Column in Rome and the twelfth century Portico de La Gloria from Santiago de Compostela.

Cora told her sons and daughter-in-law how her father read aloud city names carved alphabetically on the frieze circumscribing the court at the Victoria and Albert and indicated which ones they would soon visit. They attended a performance of *Das Liebesverbot*, an early work by the aging Wagner. Though Jones loved the source for the German's musical drama, Shakespeare's *Measure for Measure*, neither of them enjoyed the music. In Vienna they attended a performance of Anton Bruckner's *Te Deum* that Cora disliked for its heavy and somber religiosity. Like her father, she preferred Johannes Brahms.

Father and daughter spent a week in New York City before traveling home to Braddock. Cora would tell the story over and over later in life of how the receptionist at the hotel desk used speaking tubes to communicate with staff on upper floors. The pair dined at Delmonico's Restaurant. Cora remembered her father after supper lighting his new Meerschaum pipe with a friction match, the first time she had even seen one. The meal came to five dollars, a little more than a machinist's salary for two days' work at ET that year (*Unwritten History*, 1917, 110).

Electricity was making its first appearance as street lighting. Down Fifth Avenue they walked, passing Brentano's Bookstore, eyeing red and white poles announcing oyster bars, staring up at buildings that dwarfed church steeples and the snaking iron and steel of the elevated elevator trains. The Captain pointed out the office of the *New York Herald*, the newspaper that had funded Stanley's expedition to look for Livingston, who was lost in Africa. Cora remembered that their hotel room was stuffy, smelling like a Pittsburgh armoire in August.

> *Captain Bill called a towering baseball a "skyscraper" when the ball drove heavenward.*

Since her trip abroad, Cora had become more cosmopolitan; she loved the theater as her father did, although her enthusiasm was tempered somewhat by her mother's religious beliefs. Although local Pittsburgh theater thrived, it mainly drew male audiences, and the dramas dealt with topical issues, not more classical works (*Royal Blue Book*, 1913). For a long period after the actor John Wilkes Booth murdered President Lincoln, Pittsburgh and many other cities either outlawed all theater or proper society looked down on those who frequented it. Two decades after the war, many in the community still looked upon actors and musicians with disfavor.

When Cora was fifteen, Harriet was in remission from her chronic, debilitating disease, and the family celebrated the Fourth of July 1882. It was the grandest day of any year in Pittsburgh but still not as extravagant as the spectacles in Baltimore. Parading through the streets were groups of Masons in eastern attire; Irish fire companies; heavy-set men in lederhosen; Welsh choral groups with leeks in their hats; ladies of temperance and suffragettes; and war veterans in their regimental uniforms, some with ribbons of the Mexican War.

In full uniform leading the men of the 133rd and 194th, Captain Bill stepped proudly. Athletic teams in striped tank tops and cuffed trousers marched en masse before the division of the labor assemblies, like the newly formed Amalgamated union. Bringing up the rear of the labor divisions and sports teams were African Americans. Captain Bill loathed how labor and parade organizers relegated them to the rear (Montgomery 1987, 108).

Paralleling the parade were stalls with lemonade served by pigtailed friends of Cora. One booth among the concessions allowed anyone interested to receive undetermined voltage of electricity as the newest of "hits." After the parade ended at Friendship Park in East Liberty, Cora and her bosom pal, Mimi Corey, found themselves bored with the speakers on the platform, civic leaders like Tom Armstrong and Miles Humphreys and the candidates for mayor in the fall election. But the girls' parents and young William Yost listened. Yost, originally from Johnstown, had been pirated by Jones from Cambria to Braddock. He was the Jones family lawyer and would, in time, work his way into the Carnegie firm as legal counsel.

The girls maneuvered over to where the brass bands performed marches, patriotic tunes, and romantic melodies. One singer captured Cora's eye, Daniel "D. D." Gage, who was known for his tenor solos. Though small in stature, Daniel was handsome, with fine, distinct features. He often sang with the Stephen C. Foster Serenaders at such affairs. Later in the afternoon, amateur baseball teams from several mills played ball.

Nearly a half-century later in Los Angeles, John Potter explained to my father and Uncle Dan when they visited him downstairs how Captain Bill carried on watching what he described as the visitation of Apollo. He loved sport. Potter said Captain Bill called a towering baseball a "skyscraper" when the ball drove heavenward higher than church steeples, higher than the buildings Jones had seen when he visited Holley in New York. Some hits arced over the fence, clearing the bases, and then Captain Bill would throw out coins for the players. If such a ball was hit by a player from the other team, he would smash his toby into the stands where he watched the game.

One evening at the theater, Cora heard the tenor voice of D. D. Gage; she recognized him from the Fourth of July two years earlier. Although anticipating her parents' disapproval, she fell head over heels for the young man. Much later in life, D. D. Gage told his sons about their mother when he first saw her at the theater. In her European attire, Cora attracted the eyes of many young men who

D.D. Gage

slipped out of barbershops and tobacco stores to view the Belle of Braddock, the Czar's seventeen-year-old daughter. One of those up-and-coming swains was William Ellis Corey, Mimi's cousin—who much later would follow Schwab as President of United States Steel.

Cora concealed her infatuation for D. D., who had visited the home on Kirkpatrick one evening to sing, with Cora accompanying on the piano. Harriet quickly caught on. He was a singer, a performer on stage, and thus not worthy of her daughter. She barred D. D. from their home and forbade Cora to see him. Secretly, they met whenever Cora visited downtown Pittsburgh.

D. D. had been born in Oil City, Pennsylvania, one of seven children, to John Gage and his wife. John Gage was a farmer, but during the recession of the 1870s he went to Boston where he worked for a year or more. There he was influenced by the writings of Channing, Emerson, and Parker. He returned to own a farm at Cambridge Springs, where he was also a beekeeper. He became a pillar in the local Methodist Church as well as a justice of peace. D. D. traveled a great deal for his music career, but Cora's strict and class-conscious mother never came to approve of him.

Section 20: New Faces

Despite many advancements and much integration by many mills, much of the iron and steel industry still consisted of independent companies producing the various components that went into the finished iron rails. But these independently owned companies, one mining fuel, another delivering fuel, another ore, another blasting ore and fuel in furnaces into iron ingots, another pressurizing the ingot into blooms and then billets and then rails—they were becoming history. Coke was still cooked in ovens near the coal-mining site and shipped to mills, and pig iron was still produced at furnaces located throughout Pennsylvania and shipped to mills to be changed into wrought iron. Carnegie and Kloman Company had built the Lucy blast furnace in 1870 on the Allegheny River. The seventy-five-foot tall Lucy furnace was huge—surpassing in size and production potential all existing blast furnaces in the region. While the Lucy was being completed, a syndicate of small furnace owners joined together to build the Isabella only a short distance away. It was of a similar size and capability, and when the two went into production in 1870 a famous rivalry began, one in which the two American furnaces reached production levels that bested—even astounded—their European counterparts. Records were widely published and followed for years as production levels continued to their spectacular rise year after year.

Ownership of the blast furnaces allowed companies to supply their own pig iron; it also provided a reliable continuous supply. Such ownership was among the first steps taken to create vertically integrated companies. Superior even to ownership of dispersed enterprises was centralization of several stages of the production process on one site. The Cora blast furnace, which began producing in January 1880, was right on the ET grounds, not across town like Tom Carnegie's Lucy furnace; its construction had been overseen by Julian Kennedy, who remained in charge of the seven blast furnaces at ET as they were brought on line. Carnegie Steel, led by Bill Jones, was the leader in the industry; thereafter a steel works would be one consolidated factory. Both Carnegie and Jones had learned from the British the "necessity for owning raw materials and finishing the completed article ready of its purpose" (Krass 2002, 173). The economic efficiencies realized by controlling more than one stage of the production process meant vastly cheaper prices than could be obtained from a competitor or independently owned firm. For the remainder of the century, Carnegie and Phipps continued to buy or build mines, factories, and transportation in an effort to control as much of the process and delivery of their product as possible. Carnegie was the first to acquire shares in firms that were vital to his competitiveness. Jones was the genius who made it all work.

Three important developments were to influence the Carnegie Company's direction for the rest of the 1880s: 1) unions would acquire national authority that further polarized workers and management, with unions themselves polarizing skilled and unskilled associations battling for national hegemony; 2) the Gilchrist Thomas process would allow ET to purchase less expensive, nearby poorer quality ore to cut shipping costs; and 3) the Homestead open hearth process would begin to compete with the Bessemer as an effective method to produce gross steel.

During the 1870s Jones negotiated with workers in good faith, but when the Cora was installed in 1880, puddlers exhibited what he deemed elitism, a willful capriciousness, arbitrariness, racism, and sometimes graft. Jones's conflict with furnace workers dated back to Cambria. While puddlers showed they understood the devolution of their craft when they accepted hourly wages, they continued to resist each step in the verticalization of the steel making. Workers of iron, once subordinated within the whole, believed they had become working drones: "preoccupation with output at all cost [that yielded] nominal wages might be good, but unit labor costs would fall, and workers would become enslaved to the machine" (Warren 1996, 65). As one veteran of the Amalgamated reflected years later in1910:

> The union was arbitrary. "We kept men employed who ought to have been fired," said one, "and that wasn't right. But what could we do? There are many men in any mill or factory who are ignorant, unreasonable and irresponsible. There is no way of keeping such men out of the union and their votes count for just as much as those of the better sort. It was no more than natural that these men should, to some extent, have dictated the policy of the union." (Fitch 1989, 102)

Some union members contracted for fees to land jobs for third parties at furnaces. Some earned outstanding annual wages; in one case, a worker took in $25,000 in a year when his fees were added to his wages (ibid., 98). At ET in 1882, hourly salaries were: roller: $4.00; heater: $3.30; vessel man: $3.00; spiegelemelter: $2.83; machinist: $2.20; carpenter: $2.10; blacksmith: $2.00; bricklayer: $1.30; helper: $1.40; general laborer: $1.20; boy: $0.50. (ibid.) The Amalgamated would have included just the rollers, heaters, vessel man, and spiegelemelter, but not the others, although they would have greatly outnumbered the higher-paid craftsmen (ibid.).

Some have argued that Jones used building projects around the ET lot as a subterfuge, a means of laying off workers who would then be asked, as condition of re-employment, to sign a pledge which constituted a promise not to organize. This interpretation is nonsense. In 1885 ET was one of only three steel works out of eleven that did not object to an employee belonging to a union; the others forced employees to sign iron-clad oaths of nonunionism (Montgomery 1987, 31). Jones had no problem with the Knights of Labor and personally advocated a company union. He did dislike the Amalgamated Association of Iron and Steel Workers, because it could close a works with a very small percentage of the workforce upset about pay.

The new Amalgamated Association, formed in 1876, included a mix of interests that ranged from puddlers, rail workers from the Brotherhood of Rail Heaters, and rollers from the Iron and Steel Roll Hands Union. The old Sons of Vulcan were predominately Irish. When John Jarrett, a friend of Captain Bill, became the president of the National Lodge of the Amalgamated in 1880, he instilled some sense into union policy—he was reasonable and open to alternatives. Jones and Jarrett had been exploring making the eight-hour day an issue for the union to embrace, and Jarrett even entertained a radical idea of starting up an iron and steel works from which all profits would accrue to the workers, the purpose being for the national union representatives to better understand the complications faced by management (Fitch 1989, 107-8). This plan never materialized. Under Jarrett the Amalgamated reached a membership of sixteen thousand. He went on to join the Harrison administration in Washington, D.C., eventually becoming a consul in England.

By spring of 1882 five blast furnaces fed iron to ET's steel converters. Captain Bill learned that several members of the Amalgamated Association of Iron and Steel Workers had made inroads among those turning heats at five furnaces. Angry and feeling betrayed by his workers, Jones once again resigned from ET (ibid., 88). He inferred that Amalgamated's anti-Negro clause was a fundamental tenet of its raison d'être—to preserve good jobs for white Americans. Even as late as 1885 at the national convention of the Amalgamated, a minority pushed for a resolution stating that "no colored person of any trade or occupation be eligible to hold membership" (Kleinberg 1989, 18). Panicked, Carnegie went directly to William Martin, the secretary of the Amalgamated, requesting that Martin meet with Jones and himself, so that Martin could answer Jones's charge that the union was racist. At the meeting Martin explained to Jones and Carnegie that Jones had been correct, that exclusion of Negroes was in the union's charter, but at the convention of the Amalgamated in Chicago that very year a majority had voted to admit them. Temporarily satisfied, Jones withdrew his resignation (Montgomery 1987, 264; Kleinberg 1989, 4).

Of the 331 African American workers at ET, one in five was skilled labor, close to the ratio among native-born Irish, of whom 23 percent were skilled (Fitch 1989, 353). In his speech at Birmingham, Jones had specified "colored" labor in his work force. Willis Toggan, an African American, advanced in four years from his position as a custodian to the position of chemist in ET's Chemistry Department (Gaughan 1994, June 5).

In the early 1880s at the Homestead Mill, the Amalgamated made much trouble for the Kloman Company that opened the works. Andrew Kloman, who earlier had separated angrily from Carnegie, had built the Pittsburgh Bessemer Steel Company at Homestead, a few miles from ET on the other side of the Monongahela River. From the beginning, this rail mill was a direct challenge to ET and soon employed the open hearth process as an alternative to Bessemer conversion. Before the plant was completed, Kloman died. Though Homestead produced its first steel rail on March 19, 1881, trouble with labor so discouraged the owners that when, in October 1883, Carnegie approached the firm with an offer, management sold the company to him. Carnegie then organized a second Carnegie iron and steel company, Carnegie, Phipps, & Company. He built Siemens open hearth furnaces that could convert inferior iron ore and produce a greater volume of steel. Soon both mill and Amalgamated were doing well. Open hearth heats entailed labor rhythms more like furnace work, requiring twelve-hour shifts (Wall 1970, 528-32). The union's success at Homestead was never equaled at ET or Cambria.

Uncle Dan once explained the difference between the open hearth process and that of a Bessemer converter. "It takes more time to turn a heat but the open hearth can convert so much more volume of steel at one go. A Bessemer football can only produce from five to ten tons per blow at most, but it does it fast, in fifteen minutes. The Bessemers at ET produced seven-foot ingots for train rails. A good day's output in tonnage from one converter was twenty-eight heats; that's about one every fifty minutes, fifteen minutes to blow and thirty-five minutes to load and unload. At 6.5 tons, that Bessemer would produce nearly two hundred tons of rails a day. But Homestead's open hearth converters produced ortho-stats of structural steel for buildings and bridge girders, and hammered flat into vast sheets to sheath ships. Now that's the truth that makes the world run." Ultimately ET would have a Bessemer mill, a blooming mill, and an open hearth mill.

Cora remembered well the atmosphere of violence during the days when the Captain's fight with the Amalgamated came to a head. Furnace heaters were threateningly brash and aggressively pushy. Captain Bill had been fired up by a number of them, who chanted lines like "There were no men invited such as Slavs and 'Tally Annes,'/Hungarians and Chinamen with pigtail cues [sic] and fans,/No, every man who got the 'pass' a union man should be;/No black sheep were admitted to the Puddlers' Jubilee ."

One such character, David Gibson, flashed a knife at an Italian worker in the rolling mill. The Captain fired Gibson on the spot, but sometime later he ran into Gibson on the ET grounds. Jones exploded: he had fired Gibson and so why was the man on ET property? The witless Gibson answered that he was working for another company, which was independently servicing one of ET's departments. Jones's notorious temper got the better of him, and he informed Gibson that he would see to it that Gibson would be fired from that new job, too. Gibson stomped off swinging from cliché to catchphrase. He did get fired from his new job. The next week, Gibson threatened to retaliate by murdering Jones and his entire family.

One evening Cora was surprised to see her father walking, not riding in his carriage, to 817 Kirkpatrick Street. He was with Father Hickey, a priest in Braddock, who had heard that Gibson was carrying a gun and raving that he would kill a Czar for dinner. Hickey had called at the works to warn Captain Jones. At the priest's insistence, the two had trekked home roundabout, avoiding the main streets of town.

Sometime later that same night, a delegation called at the Joneses' double-turreted home. They had come to press their claims for higher pay; the Captain listened quietly as one man in particular ranted. From the upstairs landing, Cora was trying to understand the nature of the confrontation. The discussion became more heated, and the workers were unaware of Cora training a shotgun on the spokesman, ready to deal in kind should the occasion arise. When the assembly left, the Captain spotted Cora and burst out laughing, "My God, my darling, those were the good fellows!" This group of men had been trying to accomplish, through reason, what hotter heads had previously planned to attempt with lead.

Because steel rails lasted far longer than the iron rails produced until the mid-1870s, they didn't need to be replaced as often. By the mid-1800s the eleven Bessemer steel companies produced so many steel rails that over a period of years the price of rails steadily dropped and profits were threatened. The selling price for a one-ton rail in 1877 was twelve dollars less than the cost to make that rail had been two years earlier (*Unwritten History* 1917, 108). The Bessemer pool subsidized Shinn's new Vulcan plant in St. Louis to lay idle as soon as it was ready for production. To compound the problems faced by owners, railroad companies were foreclosing and laying fewer miles of track (Krass 2002, 128).

To continue his phenomenal success, Carnegie needed to lower the price on the components that went into steel: iron ore, limestone, and coke. It was his search for cheaper coke that led to his association with Henry Clay Frick.

Carnegie and Frick met each other in 1881. They soon began a business association that was characterized by brilliant management and financial success, but it ended in bitter feuding and, ultimately, the break-up of Carnegie Steel. Frick held a monopoly of the best coal in western Pennsylvania, at Connellsville, close to which his parents owned a farm. As a young man, Frick had spent a year at Otterbein College in Ohio, then held a series of sales jobs before joining up with two cousins who owned some coal land and were producing coke in small beehive ovens for steel production. Soon, Frick bought out his cousins and created H. C. Frick, Co. which, by the late 1870s, controlled the vast majority of all the coke being produced in Pennsylvania. During the depression of the 1870s, Frick had bought out his competitors. When he met Carnegie, Frick, too, was a wealthy man and had built up his own company.

The arrangement the two men made was advantageous to both of them; Carnegie guaranteed the purchase of a specified quantity of the coke and therefore received lower prices. Ultimately each man became a shareholder in the other's business. With this arrangement, Carnegie edged out competition with lower costs for fuel. But Frick was not to get involved in the management of Carnegie Brothers in a way that truly affected Jones for several more years.

Section 21: Bill Jones in Service to His Community

If one thing emerges from every aspect of Bill Jones's life, it is his complete involvement in the communities in which he lived—both Braddock and Johnstown. In many ways one can say that he spent his life trying to make Braddock a better place for his men and their families to live. He was a most civic-minded man, and probably the most recognizable person on the streets of Braddock. As portrayed by Hugh Meese, he was "a common, every-day, figure on Braddock streets, where he would stroll along eating peanuts (which often cost him 25 or 50¢ a package no change, thank you)" (1917). Yet, in England, Jones was greeted as marvel and a genius.

In total contrast with the way he did almost everything else, the Captain was quite unobtrusive in his charitable activities. Perhaps he thought those with good fortune ought to take care of those less fortunate; it was not to their credit but part of their responsibility. The Captain's annual income allowed him to live comfortably but also gave him the freedom to do what he wished. His choice was to take care of the needs of others.

Jones was not a church-going man, but he recognized churches for the role they occupied in providing community. He is remembered for saying that he was living for this world and let preachers attend to what would come after. Yet, on the day of his terrible accident in 1889, he had gone from Braddock to Pittsburgh to see Henry Clay Frick about additional funds to help retire the debt of Dr. Boyle's Methodist Church, built at the Captain's suggestion across from the new Braddock Library, on the corner of Braddock Avenue and Tenth Street. He had pledged to the minister, before construction began, that he would obtain the difference between the actual cost and the funds the church had available. The construction had been completed during the summer and had cost $28,000, "and they were short $11,000. Captain Jones went to Pittsburgh to see H. C. Frick, who gave him a check for $5,000. The Captain was not satisfied and threatened to go to Andrew Carnegie. But due to his untimely death, he was not successful in securing the money from the steel officials" (McCleary 1933, March 9).

In the Annandale Archives in Pennsylvania, in an untitled binder, is a lengthy discourse on the Edgar Thomson Works with an article stating that: "Perhaps the first library ever donated by Carnegie was one he gave through the suggestion of Captain Jones" ("Genesis," 7). Jones wrote to Carnegie in 1880:

Dr Sir

Last evening Rev C DeLong Pastor of the U B Church located in upper part of Braddock, called on me to assist him in procuring a library for use of the Sunday School connected with his church. He stated that congregation very impecunious, no library &c.

I listened carefully to his statement and concluded to do all I could to assist him. Rev DeLong is full of faith, but minus money. I told him I knew a gentleman in New York that possessed Damned little faith, but had lots of money, and was liberal in matters of this kind.

Now I would suggest to you the propriety of purchasing for the congregation on [sic] a small Sunday school library and consign to Rev DeLong, Braddock and I will have our carpenters build them a library to keep books in.

Very Truly Yours,
W R Jones (1880, April 2)

The church got its library. The Captain visited it and praised it to Carnegie in a letter: "Enclosed you will please find bill of School Library. Have examined library and must say the Rev. gentleman displayed good taste & excellent judgment in the selection of books." Carnegie also allowed Jones to build up a library at ET for the use of the men who worked there.

Captain Bill embraced his Welsh heritage. He spoke some Welsh and was an active member of St. David's Society, the Welsh benevolent organization in Pittsburgh. Each year, beginning in 1882, the society held a meeting, concert, and banquet. In 1887, at the meeting held in the Congregational Church on Fifth Avenue, Captain Bill gave a lecture. Then, at the banquet later that night in the elegant Seventh Avenue Hotel, he gave a toast to "our Welsh artists." The following year, nearly seven hundred Welshmen assembled for the Seventh Annual Festival at the English Baptist Church. The writer and poet Frank Cowan, a friend of William McKinley who had been around the world twice, gave a short address. Later, 250 people participated in the banquet at the Monongahela House. There, after other toasts and addresses, "Captain W.R. Jones answered with a toast to 'Our Fatherland' with wise and edifying observations and with a story or two (of which he is so fond) that made for great amusement" (Transcribed minutes of the St. David's Society of Pittsburgh). In the following decade, the society fell on hard-times.

Jones enthusiastically supported the society's annual Eisteddfods, competitions in poetry, literature, and song. He gave liberally in prizes and he was "noted for his readiness to encourage competitors who failed in their efforts to secure a prize. (Royal Blue Book)" The competition's results—poems, songs, books—were then sold and the proceeds used for benevolent purposes. On one occasion Captain Jones suggested to Andrew Carnegie that he support the Welsh charity.

On Christmas I visited the Eisteddfod which our Welsh friends held at Fayette Hall. I was greatly gratified at the display of talent exhibited, and felt that the efforts of this class to improve themselves morally and mentally needed encouragement and assistance. I felt it my duty as the son of a Welshman to encourage. So I agreed to be responsible for the sum of Five hundred dollars as prizes for the choral society contending. My proposition was eagerly accepted, and now Allegheny Co. is excited by bands of Welsh choristers practicing for the event which will take place on Christmas. In addition to the competition in music there will also be composition, original poetry, oratory, and recitations. . . . In appealing to you to help me in this matter, I can only say that had you witnessed the efforts of these, I may say rather crude citizens, to elevate themselves on last Christmas, you would like myself ejaculate 'This is primitive, but an earnest effort in the right direction,' and should receive encouragement. I have given them my check for $500.00. Now what shall your answer be. Don't forget that the Welsh as a class are poor, but also remember that 99% of them always vote right, and like the Scots are always supporters of good government. (1883, December 18)

Carnegie sent a check for $100. Jones not only wrote to Carnegie asking for contributions, he wrote long letters to colleagues around the United States asking them to help specific individuals get through the worst of times.

In addition to membership in St. David's Society of Pittsburgh, Bill Jones was an active member of local fraternal and benevolent organizations like the GAR and the Free-masons. He gave generously of his time and his treasure in all three. He never joined a social club.

Jones encouraged community life through the promotion of and participation in sports. He no doubt got his initial love for baseball when he served with Abner Doubleday in the Civil War, where the companies organized games. W. W. McCleary, whom Jones hired in 1873 at Johnstown, spoke to the Braddock Rotary in 1933, during which he shared memories of Captain Jones's behavior around town. He said that one of the first things Captain Bill did when he moved to Braddock was to organize a baseball club, which they called the Athletics. Even forty-five years later, McCleary could recall the names of all the best players and their exploits and specialties. Jones purchased the land on which the diamond was constructed between Eleventh Street and the furnaces. The annual Big Game was when the Athletics played Johnstown, which usually got beaten. Jones also held shares in the original Pittsburgh Baseball Club, the Alleghenies, and he went to games as often as he could. After the Pirates were established in 1882, he supported them as well.

The Captain and C. C. Teeter, ET's chief clerk, whom Jones had lured from Cambria, also organized horse races in both Johnstown and Braddock. There was an old racetrack in Braddock that had been built over the site of some former railroad tracks. Jones loved competition, loved a good game, and the men loved this about him. He believed sporting events bonded men and relieved the stress and strain of the dangerous and tiring work they were involved in.

In 1883 a Mrs. Hanna, a widow with no connection to the steel works but who lived in Braddock, appealed to Andrew Carnegie for charity. Carnegie asked Jones for advice. The Captain responded:

My Dr. Sir,

I have just received letter of Mrs. J Hanna. I judge that you have referred matter to me. I fail to see why she should ask such a favor, unless on the principle that she is a poor widow, and you are a wealthy bachelor. While she is as far as I know a very deserving woman. Yet, from the fact that her late husband was in no wise connect with any of your enterprise, I think you are in no way bound to aid her. If you are to be the chief stay of the poor widows in and about Braddock you may well pray for an immediate advance in price of steel rails. In my judgment this woman has no claim on your charity.

Wm. R. Jones (1883, December 18)

It is revealing to see Carnegie asking for the advice of his steelworks superintendent on such matters. The Captain, of course, was more involved in the local community than Carnegie, who now lived in New York. It also shows a deference, in the days before Carnegie was committed to philanthropy, to Jones's judgement.

As a philanthropist, Captain Bill was unique. He gave beyond his means, and he had totally adopted the Greek philosophy of tyche, in which anonymous giving comes back to bless the giver in manifold ways. Bill Jones's heart was even bigger than his pocketbook. "His giving," according to *The Royal Blue Book*, "was always accomplished in a most secret manner, as he thoroughly abhorred publicity, and for that reason many of his good deeds were buried in silence.... If ever a man existed who was absolutely honest in every fibre of his being, such a man was William Richard Jones" (89-90).

Section 22: A Bad Year

For a decade the relationship between Andrew Carnegie and Captain Bill had oscillated between fondness and irritation on the part of Carnegie and between hope and disappointment on the part of Jones. Jones knew that many of his own ideas about worker benefits and labor's contributions had been articulated by Carnegie in print to great acclaim. For example, in April 1886, Carnegie published "An Employer's View of the Labor Question" in *The Forum*, the first of two articles that paraphrased some of Jones's policies. The article advanced the notion of arbitration:

> I have noticed that the manager who confers oftenest with a committee of his leading men has the least trouble with his workmen. Although it may be impracticable for the presidents of these large corporations to know the workingmen personally, the manager at the mills, having a committee of his best men to present their suggestions and wishes from time to time, can do much to maintain and strengthen amicable relations, if not interfered with from headquarters (1992, 96).

At the time he wrote this article, Carnegie supported the right of workers to organize, assemble, and arbitrate with owners and his utterances appeared to be pro-labor: "Now the poorest laborer in America or in England, or indeed throughout the civilized world, who can handle a pick or a shovel, stands upon equal terms with the purchaser of his labor. He sells or withholds it as may seem best to him." At the same time, Carnegie was tiring of the 8-hour day, which had been policy for nearly a decade. Labor did not embrace the three shifts of eight hours; many preferred two shifts of twelve.

The *Pittsburgh Times* published an interpretation of Carnegie's position:

"A Scotch Yankee Socialist"

> Mr. Andrew Carnegie, of Pittsburgh, was a man of note. He made a "sensation" yesterday by proclaiming himself a socialist—in theory.... The sentiments he declared in the interview yesterday concerning "socialism" would not have been so very startling had he used instead the word "cooperation," which seems to best describe his notion of what is practicable in the way of general leveling-up mankind. Mr. Carnegie is right in saying that "socialism" is the grandest theory every presented. In its purity it is the theory of the Christian religion. When it rules the world, as Mr. Carnegie thinks it is bound to do, the millennium will indeed have come and men will be "content to work for the general welfare and share their riches with their neighbors." (Lendon1886, May 12)

One month after the appearance of Carnegie's *Forum* article, disputes over the eight-hour day precipitated a violent demonstration at Haymarket Square in Chicago. The labor movement, and especially those working in iron and steel, did not favor an eight-hour day; many preferred two shifts of twelve hours. For several days in early May 1886, a labor dispute persisting at the staunchly anti-union McCormick Harvester factory resulted in several deaths. The Eight Hour Day Association called a rally for the next day. On the evening of May 4, speeches reached a peaceful crowd of perhaps twenty-five thousand.

When the program was nearly finished, a sizeable contingent of police burst through the crowd toward the speaker's platform. The policeman in charge demanded that the group disperse: "In the name of the people of the State of Illinois, I command this meeting immediately and peaceably to disperse." At that moment someone, unknown to this day, threw a bomb toward the police. Suddenly the police opened fire and chaos reigned; at least seven police and four civilians were killed. Most of the deaths were caused by police weapons.

The press castigated the organizers for the violence, labeling the leaders of the Eight Hour Day Association vipers, ungrateful hyenas, and serpents. Eight men were arrested. Several were German anarchists, another two were German Americans. Eventually, the jury found all eight guilty on very thin evidence, and Judge Joseph E. Gary sentenced seven to be hanged, with the eighth man receiving fifteen years in prison. The case became known as one of the most dishonest trials in American history (Parsons 1969).

Public opinion blamed labor reform for precipitating violence and threatening a return to civil and class war. Labor disengaged quickly from any connection with the Eight-Hour Day Association, with both the Knights of Labor and the Amalgamated charging:

> The scenes of bloodshed and disorder which have occurred in Chicago are disgraceful, uncalled for, and deserving of the severest condemnation and punishment. Honest labor is not to be found in the ranks of those who march under the red flag of anarchy, which is the emblem of blood and destruction. . . . there is not a trade Union in America that will uphold those men in Chicago who have been engaged in the destruction of life and property. . . . The anarchist idea is un-American, and has no business in this country. (David 1958, 211)

The Haymarket riots rocked the country and focused attention on the eight-hour day. In 1881 Captain Bill had startled the engineers and scientists assembled at the Institute of Iron and Steel with his talk advocating the eight-hour day. In 1886, five years after Jones had instituted it at ET, the Federation of Organized Trades and Labor Unions of the United States and Canada met in Pittsburgh and became the first union to embrace the eight-hour day as an issue. Mention of the eight-hour day can be traced back to George Lippard in the 1840s. In his last years Lippard gave up writing fiction to organize the Brotherhood of the Union. Lippard's brotherhood was a decided influence on Uriah S. Stephens, who was an early founder of the Knights of Labor, and William H. Sylvis, an ironworker from Philadelphia, who later had a significant influence on labor issues in Illinois.

The xenophobic press then turned on Scottish-born Carnegie, who so carefully courted good public relations. Digging in his heels, Carnegie fumed at anyone associating the violence at Haymarket with his essay or with the ET labor policy. He answered the press in August with a second article, "Results of the Labor Struggle." Carnegie devoted much space to the May Haymarket trouble but rhapsodized on the eight-hour day: "Works that run day and night should be operated with three sets of men, each working eight hours . . . Each shift, of course, takes turn of each of the three parts into which the twenty-for hours are divided, and thus the lives of the men are rendered less monotonous and many hours for recreation and self-improvement are obtained" (1992, 108). He further proclaimed a series of maxims, simulating Old Testament rhetoric. One anti-scab maxim, "Thou shall not take they neighbor's job," became known as Andy's eleventh commandment. It would soon haunt Carnegie and stigmatize him as a hypocrite. He would hire those very scabs that took the jobs of others, scabs that he had scolded in a national publication (ibid., 112).

Was Carnegie a hypocrite? Or was he naive? To publicly validate the eight-hour day amidst the hysteria following Haymarket would appear naïve. Violence and terrorism were common in the United States during this period. Only five years earlier, President James A. Garfield had been assassinated. Reaction to this second article on the heels of Haymarket was fast and condemning; Carnegie's published labor philosophy elicited ridicule in the national press and from nearly every voice in the steel cartel. His board members and Frick shook their heads, baffled.

Jones was nearly alone among American manufacturers in practicing the eight-hour day. At ET, Tom Carnegie alone among senior management truly supported Jones in his belief that the eight-hour day was good for business. Nationally, organized labor had been tepid on the issue for political and technological reasons. The eight-hour day became the rallying cry of anarchical syndicalists like Emma Goldman and German immigrants in New York, Philadelphia, and Chicago, radicals too independent to be communists (David 1958, 182).

Following the trauma of public ridicule, Carnegie faced private loss and personal illness that threatened his own life. In October he contracted typhoid fever and retreated to Cresson, his mountain home only a few miles from Johnstown; many feared he would die. At the same time Tom Carnegie, weakened by hard work and long hours, contracted pneumonia. One partner predicted: "Tom Carnegie probably will die for he has been a hard drinker. But Andrew has lived an abstemious and regular life and will probably recover" (Wall 1970, 491). It proved to be an accurate prediction. Tom had been a steady and positive influence at ET, and his death produced a leadership vacuum. Harry Phipps reluctantly agreed to become the chairman of Carnegie Company. Henry Clay Frick had been invited to become a partner, and after Tom's death he soon became Carnegie's on-the-scene representative.

On November 10, one month after Tom's death, Margaret Carnegie, Andrew's widowed mother, constant companion, confidante, and mentor, died. She had been a powerful influence on Andy, the only woman in the fifty years of his life. His life-threatening illness, the death of his brother and mother, and the public's battering of him for ideals he shared with Jones resulted in Carnegie becoming a more conflicted, even dualistic, man. Captain Jones underlined the following passage in his copy of *Troilus and Cressida*, perhaps as he endured that difficult year.

Time hath, my lord, a wallet at his back,
Wherein he puts alms for oblivion,

A great-siz'd monster of ingratitudes:
Those scraps are good deeds past; which are devour'd
As fast as they are made, forgot as soon
As done . . .

Whether or not he consciously knew that the "great-siz'd monster of ingratitudes," time, was betraying him, Jones resumed his Plan by vigorously pursuing his securing of patents in 1886. On April 27 he secured a patent on machinery that fed rails in the rolling mill; on May 4, a gas furnace for the boiler-driving steam engines; and on October 12, for a process for improving the art and technology of rolling rails straight without poor joints and bad fittings when laid out as track.

Yet, none of these could defeat calumniating time any more than Holley's vessel bottom technology survived becoming obsolete as technology advanced. Other uses of gross steel began to appear, for which the Bessemer might not be the best producer. Plate for armor and other military ordnances, girders for skyscrapers, and structural steel used for the balloon skeleton of tall buildings could be better provided by other processes that could produce steel in greater volume than a Bessemer converter. In 1886 Captain Bill recommended the twenty- four-year-old Charlie Schwab to superintend the Homestead Works, where open hearth machinery could do just that.

By late 1886 the American steel industry again faced an oversupply of steel rails. As early as May 1878, Captain Bill had foreseen diversifying to produce steel products such as "steel shafts for River boats, cross heads, and all engine forgings" (1878, 24 May). In the United States in 1881, 76.2 percent of all new steel became rails, but by 1889, the percentage in rails had dropped to 44.7 percent. And by 1899, it was 21.3 percent (Warren 1996, 115).

To deal with overproduction, the Bessemer cartel apportioned quotas for each of the eleven members to produce steel to meet the country's now limited demand for track. Many heavily capitalized plants ran at a loss after filling their quotas. Carnegie's genius was his hardheaded adroitness in wresting from the pool the highest percentage allotted for rail production, reaching parity with Illinois, closer to high quality ore in Michigan, closer to western demand for steel, and his greatest competitor. Carnegie, in fact, ignored the cartel quotas and produced excess volume each year. Frick provided the lowest-priced coke in the industry. Jones's technological improvements increased production efficiency. Carnegie fought to produce the most inexpensive and highest quality rails on the market at tremendous profits.

Where Frick saw savings in decreasing wages and Jones in inventing new solutions to decrease the number of workers, Carnegie found transportation fees the means for savings. Iron ore was transported from the Mesabi Range in Michigan to Lake Erie by rail, by ship to the Pennsylvania shore, then the final leg by rail to Pittsburgh. This long haul of ore and the finished rails to the West positioned Braddock at a disadvantage. Youngstown, Ohio; Geary, Indiana; Chicago; and St. Louis, Missouri, all provided savings that ET couldn't compete with. Finished rails were now in demand primarily in the West, and Pittsburgh paid far higher rates, which were calculated by the mile, than the Midwestern steel producers. Carnegie must have felt that the railroad companies reined him in, which might account for his naming the works after the president of the Pennsylvania Railroad, Edgar Thomson.

Section 23: Death of the Eight-hour Day

The death of the eight-hour day occurred over a period of several years. When Jones and Holley had built ET, three shifts of workers labored eight hours a day pumping red molten liquid into ET's twin hearts, the grim sphinxes. A worker had to move quickly, and fatigued labor could result in injury, death, or shutting down for many days. "Good wages and good workmen I know to be the cheapest labor," as Jones wrote in a letter to Carnegie (1878, May 6). Joseph Frazier Wall concluded that Jones's genius was convincing Carnegie that sound labor policy earned profits; earning profits by taking the worker into consideration might seem to be a paradox but in fact it was sound business (1970, 522-3). Wall's conclusion concurs with that of Bridge: "[Jones's] power to manage men, joined to his inventiveness and thorough practical training, made him the most conspicuous personal element in the phenomenal success that attended the enterprise from the very first" (Bridge 1991, 79).

The leadership of the Amalgamated Association derived from skilled labor, and the national union accepted that different hours and wages were appropriate for different technologies. At ET where the first blast furnace, the Cora, was completed nearly five years after operations began in 1875, Amalgamated never gained much of a foothold. In contrast, at Homestead, the union established a foothold from the day it opened. Should ET have changed from Bessemer to open hearth conversion, its workers may have had more enthusiasm for the newly formed Amalgamated (Fitch 1989, 114).

On New Year's Day 1887, Carnegie ordered a reversion to two shifts of twelve hours for workers at ET, with a 10 percent increase in salaries. This trial run lasted until a strike in April forced a return to three shifts of eight hours. Soon, though, the price for rails dropped to $28.50, a low compared with $37.75 three years earlier (Poole). Carnegie deliberated whether to maintain Jones's nearly decade-old experiment of the eight-hour day with the same daily wage as the twelve-hour shift or to negotiate with labor to accept a sliding scale based on the average price for rails.

In early 1888 Jones agreed to negotiate with union representatives over wages, but, in addition, the union wanted the term of contracts to extend from June to June rather than January to January, as had been the case. Jones believed the issue of the calendar was capricious, that the finite issues open for negotiation were hours, wages, and working conditions, not "the color of the superintendent's tie." He may have been wrong. Late spring arbitration marginally favored labor, since the seasonal supply of workers was lower in June than in the winter months. But, should the negotiators decide to strike, it would be far easier to sustain a walkout in spring than during the cold winter months. Jones committed a blunder that he later regretted: he refused to negotiate, broke off talks, and kept the mill closed.

Because Carnegie wanted a return to the twelve-hour day, he took advantage of Jones's absence. He invited union leaders to meet with him in New York City without Jones. In March, less than a year after trumpeting the eight-hour day in his *Forum* article, Carnegie announced that labor at ET would join with every other plant in the country working in two shifts of twelve hours. He successfully convinced the workers that wages based on a sliding scale would advantage them. Consequently, the Knights of Labor accepted a 10 percent reduction in pay, in light of falling rail prices. They also agreed on a sliding scale, tying wages to rail prices. Jones responded angrily: "I candidly charge the Knights of Labor with gross dereliction of duty when, after establishing as a general rule the eight-hour day, they lie down supinely and make no effort to have it established at rival establishments" (Fitch 1989, 116). This agreement sealed the demise of the eight-hour day; it would not be reinstated for nearly fifty years at iron and steel works in the United States.

In April, Carnegie returned to Pittsburgh to finalize his sliding scale, but since the meeting in New York City, he added one component not discussed with either labor representatives or Jones. Carnegie would now require the men to sign an agreement relinquishing all ties to a national union. This position was a direct contradiction to what he had written only fourteen months earlier about the right of labor to assemble and to negotiate. Further, the new agreement specified that should one be found a union member, he would be blacklisted and prevented from working in that industry anywhere in the nation.

Captain Bill found himself in a position somewhat similar to the one he had left at Cambria. Carnegie was no longer open to his management philosophy and practices, a condition of Jones's accepting ET's superintendency in 1875. "A plague upon all your houses," Jones said of them to his family. He was bitter toward both the union and the Carnegie Company's board of directors. Carnegie had abandoned his statements in the *Forum*, his acceptance of the eight-hour day. ET's workers, too, let him down by foolishly accepting the sliding wage scale and the twelve-hour shift. And so, in 1888 Jones began to seriously invest time and energy in alternatives to working at ET and under Andrew Carnegie.

Chapter 4 Sections

Chapter 4

Cradle of Civilization

Section 24: Commemorating the War

In the 1880s a wave of nostalgia and patriotism swept the country. More than twenty years had passed since the ending of the Civil War, and the United States was taking inventory of its origins and values. The Washington Monument became a symbol of national aspirations and unity. This project to build a tribute to the first president's vision for a unified country had been stalled for nearly thirty years due to the war, lack of funds, and political bickering. The original architect, who had proposed an obelisk surrounded by a colonnade and statues of Revolutionary War heroes, was replaced by Lt. Col. Thomas Casey, an architect who designed an unembellished Egyptian obelisk of 555 feet—making it the world's tallest structure until the Eiffel Tower was constructed. The marble monument, supported by interior ironwork, was dedicated by Congress on February 21, 1885, and it opened to the public in late 1888.

During this period, Civil War veterans joined local posts of the Grand Army of the Republic (GAR) in record numbers, and it became a powerful political group in the Northern states, basing its organizational structure on the Masons and aligning with the Republican Party. It was the first successful political interest group, advocating for pensions and old age homes for veterans. It was also a major factor in the election of many Civil War generals to the presidency in the final decades of the nineteenth century. Due to GAR's influence, by 1890 most Northern states adopted Decoration Day as a May holiday to commemorate the veterans of the war; it eventually became Memorial Day.

GAR posts around the country were the major force in the erection of monuments to local men who had served in the Civil War. Monuments varied in style: many were equestrian statues; others were square mausoleums. Bill Jones was active in the Braddock GAR post: he had been elected senior vice-commander of the GAR, Post 181, for the Department of Pennsylvania. The post was active in caring for the widows and orphans of veterans. Jones also headed the committee to erect a monument high atop the bluffs overlooking the Monongahela River to commemorate the Union dead in Braddock.

Jones unveiled the elegant obelisk-like memorial, which strongly emulated the Washington Monument, on September 10, 1887. Henry M. Curry, his former comrade in war, was also active in the project, although in recent years Henry had become very distant and curiously unfriendly. Captain Bill suspected that Curry, who had stood by him before the wall at Fredericksburg then escaped with him from the blazing maze at Chancellorsville, was deserting him for corporate power and prosperity.

To commence the celebration, Roman candles, in an array of colors, were released from the promontory out toward the river. Fireworks exploded as children stood around the marble base and clapped and yelled. The monument, at the edge of the Monongahela Cemetery, is adjacent to Yost Street and can be approached on three paths. There are sixty-six names inscribed on its base and bronze grave markers for a number of Civil War veterans around its periphery.

The ceremony that Saturday was graced by the poet Frank Cowan, who recited his poem, "The Meaning of the Monument." The poem celebrated not only the Union dead but the martyred General Braddock, for whom the town was named, and the sacrifices of those in 1755 who encountered the combined forces of Indians and French under Commandant Lionel de Beaujeu. Braddock had commanded 1,459 soldiers, two-thirds of whom were killed or wounded (Fischer 1994, 379). Among those who survived were Daniel Boone, George Washington, and Thomas Gage, a remote relative of the Gage family, who was present for the unveiling of the monument (Gage 1998, May/June, 2). D. D. mixed in the crowd out of sight of everyone in the Jones family with the exception of the twenty-year- old Cora.

> Upon a height, whence the delighted eye
> Opes to the sentient mirror of the mind,
> A vast and varied vision of the Course
> Of Empire to the Gateway of the West:
> The mirky vale of the Monongahela!
> Where erst the Briton in his coat of blood
> Braved openly the Redskin and the Frank,
>
> Where now a myriad of industries,
> Within the inhulled acres of the stream
> And inwalled mile-squares of the strath, present
> A peerless exposition of the Age
> Of Fire and Electricity enthralled
> And bound unto their work with hands of steel,
>
> Upon this height, a motley multitude
> Convened from all the air's the wind can blow,
> To dedicate a monumental shaft
> Unto the glory of the nation's dead—
>
> To fit the player on the stage of life,
> To take the Patriot's and Hero's part,
> Ere he is summoned by the fates to act—
> Achieve ennobling deeds, and leave his name
> Engraved in granite by a grateful world?
> For, surely as the flow'r precedes the fruit,
> The Patriot and Hero of true worth,
> Are never such in act and deed, until
> They have been first in feeling and in thought! (Cowan 1887)

With a toby clenched in his teeth, Captain Jones stood straight and barrel-chested, as the breezes off the river lifted his wavy hair. With the Captain were Henry Curry, John Potter, and Potter's wife of four years, Margaret. With William Yost was James Gayley, an Irish American veteran. Mimi Corey, Cora's best friend, stood with Cora and others in the Jones family. Harriet was propped comfortably in a carriage, and the family posed for photographs beside the monument. Veterans in fading uniforms clustered together swapping memories, as wives mingled to share the latest news.

Section 25: New World of Steel

In the last twenty-five years of the nineteenth century, structural steel transformed building capabilities—for bridges, the height and girth of buildings, in armaments, and for ships and railroads. Steel was first produced on a large scale in England, which for a number of years enjoyed a virtual monopoly on the new metal. The Bessemer and Mushet processes, both invented by British subjects, enabled mass production of steel that required low-phosphorus iron ore. "Only 10% of the known iron ore deposits in Europe" were low in phosphorous and the vast majority were in Britain (McHugh 1980, 324). In the mid-1870s, the United States began to rival England; iron ore low in phosphorus was abundant in the Mesabi Range of Michigan and Minnesota. Its eleven Bessemer works enabled the U.S. to be completely connected by rail; protective tariffs gave American steel its own monopoly at a time of explosive growth in population and industry. When, under Jones's supervision, ET became the world's most productive mill, it helped lead the U.S. in edging out England in production supremacy.

While Jones was at Cambria, Otto von Bismarck ushered in the martial slogan "Blood and Iron." By the time that Cora and her father reached Europe, Wilhelm II of Germany had begun building an empire based on "Blood and Steel." In 1881, Alfred Krupp, the Carnegie of German steel, had invited Captain Bill to Essen. Krupp specialized in armaments and by 1887 was producing more armaments than any other steel works in the world. The company, with its many weapons systems, had a virtual monopoly and soon armed France, Italy, and Austria; in less than two decades, they would be fighting each other and extending European nations' power in colonizing much of the world. Colonialism and empire impeded the production of steel in countries outside of Europe and the United States by withholding the necessary knowledge with a secrecy exceeding later nuclear monopoly. Turkey, which might have sustained its empire but for a lack of steel, began producing gross steel in Karabuk as late as in 1937 (Sumengen, personal communication). Iran was not allowed to produce steel until the 1970s (Mortazavi, personal communication). Japan, however, experimented with its first blast furnace in 1874, using charcoal, but only established the successful Yawata Iron and Steel Works in 1901. It too was oriented toward military uses. The Captain would not live to know how his efforts led to such material progress and at the same time to such destruction in wars.

Captain Bill and Cora made a second trip to Europe in the summer of 1888 so that Jones could attend the Glasgow International Exhibition of Industry, Science, and Art. They sailed on the Cunard Line's *SS Servia*, the line's first steel vessel, which had been put in service in 1881. It operated a regular route from New York to Liverpool. On board the *Servia* he met the prominent Chicago acoustical architect Dankmar Adler, who was traveling to investigate concert halls in Europe. The two struck up an immediate friendship, documented in Adler's letter written onboard to his wife. The Captain was fatigued, the letter said, from trying to reinstitute the eight-hour day at ET. The two men had "great times," befriending the chief engineer and several officers. At the Liverpool railroad station "we had spent a good bit of time looking through and examining cars, locomotives, track . . . the result of our examination of the cars and how each was used was that each of us . . . had given up

> *Under Jones's supervision, ET became the world's most productive mill.*

our resolve to be democratic and bought a first class ticket" (Misa 1995, 67). Misa concludes that the "most significant linkage to come from this shipboard friendship was the extensive consulting relationships that developed between Chicago architects and Pittsburgh steelmakers." Chicago companies later bought a great deal of structural steel from Carnegie companies (ibid., 66).

After Great Britain, the Joneses headed for the steel works at St. Chamond, at the confluence of the Janon and the Gier rivers southwest of Lyon, in France. St. Chamond, with other nearby works, was still in an experimental phase, primarily producing railway and naval material. They then went on to Paris, where the Captain participated in the preparations for the Centennial Exposition of 1889, a celebration of the one hundredth anniversary of the French Revolution. He met the engineer Alexandre Gustave Eiffel, seven years his senior, who had won the competition to produce a one thousand-foot tower built entirely of iron, which was to be the premier attraction of the exposition. Jones inspected the tower being built, a bridge-construction angled vertically on the southern bank of the Seine. The Captain and Cora attended the opera and enjoyed a variety of fine Parisian restaurants. Cora was happy, conversing in French at their many stops.

They departed Paris on a late August afternoon from the Strasbourg Station aboard a new train destined for Istanbul, later known as the Orient Express. At one end of the platform, the newly installed Guepratte thermometer registered temperature in both centigrade and Fahrenheit. They disembarked in Munich. South of Munich, in the alpine city of Garmisch-Partenkirchen, they visited a well-known lumber concern and stayed with the owner and his family. While Captain Bill, for reasons that have been lost to history, learned about lumber, Cora enjoyed the strikingly beautiful countryside and the warm hospitality. From there, they were on to Austria.

Karl Wittgenstein and his wife Leopoldine welcomed the two Americans to Vienna. While their carriage circumnavigated the city on the new Ringstrasse, the Wittgensteins instructed Cora in the history of Viennese architecture. A circular boulevard separating the expanding suburbs from the old city, the Ringstrasse was designed by Otto Wagner with facing parallel chains of buildings, none exceeding six stories. The idea was to yield a current of horizontal activity, celebrating commerce and the newly empowered middle classes. The major buildings of the Ringstrasse were sheathed in different styles to denote continuity of the Hapsburgs back to the empire's origins in the thirteenth century. The municipal government operated out of a Gothic city hall, a style appropriate to pre-Renaissance crafts culture; a Renaissance façade adorned the university, signaling humankind's reawakening knowledge of the past; the theatre was an appropriate Baroque; and the seat of government, parliament, Greek Revival.

Karl Wittgenstein combined Bill Jones's mechanical and managerial abilities and questioning of authority with Carnegie's business acumen and Morrell's authoritarianism and rigidity. He had been director general of the highly successful Teplitz Rolling Mill in northern Bohemia since 1877, had sole rights to the Gilchrist Thomas process in the Austrian Empire, and was actively acquiring companies that produced pig iron, hardware factories, and coal mines to produce coke. He made cement with byproducts from his blast furnaces and sold basic slag, the byproduct of Gilchrist steel conversion, as fertilizer. He was one of the most forward thinking entrepreneurs of the Habsburg Empire, yet his political stance was liberal. Wittgenstein was a friend of Andrew Carnegie— Wittgenstein had visited Carnegie in the U.S., and Carnegie had come to Vienna—and they shared many beliefs. Wittgenstein was quite familiar with Jones's 1881 paper and he now wanted to learn from ET's superintendent any labor-saving techniques and ways to integrate his enterprises. Years later, Karl would show his regard for Jones's ability to see the big picture when he wrote to D. D. Gage:

> I wish also to say that the Jones-Mixer represents only a very small part of what Capt. Jones has done for the iron-industry. The chief importance of Capt. Jones was his incomparable energy and comprehension of circumstances on a large scale. The Jones-Mixer shows that he could never be intimidated by even the largest ideas. But Capt. Jones' chief merit is that by his intrepid far-seeing and energetic work he has shown new ways to the iron industry of America as well as of all other countries. (28 March 1908)

The Wittgensteins led the social life of Vienna; Wittgenstein had used his wife's and mother's money early in his employment to buy shares of Tiplitz. The fortune had since grown enormously due to his successes there and to his acquisition of other companies. The Wittgensteins were among the foremost patrons of the arts in Vienna, and musicians such as Brahms and Mahler frequented their home. They commissioned architect Josef Hoffman to do work in the halls of the Hochreith, their country estate just outside Vienna (Schorske1981). They later commissioned works by the painters Gustav Klimt and Oskar Kokoshka. Five years before this trip, Charlie Schwab had taught Cora to read musical scores by Brahms and Strauss, the Viennese favorite sons who were the rage in every European capital (Bayly 2006, 1). Dominance in steel could fortify the liberal Austrian Empire's *joie de vivre*, later captured in the 1895 drama *Liebelei* (*Loveplay*) and many other

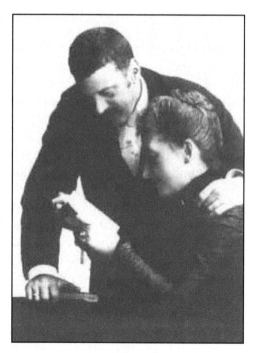

Karl and Leopoldine Wittgenstein led the social life of Vienna.

142

works by Arthur Schnitzler, who was supported by the Wittgensteins.

In spite of the lavish entertainments, there was poverty everywhere; the gap between the rich urban sophisticates and the unemployed peasants was stark. Eastern Europeans, led by those from the Austro-Hungarian Empire, had begun emigrating to the United States and Canada in large numbers in the late 1870s and early 1880s. So many were leaving Austro-Hungary that in 1881 the government had prohibited the operation of emigration agencies which advertised work opportunities in the U.S. and Canada, and such restriction increased with each subsequent year.

Before the Joneses departed Vienna, they purchased gifts for Harriet, a pistol for Will, porcelain vases, and a dining table and chair set in the formal style favored at the time. Cora bought herself an ivory brush and comb set, which my mother still used in her retirement home in 1992.

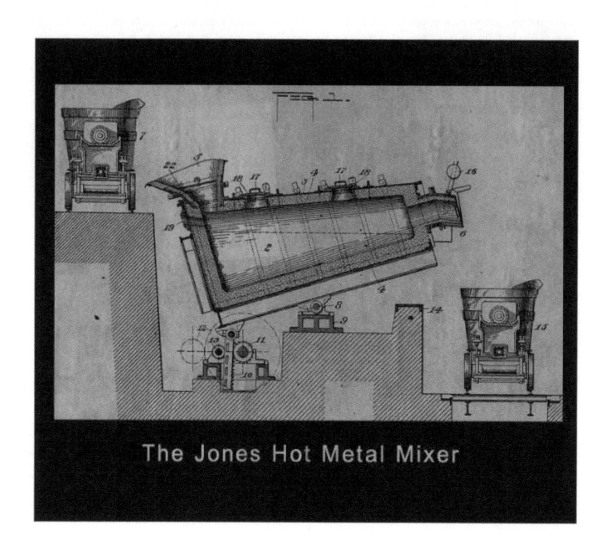

The Jones Hot Metal Mixer, called the "The Cradle of Civilization" *by author James Bridge, revolutionized steel production. Jones continued to accumulate "more patents to his credit than any single individual in the history of steelmaking" (Wall 1970, 532).*

(illustration from Jones's patent No. 404,414 "Method of Mixing Molten Pig Metal" (filed 10/31/1888 & dated 6/4/1889.)

Section 26: The Cradle of Civilization

After Tom Carnegie's death and the scare that Andrew's serious illness presented to the financial security of the company in 1886, Henry Phipps finally drew up the Carnegie Brothers & Company's "stated" policy in writing, forever and notoriously known as the Iron Clad Agreement. Neither Phipps nor Carnegie had forgotten the Shinn payout and both wanted to avoid a similar event in the future. Andrew Carnegie, protecting the company, had worked out an arrangement with Tom Carnegie's widow to pay out her share in the company over many years to prevent a lump sum withdrawal. The Iron Clad enabled those partners who owned three-fifths of the interest in the company to eject any partner from the firm and to pay that ejected person only the book value for his holdings. Subsequently, each partner entering into the Iron Clad Agreement knew that he could be voted out. Only Andrew Carnegie, because he owned more than half of the company's shares, was excluded from the provisions of the Iron Clad.

The events of 1886 and 1887—the troubles at ET, the Haymarket riots and the death of Tom and Margaret Carnegie, the implications of the Iron Clad—had fissured the relationship between Jones and Andrew. Carnegie had heretofore followed many of the beliefs of his beloved uncle who, as a Chartist in Scotland, had spent time in jail. The traumas of 1886 seemed to erode Andy's earlier liberal convictions, which were superseded by a Social Darwinism articulated by Carnegie's new friend, Herbert Spencer, who wedded the survival of the fittest to Calvinism (Krass 2002, 122-3). Carnegie's articles on labor policy in *The Forum* had been heavily influenced by Jones, whom Livesay credits with bringing "out this benevolent side of Carnegie and act[ing] as a buffer against the excesses of his cost mania" (1975, 134). But it was Carnegie's insistence that ET return to a two-shift, twelve-hour day in January 1887 that was the owner's ultimate betrayal of Jones. Carnegie increasingly became a different man, privately cynical and publicly adept at ruthless competition in business. He buttressed a conviction that the ends justify the means with his well-publicized philanthropy.

Bridge tells a story from this period about the Knights of Labor attempting to unionize women working in a totally unrelated enterprise, Pittsburgh laundries. The anti-union owners of one laundry hired scabs to work the positions of those locked out for trying to organize for the Knights. A former Cambria steelworker, whom Captain Bill had recruited from Johnstown back in 1875, was the father of two of these scabs. Several members of the Knights of Labor approached Captain Bill, demanding that he discharge his loyal ET employee simply for being the father of daughters who worked as scabs. Reacting to this demand, the Captain exploded and physically threw the men out of his ET office. Undeterred, the men went directly to Carnegie. Carnegie endorsed their plea that the father needed to learn how to manage his daughters by firing Jones's old comrade from Cambria. Carnegie justified his actions to Jones: "We cannot afford a strike for a principle" (Bridge 1991, 118). To placate a national union having nothing to do with iron or steel production, Carnegie fired a good ET worker.

Carnegie's capricious behavior nearly cost him his developing relationship with Henry Clay Frick as well. In early 1887 all the coke companies near Connellsville were hav-

Flow Chart of Steelmaking

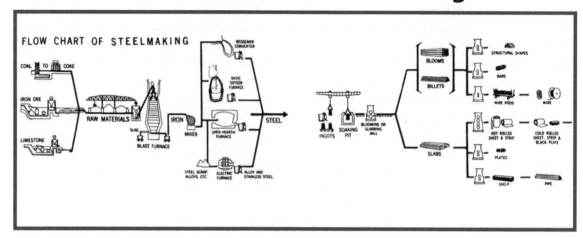

Key to any steelmaking is the Jones Hot Metal Mixer, *positioned (in red) as bottleneck for converting hot iron ore into steel, whether by Bessemer, Basic Oxygen Furnace, Open Hearth Furnaces, Steel Scrap Alloys, Electric Furnace, and Alloy or Stainless Steel products. The mixer, refered to as the* Cradle of Civilization, *and the Jones process established an essential bridge between iron and steel still used in today's steel production.*

(chart,1930, from Gaughan; film: The Making of Steel, Delft Univ. of Technology, 2009, via YouTube))

ing serious labor problems. A board of arbitration had arranged a wage settlement which had been accepted by the national unions. But the local workers did not return to work. Frick then achieved unanimity among the owners of coke ovens not to bend to the striking workers and to hire scab labor, if necessary. It was Phipps and John Walker, the chairman of Carnegie, Phipps, & Co., who notified Carnegie, in Europe on his extended honeymoon. Carnegie, who now owned a majority of the stock in Frick's own company, and in need of his coke for the strong steel market, prevailed upon Frick to give in and pay higher wages to his striking workers. The other owners of coke companies branded Frick a traitor. Frick was humiliated and so angry with Carnegie that he resigned from the presidency of his own company, in Jones-like fashion (Wall 1970, 494). Six months later Frick was re-elected to the presidency and returned to that position. His company, like Carnegie's, made enormous profits. It was the one company in which Bill Jones owned stock; he owned one hundred shares, but this investment did not tie him to the company, as would be the case if he accepted shares from Carnegie. Carnegie should have been forewarned; Frick would not always do things Andy's way for within a dozen years of Jones' death, Carnegie would lose, as Wall summed up, "The future would belong to Frick and Schwab, and even Andrew Carnegie had become something of an anachronism." (ibid. 534).

Why did Carnegie intervene in both these cases, going over the heads of the two men he needed most? Jones challenged anything that impeded a practical solution, including lofty idealism. In public, Jones called Carnegie "an oatmeal-eating son of a bitching Scotsman" (Holbrook 1939, 214). Jones looked after the workers' interest, but Carnegie's romancing the unions was opportunistic and hypocritical. More than anything he apparently wanted to be liked, coating his ruthlessness in joviality and public philanthropy.

By 1888 the structure of Carnegie's companies was changing rapidly as Andy acquired more and more businesses and consolidated them. Captain Bill needed to sustain his authority against a fickle Carnegie, particularly after the loss of the eight-hour day. Jones continued to accumulate "more patents to his credit than any single individual in the history of steelmaking" (Wall 1970, 532). If things continued to deteriorate at ET, he could join Shinn in St. Louis, John Fritz at Bethlehem, Robert Hunt at Troy, or even John Fulton at Cambria in Johnstown now that Morrell was dead. Most promising, Jones was considering the launch of a new works at Youngstown with Joseph Butler (Butler 1918, 56).

On October 31, 1888, Captain Bill delivered to the post office the patent letter for his greatest invention, the Jones Hot Metal Mixer; he concurrently filed a patent for the Jones Direct Process. He had installed the first mixer at ET earlier in the year. The mixer was a mobile, elephant-sized cradle, initially capable of rocking 250 tons of liquefied iron. By 1888 ET had seven blast furnaces; each produced forty tons of pig iron of differing quality and of slightly different proportions of limestone, coke, and iron, so that the resultant steel from each furnace lacked uniformity. Until the Jones mixer, pig iron had been cooled after the blast furnace, then pigs were grouped by chemical similarity and reheated in the cupola furnaces before being fed into a converter. With this new invention, the mixer tapped a blast furnace, then rocked its way down the track from that furnace to the next and so on until it reached the steel converter. During this journey, the mixer was always nearly half full of molten iron from several furnaces, which it processed and homogenized on its way to the converter.

The mixer eliminated the second heating and produced a consistent mass of pig iron. Such quality control of metal destined for conversion to steel was unprecedented. It saved enormous amounts of time, fuel, and labor, and produced a steel of greater consistency. It was worth literally tens, if not hundreds, of thousands of dollars to a steel works each year, not to mention its value to the patent holder.

Section 27: Utility of the Cradle

The mixer had resolved an important problem that all mills shared, and thus became an essential intermediate step between the blast furnaces and the converters. In time virtually every mill in the world used the mixer, with each needing to purchase rights to use it from the patent holder. At first glance the revolutionary implications of this invention may not be apparent. Without uniformity, steel still had limitations on its use. It was stronger than iron, but any given batch could produce inferior products. The mixer made possible large buildings and other stress-sensitive projects. Uniform high-quality steel now enabled more durable, safe bridges, skyscrapers, and other massive construction heretofore impossible.

In 1903, James Howard Bridge rhapsodized about the Jones Hot Metal Mixer in *The Inside History of the Carnegie Steel Company*:

> And who shall tell of what goes on in the giant chest where two hundred and fifty tons of liquid iron have just been poured, to be rocked to and fro, a seething, swirling, bubbling mass? In one aspect this is the cradle of civilization. Here, in the Jones mixer, goes on the first of the processes by which is made the steel of locomotives, rails, and ships that link race to race throughout the world; of the engines of mines and factories; of the machines of thousands of mills; of the reapers and harvesters of farms; of the beams and angles and bars of which modern cities are largely built. Here rocking in this huge box are the springs of chronometers that keep pace with the progress of the stars; the needles that point the mariner's way; the tubes through which the astronomer watches the birth of worlds; the disks that talk through a thousand miles of space; and most of the other miracles that make the sum of modern civilization. To the intelligent onlooker there is as much poetry in Jones' box as there was in Pandora's; and even this does not contain all the wonders of the beautiful transformations which have given Pittsburgh a yellow crown of light. (1991, 144)

What Bridge called the cradle of civilization was about to rock, as cities stretched skyward and military empires were built on the new steel.

The mixer and the Jones process established an essential bridge between iron and steel. It did not matter whether steel was produced from the open hearth, the Bessemer, the basic oxygen furnace, or future electrical furnaces, the latter a process Jones could never have imagined. Subsequent to his invention of the cradle, all future methods of making steel would rely upon the Jones Hot Metal Mixer or a modification of it and the progression of the Jones Direct Process before steel conversion (Gaughan, personal communication).

Rail prices continued to fluctuate dramatically, and each of the senior players worked on different strategies to remain competitive. Carnegie continued to devise schemes to cut railway fees for transporting ore from the Great Lakes to Pittsburgh and limestone and coke from Butler County, Pennsylvania, in the north, and for delivering finished rails to all points east and west. He went into full-scale battle against the Pennsylvania Railroad, which he believed was charging the Carnegie companies excessive rates, particularly given the volume of business they were giving the railroad. Jones worked on technological solutions, inventing machinery that short-cut steel forging processes and rail-shaping procedures, such as his automatic roller table that replaced several hook-and-tong men with a single operator (*Unwritten History* 1917, 108).

Frick, after 1888, gradually assumed more and more duties for Andrew Carnegie. On January 1, 1889, Carnegie formally appointed him chairman of the board and general manager of Carnegie Brothers (Wall 1970, XV), after which Frick had more frequent interaction with Jones. Frick was Carnegie's point man, allowing Carnegie to stay in the background. Frick's ruthless treatment of labor, including lock outs, cutting wages, and blacklisting union members, led to unfavorable press. (Krass 2002, 174). Warren reports that Jones let Frick know that he wanted to run the works his own way. In March he wrote Frick to protest plans of the Pennsylvania Railroad to lay another track through ET. He wrote Frick again that summer with an optimistic outlook for the rail production that year (1996, 58). They were surely two different personalities, with completely different management styles. But they were the two most effective men ever to work for Andrew Carnegie.

Since the installation of natural gas earlier in the decade, one laborer now performed the work of eighty-two coal heavers (Krause 1992, 76). In a workforce of 3,500 men, a displaced tong man or coal heaver would be reassigned to another position, unless demand simply did not require production. Captain Bill rigorously maintained the policy of steady work for laborers that he had declared in 1875 (Bridge 1991, 81). In early 1889, the Captain had an appointment to meet with Carnegie in New York. He stopped by Bradford Gilbert's new building constructed of Homestead steel, the first building in history to exceed six stories. The surge in steel girders would soon enable buildings to reach forty or fifty stories, overtaking the Egyptian pyramids, until then the tallest human-made structures. The weather that February day was stormy; a hurricane had moved up the coast, bringing heavy rains. On the soaking sidewalk, he encountered Gilbert in front of the scaffolding of his ten stories, praying that the structure would survive the storm's winds. According to the family lore, the building was of a height equal to the towering arc of a "skyscraper," one of those pop flies hit by the sluggers on the Captain's baseball team, the Athletics. Bill Jones contributed the baseball moniker to its lasting association in the English language with tall, narrow buildings of steel .

A man who was to play a key role in the Jones family story, James Gayley, said that Captain Jones's inventions were fully as significant "as [those of] Mushet or Sir Henry Bessemer" (*Royal Blue Book,* 1913, 88). The importance of the Jones Hot Metal Mixer and Jones Direct Process to the steel industry can be seen by comparing their longevity with that of the Bessemer converter. The Bessemer process was phased out of most mills early in the twentieth century. In contrast, the Jones inventions are still required for all steel making, except the ancient cementation or crucible processes for small volumes of steel and the recycling of scrap metal. In Pittsburgh, one can see Jones's cradle today in the engine-driven torpedo cars glowing golden in the early evenings on the way to converters.

Section 28: The Joneses' Social Life

"Bill Jones built a new home for his family when he had been at Braddock for perhaps two years, a two-storied Victorian shingle at 817 Kirkpatrick Street. It became a social center in the town," my Aunt Margaret recounted during a visit to Sacramento to see the portrait of former governor Henry T. Gage. "Jones was the Baron of Braddock's Field—

Bill Jones built a new two-storied Victorian shingle at 817 Kirkpatrick Street in Braddock, PA.

Schwab called him the Czar." The Captain was an extrovert and loved people and parties. The Jones family usually attended concerts and supported the Welsh community's Christmas Eisteddfod, a festival of poetry and song. Jones hosted many parties, musical events, and lavish dinners. A variety of artists, intellectuals, and future leaders of industry frequented the Joneses' oak dinner table. The Captain brought to his home both his colleagues from ET and many visitors who came to the works. James Howard Bridge dined often with the family. Jones and Bridge, or another visitor, discussed literature or politics, while Cora played Schubert and Brahms on the piano.

The Captain supported a number of young, struggling authors, including the poet and fiction writer Frank Cowan, who, like Jones, was Welsh American. Cowan had a well-groomed white mane and spoke carefully enunciated schoolboy English. He enjoyed hearing the Captain read poetry and dedicated his book, *Short Stories from Studies of Life,* to Captain William Richard Jones (1878).The Captain also championed the Tennessee author Mary Noailles Murfree, who wrote under the pen name Charles Egbert Craddock. The Captain had met Mary earlier after he had read her articles and stories published in the *Atlantic Monthly* (Bridge 1931, 40). She captured the dialects and regional lifestyle of the mountaineers in the Cumberland Mountains of eastern Tennessee in the novels *In the Clouds* and *Where the Battle was Fought*, and in a collection of short stories, *In the Tennessee Mountains.* She revealed her identity as a woman only in 1884, by which time she was already a well-known regional writer. By 1887 she had published seven books.

Andrew Carnegie also sponsored artists, particularly John Hammer; social theorist critics like Herbert Spencer; and the poets Edwin and Matthew Arnold (Wall 1970, 387). Carnegie brought these men to Pittsburgh to meet the Captain and see the great ET and hosted them at Cresson. Carnegie had given Captain Bill two of John Hammer's watercolors, *Waterfall* and *Old Portage Road*, which depicted the area near Carnegie's home at Cresson. Jones went on to introduce Hammer to Joseph Butler of Youngstown, who specialized in collecting American art.

The parlor of the Kirkpatrick Street home smelled of burning anthracite, and the dark walnut panels often resonated with music. The piano was framed by Belgian tapestries and vases, with wing-backed chairs and other furnishings the Captain joked about as his loot from Europe.

One of Cora's suitors, the Captain's favorite, was William Ellis Corey, Mimi's cousin, who frequently visited the Jones home. Corey had been working as a chemist at ET's laboratory. One day the manager of the lab became so enraged at young Corey that he kicked him through the doorway. Corey landed smack in the iron gut of the Captain, who had just arrived in the doorway. Corey picked himself up without looking at his backstop and yelled at the manager, "You go to hell, you old son of a bitch!!" Corey then gathered himself together, never having seen the Captain standing there. The Captain instantly liked Corey and sent him over to Homestead where Charlie Schwab gave him a job on the spot (Whipple n.d.). Years later Corey was to follow Schwab as the second president of United States Steel.

Corey was a bird enthusiast. He and Cora with Grandmother Mary went bird watching along the Monongahela to survey the migrating ducks and geese. Cora and William remained friends for many years. Harriet often told Cora that she would have been pleased with William Corey as a son-in-law.

Harriet had for many years had spent much of the time in her bedroom. She had certainly stopped being a sexual companion to Bill by the mid-1870s, sometime after the birth of their last child. Bill was still a vibrant man—extremely social and full of extraordinary energy, attractive and engaging to all who met him. One can only speculate on where he went for feminine companionship.

Bridge, writing many years later, gives a vivid picture of Bill Jones at work and at home during the 1880s.

> Captain "Bill" Jones ... was another mixture of gentleness and harshness. He had the most lurid gift of invective of anybody I ever knew. On his office door was the sign: 'Any oil-drummer found on these premises will be promptly bounced'. I once witnessed the bouncing of an 'oil-drummer'. If it had been the oil itself it would have caught fire! A few minutes later when we reached his house—for I was staying with him in his Braddock cottage—he was the gentlest, kindliest man imaginable. His wife was life-long invalid, and his was a life-long devotion to her. His voice was low and sweet, and full of loving inflections, so that one wondered at his rough exterior ... (2008, 56)

Although Harriet had forbidden Cora to see D. D. Gage, Cora found opportunities during the year to take the train into Pittsburgh to meet secretly with D. D., who sang with choral groups in and around Pittsburgh. They met behind frosted glass swinging doors of new, fashionable drug stores. But word of Cora's meetings got back to Harriet in Braddock. So Harriet organized parties and invited the up and coming swains to meet Cora and listen to her play the piano after dinner. On these evenings, Harriet's five servants met Cora's every wish, as the doting parents did everything in their power to foster some spark between the guest and the defiant Cora.

Harriet and the Captain held a gala party for Cora's twenty-first birthday on January 4, 1888. The house was adorned with Chinese balloons and other festive decorations. A small orchestra played for nearly a hundred guests from beyond Braddock and as far away as Johnstown in the east and Youngstown in the north. Horse-drawn carriages deposited young women with chaperones and gentlemen dressed in wool and fur caps to protect them from the Pittsburgh-sooted snow. W. W. McCleary, with taproom nose a-glowing, brought his daughter Lizzie. John and Margaret Potter remembered the gala event years later. James Gayley and his Julie arrived late. D. D. Gage, of course, was not invited and nothing could brighten Cora's spirits because of that.

Cora moped throughout the evening. After dinner and birthday cake, she opened presents. Dazzling treasures were bestowed on the Czar's daughter by the guests in an effort to upstage one another at the party. Cora received bracelets, rings, music scores, perfumes from Paris, and cameo pins. When Lizzie McCleary gave Cora a silver locket and chain, Cora dashed it to the floor. She felt Lizzie mocked her because she could not put D. D.'s picture in it. From her father, she received a painting by the German American artist John Hammer of a young girl picking flowers in a bucolic setting. Cora told her sons and their wives, forty years later, how badly she still felt about her behavior that night. In fact, she had displayed all the attributes of a spoiled, self-centered young woman.

By 1888 the family was discussing a move, as Bill Jones looked for an alternative to his situation at ET. Harriet thought a move to Ohio might distance Cora from D. D. Gage.

Section 29: Of Innovations and Homogeneity

In 1888 a rival steel works was built four miles upriver from Homestead at Duquesne. This new works used a novel method for producing rails, which the Duquesne owners ambiguously referred to as the direct process. The Duquesne direct method differed from the Jones Direct Process. Jones's direct process took place in the pre-conversion stage; the hot molten pig iron was moved directly from iron furnaces to the steel converter without reheating. Duquesne's direct process referred to a stage after steel conversion, with molten Bessemer steel moving from the converter directly to billets and rails from the soaking pits. It, too, eliminated a second heating, which resulted in significant savings.

By February 1889 Duquesne was producing rails. Carnegie realized this new competitor would cut costs in production (Bridge 1991, 174). Aware of Jones's pending patent for the pre-conversion direct process, Carnegie wrote to purchasers of railroad goods, stating that Duquesne rails were defective, lacking in homogeneity. Alarmed, rail purchasers were wary, and Duquesne could not sell its cheaper rails to anyone. Within a year the new owners sold the plant to Frick for paper in one of his greatest business coups; these bonds amounted to a million dollars but earned six million dollars for Carnegie Brothers in five years (Bridge 1991, 174-183).

Historians have focused on Carnegie's wording about direct process on the flyer to the rail consumers as an example of his duplicity. In 1903, Bridge stated that Carnegie had fibbed in late summer of 1889 by slandering the rail products of the new Duquesne Works (ibid., 174-183). Nearly seven decades later, Joseph Frazier Wall sustained Bridge's opinion by elaborating on why Carnegie criticized rails produced by Duquesne's direct method:

> Carnegie immediately saw the cost threat of this invention [Duquesne's post-conversion direct method] and before the first rail had been rolled at Duquesne he had drafted a circular to railroads throughout the country warning them that the process being used by [Duquesne] would result in defective rails, because for lack of a second heating the steel in the rails would not have "homogeneity" of structure. No one in the Carnegie mills knew what this meant, but it sounded impressive, and the railroad purchasing agents were reluctant to take a chance on rails which lacked "homogeneity". (Wall 1970, 498)

Contrary to Bridge's and Wall's assertions, Carnegie was not guilty of misinformation or deliberate ambiguity; Carnegie knew exactly what he was saying to the rail consumers, and he was accurate in stating that Duquesne rails lacked homogeneity. The Duquesne owners' usage of the phrase direct process is what is ambiguous, for their process refers to the post-conversion stage of rolling molten steel ingots directly into rails. Without the mixer, iron from a single furnace at Duquesne went into the converter and from there, as steel, it moved directly into rails. Any steel from a works that does not use the Jones mixer lacks homogeneity, unless, of course, iron from several furnaces is cooled and then reheated in a cupola furnace, but salaries of labor and fuel for reheating would increase costs. Herein lies Carnegie's deception: as soon as Frick had acquired the Duquesne works, the direct method used there was installed at ET and Homestead.

That same year, John Potter was transferred to Homestead, where the open hearth process was yielding a higher quality steel in greater volume than the Bessemer batches at ET. Unlike Schwab and Corey at ET, Potter shared the Captain's mechanical inventiveness (Gaughan, personal communication). He had also become something of an expert in the fabrication of armor. Incidentally, this accounts for Homestead fulfilling the Czar's order to construct the Russian naval fleet in the following decade. (conversation with Gaughan in company of Professor David Demarest, June 4, 1994).

Carnegie understood the potential of the Jones mixer, and with Frick in place of his brother, Tom, he had already co-opted some of Jones's authority with labor by dictating the length of the work day. In spring of 1888, Jones had corresponded with Robert Hunt at Troy, John Fritz at Bethlehem, John Fry at Chicago and, especially, a number of people in Ohio. Joseph G. Butler, Jr. in Youngstown and Henry Wick were keenly interested in building a new plant that would utilize both Bessemer and open-hearth processes that could rival ET and Homestead (Higley, 1953, pp. 123-5).

At about this time, Jones was promoted to chief engineer for all Carnegie operations, in addition to continuing as superintendent at ET. He was being drawn further into management.

Andrew Carnegie withdrew more and more from operations in Pittsburgh, which he largely delegated to Frick, although the two were in regular communication and Carnegie never relinquished ultimate control. Carnegie spent increasing amounts of time in Europe and had become quite involved in British politics. In the early 1880s he had bought a number of newspapers there and used them in an attempt to revive the Chartist movement against hereditary privilege—including abolishing the monarchy and the House of Lords. These activities may seem contradictory to Carnegie's own single-minded pursuit of wealth and power, but they are quite in line with his Social Darwinist beliefs. His primary home in the United States had long been in New York, but when he did visit his mountain estate at Cresson, near Pittsburgh, and the South Fork Lake Fishing and Hunting Club above Johnstown (McCullough 1968, 46), he often invited American politicians, intellectuals, and industry magnates as his guests. He was also increasingly involved in politics in the United States.

The new year, 1889, got off to an inauspicious start. On January 9, a tornado ripped through Pittsburgh, Braddock, and McKeesport deracinating sycamores, oaks, and elms. In Pittsburgh seventeen people were killed, crushed beneath collapsed buildings. At ET, the tornado damaged blast furnace C, putting it out of commission for a week. Roofs were ripped from sheds and newly-planted telephone poles were downed, with dangerous electrical wires entangling flat cars on the Ohio and Baltimore tracks. It took two weeks to clear the mess.

Section 30: Flood Path to Johnstown

In May 1889 a stationary front with accompanying thunderstorms plagued western Pennsylvania. Heavy rain started on May 29. On May 30, the rain became so heavy and continuous that it disrupted Decoration Day festivities. In the mountains surrounding Johnstown seven inches of rain fell over two days. Fourteen miles out of Johnstown perched the South Fork Lake, the reservoir formed on the Little Conemaugh River, held back only by a dam which had been neglected for many years.

Filius Heyer had reported in 1879 that a group of laborers had arrived by train in Johnstown before traveling by horse-drawn wagons up to the lake at South Fork. Heyer surmised that Pittsburgh money was financing the construction of what would become the South Fork Lake Fishing and Hunting Club. He told of lavish cottages, some three stories high; a club house the size of city hall in Pittsburgh; and sailing boats on the lake like "you'd find in Newport, Rhode Island—yachts in the middle of the Allegheny mountains," crowning the mountains four hundred feet above Johnstown (ibid., 39-78). Henry Clay Frick and Benjamin Ruff, his colleague in the coke business, founded the club and bought the land for it. They then invited prominent businessmen from Pittsburgh to join. Henry Phipps, Jr., John G. A. Leishman, Benjamin Thaw, Andrew Mellon, and Andrew Carnegie were among the prominent Pennsylvania men who were members. The club was quite secretive and exclusive. Despite the construction for cottages and club buildings, only limited repairs were made to the dam in 1879.

Earlier in the 1870s, Daniel Morrell had asked Captain Bill's friend, John Fulton, to analyze the dam that corseted the increasing volume of water above Johnstown. Fulton identified many structural problems. For more than twenty years, hunters and vandals had robbed piping from the spillway for their homes and shops down river. When the Pittsburgh owners bought the property, they estimated the expense of rebuilding the derelict dam, and, ignoring Fulton, they filled in the earlier break with what could be found— rubble, tree limbs, straw, and horse manure (ibid., 55). Now living in Johnstown after his tenure in Congress, Morrell was adamant that the dam needed attention; he, too, was a member, primarily to enable him to stay informed about the club. But Morrell's health was failing, and the dam was not his highest priority.

Filius's neighbor Cyrus Elder also was a member of the club; he was attorney and chief counsel for the Cambria Iron Works. His brother, James Elder, had mustered out young Bill Jones from the 133rd in May 1863. In the early 1880s, Cyrus had asked Captain Bill to join the club, but Jones had declined.

On the last day of May, 1889, the rain fell like Niagara. Rain-bearing black clouds seemed to be sucked into river valleys that fed the Little Conemaugh. Cora remembered talking with the stationmaster in his straw hat at Bessemer Station, adjacent to the offices of ET, when word came in that Johnstown was enduring a terrible rainstorm. He had relatives in Johnstown, as did the more than 200 former Cambria employees who come to ET in 1875.

By the third day of rain, the lake was brimming full; approximately twenty million tons of water was pushing against the neglected dam four hundred feet above Johnstown,

The 20-mile per hour wave carried houses, people, trees, machinery, a locomotive, passenger cars, and miles of wire.

a city of some thirty thousand residents, most of the men still employed at Cambria. At around three in the afternoon, a ten-foot notch in the dam gave way causing the middle of the dam to burst. A massive wave swept down the valley toward Johnstown, cresting some ninety feet above normal level at the narrowest point in the canyon leading to the city (McCullough 1968, 58). The contents of the reservoir emptied in less than an hour, and the deluge gathered force as it swept along at twenty miles an hour over the fourteen miles to reach Johnstown (ibid., 54.).

The wave followed the course of the Little Conemaugh, whose bed had been silting up with each year's flood and with each reclamation of the embankments. In years past, Captain Bill had gauged the flood danger by measuring the high water mark of each year's flood at the home of Colonel John P. Linton, a comrade from the war (Jones 1889, June 7). The wave first struck the upstream town of Woodvale, destroying 225 houses and drowning 314 people (Brown 1989, 96). When it hit Johnstown at about four o'clock, the wave carried houses, people, trees, machinery, a locomotive, passenger cars, and miles of wire, all washing up perpendicularly against the massive face of the hog-back.

This collision of water against mountainside caused a backwash wave of nearly equal height and violence. It returned back up through the town, before gravity and inertia drew the mass of debris and bodies back whirling up into Stony Creek River and down the Conemaugh to the Stone Bridge, which functioned like a plug. Blocked with refuse, the streams beneath the bridge caused another backwash up into the city, creating a rising lake over areas of Johnstown. The Stone Bridge held against the downhill force while a mountain of debris amassed up against its rock foundation until the waters crested at twenty feet.

Three to four feet of mud, debris, and death layered the area from the Little Conemaugh to the Stony Creek River dam where Jones and his young family had so often swum and picnicked down by the bridge. A treacherous mass of steel cable and barbed wire moved downstream, wrapping around bodies and parts of buildings until it was wedged against the bridge. Witnesses described nearly three hundred people caught in the debris who perished while the onlookers could do nothing to help.

Mired within were human bodies, houses, cows, telegraph poles, parts of bridges, and barns in the aftermath of the great wave.

Downtown Johnstown was turned into a wasteland of sand and debris, deposited by the great wave over parts of homes, shops, churches, and schools. Mired within were human bodies, houses, cows, telegraph poles, parts of bridges, and barns. As the water receded on Washington Street, an ironclad, brick-lined boiler emerged dripping wet in a yard at least three miles from its source, the Gautier plant in Woodvale up the Little Conemaugh. Steam pumps, each weighing fifty tons, had been driven more than three hundred feet. Thousands of bricks lay along the river's edges for miles.

When the dam broke, Captain Bill was finishing the day's work at the ET office, preparing to leave for home. In 1878 the waters of the Mon, as he referred to the Monongahela, flooded into the works. The five-foot barbed wire fence between the Baltimore and Ohio tracks and ET property had been under water. Earlier in the evening, Superintendent Robert Pitcairn, an official in the Pennsylvania Railroad in charge of the western region of the state, traveled east, worried about the South Fork dam. He telegraphed the first message about the catastrophe from Sang Hollow, four miles from Johnstown, around 6:00 p.m., and word reached Captain Bill via Bessemer station.

Jones immediately telegraphed the chamber of commerce in Pittsburgh for two thousand volunteers to assist Johnstown (Shappee 1940, 98). He ordered the closing of Edgar Thomson Works and dashed into the mills and sheds telling workers to drop what they were doing and alert their families that they were drafted to help the survivors of the flood. Captain Bill rounded up 170 men from ET, half of whom were Hungarians, and drew from the relief fund, which he had instituted at the firm (*Pittsburgh Post*, 1893, September 27, 4).

Closing ET meant a loss of $15,000 per day, and even more costly would be the wear and tear on equipment. Once the furnaces cooled, it would take several days to reheat them for the next blast of ore. Cooling also caused premature aging of the brick-lined walls of boshes, the lower section of the furnaces, but Jones made the executive decision to put human life before financial gain. One must wonder if this decision to cease production and allow the furnaces to cool may in part have accounted for the explosion that was to occur at ET's furnace C four months later, injuring Jones.

Jones enlisted his brother-in-law, William Lewis, and William Yost to travel sixty miles to investigate the extent of flood damage. By Saturday morning, June 2, Jones learned in detail the situation in the Conemaugh Valley. Train service had been restored to Johnstown, and by midafternoon, ET workers had stacked cots, mattresses, and coffins on three Pennsylvania Railroad boxcars at Bessemer Station. Just forty-eight hours after the mountain of water hit Johnstown, the rescue train was on its way. The entire town of Braddock followed Captain Bill's lead, and by late Sunday another five boxcars loaded with food, medicine, bedding, soup kettles, and clothing departed for the stricken town (McLaurin 1890).

Debris and devastation washed against Stone Bridge in the wake of the Johnstown Flood. (Public Domain.)

Cora wanted to accompany her father to Johnstown, but he did not permit it, instead, suggesting that maybe later in the week she could join him. Cora wondered about the fate of the town of her birth and about her childhood friends, with many of whom she remained close by attending parties (Daniel Gage, personal communication). Her Braddock neighbors, Ann Cadogan and her mother Mary Cadogan, had gone to Johnstown to participate in the Decoration Day festivities.

No one yet knew what havoc reigned in the mountains. Harriet ordered two servants to boil all drinking water in fear of typhoid and asked the remaining household staff to collect clothing and towels for the survivors. Early on the morning of Sunday, June 3, Jones and other members of the Pittsburgh Relief Committee traveled east from Bessemer Station. The Pennsylvania steam engine passed Greensburg and traveled on to Latrobe. At each station, early morning crowds swarmed the platforms, waving as the train roared by. At Bolivar, the train reached the Conemaugh River. The river was still high, but Jones could see the crest mark of Friday's wave some twenty feet above the current water level. Telegraph poles, tympana of houses, dead livestock matted both sides of the banks as the train chugged up through Laurel Hill past Nineveh and into Sang Hollow. The telegraph agent at the station had just wired to Pittsburgh: "Physicians are not needed; send as many undertakers as possible" (McLaurin 1890, 251).

The train could go no farther, so Jones's 170 men shouldered their backpacks and disembarked with shovels and crowbars. The Captain led the group up through the pass above Johnstown. At the summit, the rescuers looked down into a hole of death. Smoke rose from fires burning in the mass of debris near the Stone Bridge. The Cambria furnaces, on higher ground, stood firm, but Jones could not see any sign of the adjacent buildings on what had been Locust, Main, and Lincoln, and other streets in town. From where his band of rescuers stopped, the scene of what had once been a city was now a vast lake with only a few spires of churches and brick buildings on stone foundations remaining. Below was Grand View Cemetery where his infant son Charles was buried. For fifteen years he and his family had lived and enjoyed life here.

Cambria's main works sat north above the protective Stone Bridge, with only a few buildings damaged. Most of the 7,100 men working that Friday survived, but a three-foot veneer of mud spread for acres along the river. A temporary lake of filth, rubble, and disease stretched from the burning debris backed up from the bridge and up beyond Stony Creek. Fires from gaslights had ignited the soggy wood and oil in the detritus against the bridge and those not drowned burned to death (McCullough 1968, 145-204).

Along the Little Conemaugh, only a few buildings and parts of others were standing. The exception was on high ground like Prospect Hill, where there were now many temporary sheds and lean-tos, rapidly erected to shelter the thousands without homes.

Jones's workers marched down into town. By around six in the evening the rain finally stopped. A mud-smeared crowd of overwhelmed residents watched the men set to work. Already, reporters from the *Pittsburgh Post*, the *Pittsburgh Gazette*, and the *Clearfield Raftsman* were writing their stories, using coffin tops as desks. As part of one of the first rescue groups on the scene, Jones ordered debris removed to enable the setting up of soup kitchens and a mess area near the Cambria Iron Works. A telegraph line was open at the company office. Jones wired the War Department in Washington for a thousand feet of pontoon bridges, and for competent engineers to build them so the rescuers could cross the lake that had filled one half of the city (Connelly and Jenks 1889, 193).

By Monday morning a regular army kitchen occupied the high ground away from the smoke and the smell from the bridge. Jones wired orders back to the Pittsburgh Relief Committee that they needed equipment and people who specialized in emergency relief. By noon the Jones brigade was able to feed six hundred workmen who had filed down from Sang Hallow and volunteers from other towns and Pittsburgh factories, like the National Tube Works at McKeesport. A thousand men were working on the ruins. Captain Bill knew that they needed shelter, for few slept well under the stars.

After organizing what could be done for the living, on Monday, June 3, Captain Bill directed W. W. McCleary to address the dead. Already on the previous day, many bodies had been carried by family and friends up Prospect Hill where they were laid out in long files, now awaiting burial. The smell was becoming overwhelming. McCleary's men found arms and legs protruding from under the clapboard sides of houses. Among the mounds of debris, legs straddled inverted window frames. Further up the Little Conemaugh, they found the body of a woman twenty feet up in the branches of a tree. His team found entire families in open cellars now sealed to the outdoors by mud. Each basement had to be completely dug out, the most gruesome of their tasks.

Progress was slow. When a body was brought to light, a mob of grief-stricken residents approached the corpse, in hopes of identifying the body. Extricating some bodies proved nearly impossible for they were entwined in Gautier wire. The stone foundation of the schoolhouse had withstood the flood waters and the classrooms were turned into a coffin-filled morgue. McCleary's men bore stretchers through the waist-deep muck. Frightfully contorted bodies were forced awkwardly into pine boxes. Glassy eyes and rubbery complexions would haunt many of the Braddock volunteers for the rest of their lives.

The Pennsylvania station became the next site Jones co-opted for a sepulcher. For sanitation, many bodies were placed in trenches. To distinguish rescuers from dazed townspeople, the Captain used strips of yellow ribbon Harriet had provided him as badges. An increasing number of tourists and relic hunters descended on Johnstown from Cresson and Pittsburgh. More than two hundred gawkers with cameras picked their way through mud and debris as early as June 3. But relief workers by the hundred were also arriving (McLaurin 1890, 256).

During the day more than four hundred coffins from Johnstown were ferried across the deluged city to the rows of the dead, then hauled up the hillside, where they were buried in shallow graves. The bodies of some of the missing would not be found until years later—two were discovered downriver as late as 1906 (McCullough 1968, 196). The Captain joined McCleary in dressing the dead, for decayed bodies would quickly poison the water flowing downriver to Pittsburgh and on down the Ohio. In fact, typhoid did break out, and some fifty individuals died from it.

On Tuesday morning, Captain Bill heard a voice in the desperate crowd: "Captain Jones!" Jones did not recognize the man covered in mud. "Hello, Bill!"

The Captain looked at the survivor, and then uneasily stated: "You'll have to tell me who you are."

"I'm Pat Lavell," came the reply.

The stunned Captain Bill embraced Lavell like a brother. "How did it go with you?" The Captain asked the dreaded question as he so often had that week.

"Lost everything," answered Lavell, "my home, my savings—everything; but," his eyes suddenly beamed below the mud-caked forehead, and Lavell exclaimed "I'm the happiest man in Johnstown, for my family's all right."

Religious zealots disrupted Jones and his men, crying that God had cleansed Johnstown of its bawdyhouses and its ninety-five saloons. Some survivors, drunk from the half-submerged whiskey kegs found in the mud, joined in the mayhem. One waved his cup and sang bawdily from the top of a piano (McLaurin 1890, 262). Word had spread about treasures from Johnstown's four jewelers, who had perished in their shops. Prospectors dug frantically around Clinton and Franklin Streets, obstructing some efforts to help survivors. The business district, in fact, was largely destroyed. California Tom's tavern was gone, as were the Eagle Hotel and the St. Charles Hotel, which had been full of guests attending Decoration Day festivities. Over fifty perished at Hulbert House Hotel alone.

Jones found Colonel John P. Linton among the survivors, but his daughter had drowned. The Linton home on Lincoln Street had been rebuilt following the 1862 flood, with the first floor elevated above the usual flood mark. Because trees had been clear-cut all along the fourteen miles northeast to the South Fork Lake, silt had filled the riverbed. On the Friday before the dam broke, Colonel Linton's first floor was covered with three or four inches of water. When the dam broke, the initial wave carried a section of an iron bridge,

> *The loss of children in the flood was staggering.*

which bisected the house (McCullough 1968, 185).

Within a day, a well-provisioned tent camp and a commissary were set up to house some nine hundred under William Flinn, a demolitions expert, who arrived Wednesday. (Flinn, with Christopher McGee, constituted the political machine that ran Pittsburgh and Allegheny County during the 1880s; they were renowned for favoritism and graft (Connelly and Jenks 1889, 191-4).) Captain Bill wired Harrisburg, imploring Governor Beaver to organize a military unit to come to protect survivors and feed six thousand workers who needed food and shelter (McLaurin 1890, 226).

Soon Captain Bill and his men could not distinguish survivors from looting ne'er do wells. The scale of the disaster and the ensuing confusion were enormous. There were cases of theft, but out-of-town newspapers exaggerated an already tragic situation, often blaming foreigners, particularly Hungarians, for looting and theft, even though fifty-eight Hungarians died in the flood (ibid.). Cora later recounted that Captain Bill was as angry as a hornet's nest with the newsmen because the Hungarians from ET outperformed all in their efforts to help survivors—one, the father of Cora's friend Sarah Wolf, contributed $1,000 out of his own pocket for relief. The Cambria county sheriff deputized many with tin-tags, crudely cut from canned food lids (ibid., 264). But some deputized residents challenged many of Captain Jones's workers, half of whom were Hungarians. The Captain's friend, Tom L. Johnson, deputized his former mill partner, Alexander Moxham, as dictator; Moxham spilled all the liquor his squad could find and replaced the tin-taggers (ibid.).

Many of the Jones's friends and former neighbors had suffered terribly. Gertrude and Filius Heyer could not be found, then Jones learned that the couple had been out of town and were desperately trying to return. The grandchildren of Colonel Bowman, who had once run the *Johnstown Tribune* and was a supporter of the Union League, were lost. James Elder's niece and sister-in-law had perished. Cyrus Elder had returned from Chicago on the day of the flood and told his story to Captain Bill in short, matter-of-fact sentences. At around three o'clock that Friday afternoon, Cyrus had exited the train car and had tried to wade from the station to his home on Walnut Street. He could only call to his wife and daughter, because the water was so deep he couldn't reach his house. He waded to his brother's house, higher up the hillside, and was changing into his brother's clothes when the first wave hit the city. He had heard a locomotive whistle screaming continuously, followed by a thundering roar of water. From the doorway of James's house, the two Elders watched a black wall below sweep Cyrus's house down the river without any sign of his wife or daughter. Neither woman was ever found. Houses and other features from the lower section of Johnstown constituted much of what piled up against the bridge. Panicked, the brothers made their way toward the bridge and hunted in vain until, paralyzed by horror, they witnessed gas pipes exploding and saw the debris amassed against the Stone Bridge catching fire. In addition to his personal loss, Cyrus Elder would carry much of the brunt of his neighbors' rage, for everyone knew that he was a member of the South Fork Club.

Water around the bridge subsided considerably. The cars from the Day Express, which had been swept down from the Little Conemaugh, surfaced. Word had spread that the wife of Lew Wallace, Jones's commanding officer in Baltimore, was in one of those cars. When the parlor car was excavated it was full of bodies but Mrs. Wallace was not among them. She had apparently missed the ill-fated train (ibid., 269).

The loss of children in the flood was staggering. At three in the afternoon on Wednesday, young Eddie Schoefler, having survived under entangled debris for six days, was found alive. His mother had resigned herself to her son's death and was nearly mad; his father embraced W. W. McCleary and the Hungarians who heard Eddie crying beneath a half ton of splintered buildings and debris (McCullough 1968, 210).

On Thursday evening, June 6, Captain Bill decided to hand over his responsibility and to return to Braddock (Connelly and Jenks 1889, 194). Arriving home, he learned that charitable groups from Pennsylvania and around the country were giving generously to those who suffered, including the Italian Brotherhood of Pittsburgh, which donated $200; the City of Chicago, $5,000; and the Pennsylvania Railroad, $25,000 (*Pittsburgh Press*, 1889, June 7). But the Captain was again shocked and angered by the xenophobic press hysteria. In spite of donations made to the relief effort by various ethnic groups, headlines screamed of Hunkies pulling gold teeth from the jaws of the dead and cutting off fingers for rings, and of Irish and Italians robbing household chests found in collapsed houses. Jones castigated one reporter at the *Pittsburgh Press* and challenged him to correct the misinformation being printed. He hoped that people would consider well the source of the tragedy but knew the truth of Shakespeare's cynicism: "One touch of nature makes the whole world kin,/That all with one consent praise new-born gawds" (*Troilus and Cressida*). I tell you what you might say; you might say that the Hungarians of Johnstown are the most abused people on the face of the earth. They are being outrageously persecuted on account of a lot of lies that have been circulated at their expense. That some of them have not been lynched is not the fault of the hoodlums who are hounding them or of the newspapers which have been describing their imaginary atrocities. I don't blame correspondents who credited the first statements concerning them, when it was impossible to fully investigate the facts, but I hold that they should all follow the example of the Press in doing them tardy justice, now that the truth of the matter can be so easily obtained. The only cases of pilfering which came under my observation at Johnstown were two, in which Native Americans were the offenders. One of them had picked up a few articles of trifling value among the ruins of a dwelling, yet I had the greatest difficulty in preventing him from being lynched by the furious mob by which he was pursued. He was terribly beaten as it was. I had him sent out of town with a warning not to return. The Hungarians, who formed a large portion of my relief corps, worked silently, faithfully, and intelligently, and when the meeting was held at Braddock on Saturday to consider measures of relief, were among the first to contribute a day's work. Joseph Wolf, a Hungarian and one of the best citizens of Braddock, has been most active in the work of relief and contributed $1000 outright out of his own pocket.

The South Fork Hunting and Fishing Club kept a low profile after the flood. Many members sent relief money; Frick was the most generous, sending a personal check for $5,000. Carnegie, however, later made the splashiest donation—during a visit to the city, he promised the rebuilding of the Johnstown Library, to great acclaim. The survivors in Johnstown, however, blamed the club and many suits were brought against it and its members. In every case the court decided that the disaster had been an "Act of Providence", with no responsibility involved.

Once back in Braddock, the Captain caught up with mail that Harriet had received, including an envelope from the Department of Interior. The Government had granted Jones the exclusive patent rights for the Jones Mixer and the Jones Direct Process.

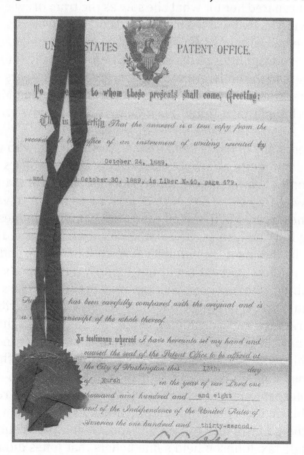

The patent awarded for Captain Bill Jones' greatest invention, the Jones Hot Metal Mixer, still in use in today's steel industry.

Section 31: At the Commissary

On Friday, June 7, Cora met Captain Bill at Bessemer Station with a half dozen cigars from McDevitt's store. She questioned him about the flood survivors. He told her the school on Adams Street was among the few buildings standing. He had seen Mimi Corey, who was safe, but none of her other friends.

Jones spent two days at the ET office, wiring Carnegie in Paris, the state capitol in Harrisburg, and President Benjamin Harrison in Washington, D.C. He took care of matters at ET that had to be addressed and spent hours explaining to the press and leaders of Braddock what had happened at Johnstown and what Braddock might contribute to the effort. He confided to family and close friends how angry he was with the negligent owners of the South Fork Club.

On Sunday, June 9, Jones returned to Johnstown with Cora to see how relief efforts were progressing. Although he had described to his daughter the devastation and horror at Johnstown, nothing prepared her for what she saw as the train drew over the pass, and she hiked down into town. The two walked past crowds of relief workers, displaced residents, tourists, and militia, who were now standing guard over the somewhat peaceful but ruined city. Cora assumed responsibilities at the soup kitchen. Old Kelly, a former slave who had escaped from the South in the underground railway, greeted her. Years earlier the Reverend Lloyd had looked after Old Kelly at his Johnstown parish. Cora and Mimi visited the fresh grave of their friend Kate Fritz at Grand View Cemetery. The new graves stretched on by the hundreds.

Cora consoled many of her grandparent's Welsh friends who were in dire circumstances. The Welsh community as a whole lost over a million dollars in assets (McLaurin 1890, 225). Many homes near her grandfather's former church at Main and Locust streets had been washed away. On Friday, Cora's D. D. arrived and went to work for the Captain. During the week, Jones treated D. D. warmly and with genuine fondness.

One evening D. D. arrived at the commissary looking grave. He had been helping retrieve bodies in Millville, a settlement upriver from Johnstown, and had recognized the bodies of two whom others present could not identify—the Jones's neighbors, Mrs. Cadogan and her daughter, who had been visiting from Braddock. Years later, D. D. and Cora would break down in tears recounting what they witnessed that terrible week.

Amid the wreckage and nonstop cleanup, the Captain caught up with his friend, Tom Johnson, who now lived in Ohio but was building streetcars in a factory he owned in Johnstown with his partner, Alexander Moxham. Moxham and others from Johnstown eventually approached Captain Bill about returning to Johnstown to restore the damaged works there. Johnson spent many weeks in Johnstown on relief and rebuilding, an experience that modified his political philosophy. Both Tom and the Captain shared a knowledge of and respect for the philosophies of George Lippard and the economist Henry George, who proposed a single tax. Johnson held some beliefs that Jones did not share, especially Johnson's disapproval of high tariffs for steel, which he believed benefited the industrialist at the expense of the average citizen.

One evening at the commissary the two men smoked and discussed politics after long, exhausting hours spent on relief and rescue work. Johnson berated Carnegie and Frick, citing how the two and their friends were responsible for the flood. He scoffed at Carnegie's public charity as nothing more than a rich man's salve for the disease that greed had caused. Puffing on his Meerschaum pipe, the Captain told Tom about negotiations to build a new steel works in Youngstown with Walker Kennedy and Joseph G. Butler, Jr. The two discussed how Carnegie might react to the loss of Jones and his patents if the Captain were to leave the company.

Cora remembered Tom Johnson mocking Carnegie over the dedication in Braddock of the first Carnegie Library the previous March. He had proclaimed the Braddock Library " . . . a center of light & learning—a never failing spring for all good influences" (Johnson 1911, 36-7). Johnson knew that Captain Bill had inspired some of Carnegie's largesse; prior to the Captain's prompting, Carnegie had donated funds only for a pipe organ in his parents' Swedenborg church in downtown Pittsburgh and a swimming pool and a library for his hometown of Dunfermline in Scotland (Wall 1970, 815). Carnegie had claimed that Homestead, too, could get a public library if it had no labor unrest, an assertion that Tom called extortion.

As described above, Carnegie, Frick, Phipps, and Rush had spared nothing in building cottages and a clubhouse at South Fork. But they had failed to adequately address the faulty spillway that lead to Johnstown's destruction, which could have been repaired at a cost that would have been equivalent to the wages of one company machinist, working for six and two/thirds days. Instead, so that two carriages might pass over the dam simultaneously, the club manager had widened the road on the top of the dam (thereby lowering and weakening it) at a cost much greater than that of repairing the spillway. Ignorant of engineering, these wealthy amateurs lowered the middle of the span rather than the sides: when a dam breaks, the middle goes, and the entire lake evacuates (McCullough 1968, 75-7). Both Johnson and Captain Bill remembered Fulton's report, written five years earlier, which explicitly stated the following:

> Two serious elements of danger in the dam. First, the want of a discharge pipe to reduce or take the water out of the dam for needed repairs. Second, the insubstantial method of repair, leaving a large leak, which appears to be cutting the new embankment.
>
> As the water cannot be lowered, the difficulty arises of reaching the source of the present destructive leaks. At present there is forty feet of water in the dam, when the full head of 60 feet is reached, it appears to me to be only a question of time until the former cutting is repeated. Should this break be made during a season of flood, it is evident that considerable damage would ensue along the line of the Conemaugh. It is impossible to estimate how disastrous this flood would be, as its force would depend on the size of the breach in the dam with proportional rapidity of discharge.
>
> The stability of the dam can only be assured by a thorough overhauling of pres-

ent lining on the upper slopes, and the construction of an ample discharge pipe to reduce or remove the water to make necessary repairs. (McCullough 1968, 73-4)

Although hundreds of thousands of dollars—eventually millions—were pouring in to Johnstown, as were food, furniture, and all manner of durable goods, Johnson railed against wealth and charity. Twenty years later, he was still angry when he wrote his autobiography. "What did charity from all over the world do for Johnstown? It was powerless to restore children to parents, to reunite families, to mitigate mourning, to heal broken hearts, or to bring back lost lives" (Johnson 1911, 45).

On Sunday, June 16, Captain Jones met with Adjutant General Hastings, who had arrived on June 8 with five hundred national guardsmen and was now charged with maintaining order in the chaotic city. The two escorted Governor Beaver, who arrived that evening, in a survey of the destroyed city.

In the month following the disaster there was talk of Captain Bill being groomed by the Pennsylvania Republican Party for a political career. The leadership qualities exhibited by men during the flood relief efforts gave them much positive press and eventually led some to elected office. William Flinn and General Daniel Hastings were elected, respectively, to a state senate seat and as governor of Pennsylvania. Tom Johnson was elected to the U.S. Congress and, running as a Socialist, to the mayoralty of Cleveland, Ohio.

When Jones and Cora returned home after a second week in Johnstown, Harriet met them, screaming abuses that Cora never forgot. Her beefy brother, Will, had told their mother that D. D. Gage was also in Johnstown. Harriet called D. D. an immoral actor, and Cora, a slattern. She forbade Cora ever to see D. D. again.

During the last summer of his life, much of the Captain's time was taken up with his continued efforts to help flood victims in Johnstown. He wrote dozens of letters to fellow steelmakers about the plights of those who survived, including the following:

Mr. Wood, Gen. Supt. Penna Steel Wo.

My Dear Sir

Mr. Alex Hamilton Supt of the Cambria Mills suffered severe losses from the appalling calamity that befell Johnstown, having lost seven of his family and making a wonderful escape with himself and wife. They had sought safety in the attic of Mr. Geo Randolfs residency, and when discovered found Mr. Hamilton and wife almost exhausted. Mr. Hamilton was completely worn out in his superhuman effort to keep his wife's head above water, and had not a friendly log pushed its way through the building and assisted Mr. Hamilton in sustaining his wife by having her throw her arms around the log both would have been drowned. They were discovered in the nick of time, and pulled onto the roof of the house a few minutes before the house was completely wrecked, and they in conjunction with twelve other persons were carried off in the flood. They were carried up the river some two miles and in their journey rescued forty-two persons and finally succeeded in crawling over debris into the upper story of the 6th Ward schoolhouse. The awful scenes through which Mr. Hamilton and his wife passed, and the terrible loss of seven of their family have broken them down, and I am of the opinion that they will never recover. Mr. Hamilton is in straightened [sic] circumstances and I have made an appeal to the trade at Chicago, who have nobly responded in helping to raise a sum to enable the old gentleman and his wife to pass their few remaining days in peace, and not be harassed for want of comforts.

May I ask you to contribute to the fund—recollect he is probably the oldest living representative of the rail trade, and I think those of us who can afford it, should make his few remaining days, days of peace.

Very truly yours,

W. R. Jones (1889, August 8)

Such appeals were typically answered within the week of his writing.

Pennsylvania Steel Company
Office of the General Manager
Steelton, Penna
Capt. W. R. Jones Genl. Supt. Braddock Pa.

My dear Sir.

I found your letter of the 8th on my return after an absence of several days.

Mr. Hamilton had my deepest sympathy in the dreadful misfortune that has befallen his family and I thank you for affording me the opportunity to contribute a little to the fund you are raising for so praise worthy a purpose.

Yours very truly, H. W. Wood

chk. #280 for $25 Encld (1889, August 16).

A note appears upon this receipt:

"Many thanks for your charity. Have received today $875, which will give the old man a lift. W. R. Jones"

Cora later told of her father's growing frustration that summer over the ignominy of those responsible for the flood and the side-stepping of Carnegie. The Captain raged at how Andrew postured about the plight of the flood's survivors, and how he, while safely abroad in Paris, gave a new library to the city, never acknowledging any association with the South Fork Club (McCullough 1968, 256). Since the beginning of that year, Jones had witnessed a degree of hypocrisy in Carnegie unequaled in their fifteen years of doing business together. At the Braddock Library commemoration, Carnegie, who a year before engineered a return to the twelve-hour day with a sliding scale, had the gall to state in Jones's presence: "It is highly gratifying to know that the hours of labor are being gradually reduced throughout the country—eight hours to work, eight hours to play, eight hours to sleep" (1889, March 30).

Historians agree that the South Fork Fishing and Hunting Club was singularly responsible for the disaster in Johnstown. Although the newspapers of the time were full of condemnation, no names of the club's members were printed. The powerful intimidated. It was well known that when the dam broke, the few club members at the lake escaped east to Altoona, with not one going to Johnstown to help out. Initially, the club members drew the wrath of those left alive, until, as described above, the press in Pittsburgh and New York targeted the Hungarians as villains (McCullough 1968, 264-6).

Cora and D. D. always suspected that the press invented the stories about the Hungarians' atrocities to divert attention from the club members, whose names were not revealed, and the fact that they did not assume any responsibility for the tragedy. McGough's recent treatment of the flood would seem to confirm this (2002). The diversion was successful, for by the early fall, newspapers had turned their focus to the forthcoming election between Grover Cleveland and Benjamin Harrison.

By July's end, the first lawsuit against the club was filed by Johnstown's foremost lawyer, Colonel. J. P. Linton. In Paris, Carnegie gathered crowds to proclaim the magnitude of suffering, keeping secret his membership in the club, and typically commanded the headlines with announcements that he would contribute $10,000, with a total of $30,000 including the company's contributions (*Pittsburgh Post* 1889, 7 June).

In the end, every lawsuit filed—and there were many—came to nothing, except for one Philadelphia distiller who sued and collected compensation for dozens of kegs of whiskey transported on the Pennsylvania Railroad, possibly the whiskey drunk by the lout dancing on the piano that Captain Bill had seen the day he arrived. Those who suffered loss of homes and family members recovered nothing through litigation (McCullough 1968, 264-6).

The Pittsburgh lawyers representing the South Fork Club convinced the judges that the catastrophe was an act of Providence. This verdict made Captain Bill fume at the willful ignorance of the public and the manipulation of the authorities. Jones condemned the club for failure to address the accident that was just waiting for a good rainstorm.

At home, Cora shared the press coverage of the events with Harriet. They talked about the Captain's difficult decision to leave Carnegie. Lately, her invalid, bedridden mother relied upon laudanum to relieve her suffering. At first the drug with a little quinine helped her sleep, and she would wake invigorated. But eventually she became indifferent. When posed a question, she never answered directly but eventually established what she wanted Cora or the Captain to understand by circumlocution. During these years, the family worried that in addition to her multiple sclerosis, she was going mad, perhaps from years of taking laudanum. Harriet, probably a long suffering victim of multiple sclerosis, was in no state to handle matters of any kind, whether her daughter's choice of interest in love or business. She demonstrably relegated all authority to the family lawyer, Yost, Mimi's father.

Chapter 5 Sections

32. Good Timing
33. The Accident
34. The Theft
35. Cora and D. D.
36. Carnegie Company
37. Carnegie and Frick Unite
38. Last Chapter in Braddock

CHAPTER 5

EXPLOSIONS AT ET AND HOMESTEAD

Section 32: Good Timing

Even though Bill Jones and Andrew Carnegie had similar basic beliefs about social reform and how to improve the world, Jones clashed with his boss from the very beginning of their association. Jones's early filing of patents distanced the Welshman from the Scot's hegemony. Jones had relied upon Alexander Holley to help secure him a sound salary; subsequently, in business dealings he watched Carnegie's every step. For a number of years, as we have seen, Jones was given free rein to institute and uphold his own labor policies. But, following the events of 1886 and as his business holdings expanded and the steel industry became more competitive, Carnegie abandoned his promises to Jones to ensure his own supremacy in the steel markets. By the late 1880s, Carnegie was committed to a tough position toward both his own employees and toward unions (Nasaw 2006, 325-56).

During the spring and summer of 1889, Captain Bill explored the possibility of relocating to Youngstown to form a new business in partnership with Joseph G. Butler, Jr., in what was to become the Ohio Steel Company. He intended to keep his negotiations with Butler a secret from Frick and Carnegie until the very end.

Joseph Green Butler, Jr., the Nestor of Ohio's Valley of Iron, had worked at the Girard works in Youngstown (Warren 1996, 268) and came from a family of ironmongers. His grandfather had built and operated an early blast furnace in Pennsylvania, and his father was an iron manufacturer and blast furnace expert. The family had moved to Niles, Ohio when Butler was a young boy. Butler was an inch shorter than the Captain, with a deep, rich laugh that echoed as if he were in a cave. He had taught himself Welsh and spoke it better than Jones.

Jones traveled to Youngstown to inspect the site of the proposed new steel works, the Mahoning Valley, midway between Cleveland and Pittsburgh. From the Youngstown area, the Mahoning flows east to join the Shenango River, ultimately entering the Ohio River in Pennsylvania. There were already a number of blast furnaces in the valley, and it was a major producer of pig iron. The valley had extensive coal reserves and early became a center for coke and iron production, but now was dependent on Pennsylvania coke. Youngstown is, of course, closer to the iron ore in Michigan than is Pittsburgh. Joseph Butler was a student of the steel industry in the Chicago and Pittsburgh areas and acutely aware of the shortage of local pig iron production in Pittsburgh. He had observed how Youngstown sent pig iron to Pittsburgh, where it was converted into steel billets, which were then shipped back to Youngstown to be made into finished products. Butler knew that the elimination of this double transportation cost provided an opportunity for Youngstown investors. The Carnegie companies, for example, bought from Youngstown furnaces, some sixty-eight miles to the northwest, much of the pig iron that they lacked the capacity to produce.

Butler and Jones were in final negotiations that would result in Jones leaving Carnegie to build the new works in the Mahoning Valley, where Jones would be given complete autonomy to create a new works deploying both Bessemer and open hearth methods. Butler was convinced that the Youngstown Works would compete favorably in less than a decade with Carnegie and Illinois, the country's leading steelmakers. In fact, by 1901, National Steel in Youngstown had an annual capacity for producing six hundred thousand tons of

Bessemer rails in comparison with ET's annual production of 650,000 and South Chicago's of 675,000 (ibid., 383). Had Jones lived to build a state-of-the art facility, Youngstown surely would have captured significant market share in the 1890s because it could sell steel more cheaply than Carnegie could. Youngstown would also possess the Jones Hot Metal Mixer, as well as all the other Jones patents, which would have introduced still greater economies as well as quality.

Another factor in Butler's and Jones's considerations was that in 1889 the markets were changing. When Carnegie began, Pittsburgh was the outstanding location with its nearby shale, coal beds, and excellent water and rail transportation for hauling ore and distributing products. Rails were the product in highest demand, and Carnegie, by cartel allotment, supplied 30 percent of the market. By 1889, rail demand had dropped. Carnegie's position in the industry, while still dominant, was changing; the Homestead plant was being fitted for larger pieces of structural steel, which would be increasingly important. Chicago and Pittsburgh were now competing to supply the growing Western market, which included high demand for bridges, agricultural machinery, and steel for buildings. Chicago was experiencing a building boom and was a major consumer of Homestead's structural steel. On the East Coast, Carnegie would soon have additional competition from works being built at Sparrow's Point near Baltimore. Located on the seaboard, this company would buy its iron ore from Cuba. Carnegie was losing markets.

Bill Jones was ready to break with Andrew Carnegie.

Although the steel cartel elicited an agreement from both Carnegie and the Illinois steelworks to supply an equal limited percentage (30 percent), Illinois was making a run for the lead in profits. The distance from the ore source would be Carnegie's Achilles' heel. Youngstown, like Illinois, would be closer.

To run a three hundred-ton blast furnace each day for a year required forty thousand tons of limestone and one hundred thousand tons of coal times 365 days a year (ibid., 197). In 1894 the Pennsylvania Railroad estimated comparative costs of transportation of ore, limestone, and fuel to the two locations. The transportation costs of a ton of Michigan iron ore to a Carnegie plant in Pittsburgh was $1.15, but to Youngstown, it was only $0.675. The freight cost for 0.4 ton of near-by limestone to Pittsburgh was $0.80 but to Youngstown was $0.30. However, the cost of transporting 8.5 tons of Frick's coke to Pittsburgh was only $0.55 compared to Youngstown at $1.25. In terms of total expenses for producing a steel rail, Carnegie's Pittsburgh plants spent $3.335 compared to a Youngstown works that would spend only $3.148.

Jones and Butler envisioned installing two ten-ton Bessemer converters at the 171-acre site that had once been the Hawkins Farm on the west bank of the Mahoning River (Butler 1918, 56). The venture was postponed because of Jones's death, but when the

Homestead Strike occurred, Butler and Henry Wick followed through with Jones's idea to form the Ohio Steel Company, with Bessemers. It began producing steel in 1895 and soon thereafter added two blast furnaces.

Although Bill Jones was ready to break with Andrew Carnegie, he had concerns about Youngstown, which, like Johnstown, was more provincial than Pittsburgh. He worried Harriet might cause trouble about the move; perhaps in her state of mind she might even give away his plans, deliberately or in incoherent ramblings. He had much to lose. Jones would miss their home on Kirkpatrick Street, the panorama of boats and tugs flowing on the Monongahela. He had spent fourteen years perfecting the world's greatest steel plant only to pull up stakes and begin again. ET was now fully integrated. From raw ore being blasted into pig iron through the shearing of billets into rails ready for delivery, every step was completed on the grounds. It was the most efficient, well-designed plant in the world. But Jones had been working almost round-the-clock through the summer on various issues in the community and at the works (Whipple n.d.). He was ready for a change.

Section 33: The Accident

In the days preceding September 27, 1889, Andrew Carnegie had come to Pennsylvania after being in Europe from May until the end of the summer. He stayed at Cresson toward the end of September, and from there he had made a quick trip to Johnstown to survey the damage; this is when he announced his plans for additional new libraries around the area. On the morning of September 27 he had gone to Allegheny City to review the progress on the library and music hall he was building there (McCleary 1933, 9).

On that day, the sun shone through the industrial overcast of Slag Town, though storm clouds gathered in the west over the three rivers area. Captain Jones had been out seeking donations for those who had suffered so from the flood in May. He also had visited Henry Clay Frick, who gave him a check for $5,000 to help retire the debt of Dr. Boyle's Methodist church. After seeing Frick, the Captain returned to Braddock and ran into Charlie Schwab. There had been some trouble at ET but Charlie wasn't sure how serious it was. Continuing down toward the works atop his carriage, Jones entered the grounds as several workers rushed to meet him, yelling from a distance that furnace C had chilled during the afternoon heat.

The Captain entered the iron shed that nested furnace C to find James Gayley, a blast furnace expert at ET since 1885, who waved him on to join the others on the scaffolding. Gayley, the inventor of bronze cooling plates, knew his furnaces. John Lewis Jones, five years the Captain's junior, saluted his brother, as a group above huddled around the appendage known as the monkey, the furnace cooling port through which one could monkey with a rod to agitate the near-percolating iron to a boil. Against the bosh were pails of water that workers drank during shifts. The air itched with acrid fumes. Above, Edison's new electric lighting allowed adequate visibility, a major improvement from just three years earlier when such work was lighted by dangerous gas.

When Captain Bill arrived at the shed, he would have seen on the scaffold Michael Quinn, the foreman of the furnace, and Andrew Harrilla working with a four-foot tamping rod at the hole leading into the twenty-foot diameter base, near the widest section of the bosh. John Lewis Jones remembered seeing his brother climb two steps at once into the clouds of steam to join those on the scaffolding. Someone thrust the rod into an opening to jiggle the forty tons of molten iron, just gingerly enough for the hang to drop and percolate like coffee.

The heat had chilled, or what the Hungarians called hanged, sometime after lunch, and now at 7:00 p.m. the second shift was arriving. Harrilla swore in his native tongue and yelled over the roaring furnace to the boss and jogged in place in clogs that elevated him two inches.

Patrick Burns, a former puddler who had worked with Jones at Cambria, chattered among the stooping laborers, tired after nearly a day of breathing iron fumes. No doubt the men of the crew were looking forward to an evening bucket of beer. Thankfully, the summer rains and muggy heat would soon pass, and fall would come. Quinn had just dumped in some cakes of iron ore from above, hoping the weight would break through the hang that plugged the chimney and drop into the fiery mass of shale, coke, and ore to brew normally. Blasting iron in the bosh, the bottom of the lamp-shaped furnace, is like boiling coffee grounds in water; if the mix rises too rapidly, coffee grounds spill all over the stove. In the case of a furnace, the excessively hot molten mix rises too quickly into the cooler neck of the narrowing chimney, chilling into a wad rather than allowing exhaust fumes to be expelled skyward. That afternoon the cooler bricks of the chimney had chilled to wedge a solid plug. Gayley ordered Quinn, Kerr, and Harrilla to monkey and probe the blast.

John Lewis Jones remembered an episode at Henry Curry's Lucy furnace years before when a hang shut down the furnace, which took a week to cool. A team then entered the bosh, with a nearby Civil War relic, a cannon, and aimed it vertically. The shot fired into the clotted ceiling brought the hang crashing down. It became a local legend among iron and steelworkers.

Iron and steel work posed a multitude of dangers. Heat from blast furnaces and steel converters turned water into fire. Many men died from hot metal explosions, asphyxiation from furnace gas, electric shock, falls into slag pits, and mistakes when operating rolls (Fitch 1989, 64). Nearly a quarter of the 415 men killed in iron and steel work from 1870 to 1900 were skilled workers facing exactly this kind of danger (Kleinberg 1989, 29). On that Thursday, if anyone could have averted a horrible accident it was Bill Jones. It was not to be.

That day Gayley's men had tried to work the rod through the cooling system, behind which a crust had formed. After Captain Bill climbed the scaffolding and wrested the rod from Harrilla, he attacked the bricks protecting life from the roar within. These veteran laborers had been working for hours, but few at ET, or the nation, had the forty years' experience of building and working furnaces that Jones had. Listening momentarily to Harrilla, the Captain tried "to physic" the hang surgically to agitate the load free from the cooling mantel.

As the Captain worked the hole, a sudden roar—louder than the South Fork Dam breaking—thundered, exploding forty tons of molten iron though the protective furnace wall. Hot coke, limestone, and ore shot through a twenty-three-inch hole, firing incandescent metal like a cannon, flooding the platform and pit below with glowing red iron and penumbral cinders turning black. The deluge threw Jones forty feet below, where he landed and quickly scrambled behind a protective Modoc car. Nearby, Andrew Harrilla landed in another car. Still others, like propelled grapeshot, landed in the illuminated pit: Nee, Harry O'Connell, Pat Burns, and Michael Quinn were all badly burned but alive, while Gayley and Kerr on the scaffolding had dived to the right, avoiding the explosion.

For a full minute nearly two dozen workers froze in the white heat, staring in horror, before John Lewis Jones dashed across the glowing cinders of the fiery sepulcher to help his brother. He passed Quinn—every inch of clothing stripped off along with the flesh from parts of his body, webbed muscles hanging from bones. John Lewis found his brother nearby.

"John, is anyone hurt? My eyes are okay." The Captain's hair was burned off on one side and his eyebrows singed. His right hand and arm to the elbow smoked of burning flesh. His trousers were torn off. He was frightfully burned up to his abdomen but conscious, talking to his brother (*Commercial Gazette*, 1889, September 27).

Someone ran to get the Captain's carriage while others laid planks for a pathway over the cinders so that John Lewis Jones could retrieve his brother, and the wounded could be evacuated. In smoking shoes, Attila and Alexis Harrilla began calling in Hungarian for their brother, Andrew. John McCabe, who was only slightly hurt, was helping John Nee, whose face and limbs were badly burned. Near Gayley, still up on the scaffolding, was Patrick Burns, clinging to the platform, screaming above the wreckage that he was blind. Harry O'Connell wandered dazed among the cinders, escaping his rescuers, his face dissolved in a mass of iron and flesh (*Commercial Gazette*, 1889, September 27).

"Andrew!"

"Andrew!"

"Where's Andrew?" The brothers yelled out and began to look among the no-longer glowing sparks. McCabe, writhing in pain, yelled that he had seen Harrilla with Jones hurtling through the air, disappearing among the cars below. A blackening crust layered the pit floor. But Andrew was nowhere to be found.

> *As the Captain worked the hole, a sudden roar thundered, exploding forty tons of molten iron.*

Among the Modoc cars—ore buggies that extracted slag—rescuers found two cars full to the brim with glowing red iron seeming to pulsate, too hot even to approach. All went numb, mute. Like a siren's crescendo, the Harrilla brothers' wail amplified to nearly challenge the scream of the explosion: there, fingers clutching the bucket's rim—from within—and there, in the steam of the lava glow, they could see Andrew's head in profile, like that of the effigy on a knight's sepulcher.

The furnace malfunction could have resulted from the early February tornado that ripped through the city, stopping continuous furnace heats and Bessemer conversions for two weeks. Or maybe it resulted from the Captain's banking the furnaces for more than a week in June to take his 170 rescuers to Johnstown to help others in need.

The Captain's carriage drew up to the entrance of the furnace house, as John Lewis Jones and three others lifted and carried the muscular body of the fifty-year-old Jones over the planks to the waiting vehicle. Captain Bill's legs were badly burned, but he kept repeating that his eyes were fine, that he could see, and for his younger brother to tell Harriet that all would be well. At the company office two doctors, W. A. Sandler and A. W. Schosbey, bathed his wounds with chamomile oil, an antiseptic and antibiotic. Then, the five prepared to meet the soon-to-arrive train bound for Pittsburgh from Bessemer Station (*Pittsburgh Post*, 1889, September 27).

Later Charlie Schwab reflected upon that evening: "I was going to Chicago, and when I left [Jones] that night, I went home to pack. He went to the plant. Ordinarily I would have gone home before with him. I went west to Pittsburgh to take the train to Chicago. As I lay in berth there was a commotion outside, and I saw them taking a stretcher up past me. I didn't know it, but the man on the stretcher was Bill Jones" (Whipple n.d., 21).

Word-of-mouth in Pittsburgh reported the Captain dead, and crowds in search of information had gathered at the downtown station of the Pennsylvania Railroad. Rushing up to the train, they nearly broke through the windows of the compartment carrying Jones (*Commercial Gazette*, 1889, September 27).

Dr. McClelland gave his opinion. He said: "There is no immediate danger. He is a big strong man."

John Lewis Jones, his sister Mary Bowman, and William Yost followed on to Pittsburgh and visited the Captain's room at the Homeopathy Hospital. The doctors in attendance, McClelland and Willard, told John Lewis they expected his recovery. The Captain spoke with his brother. The little group left in tears at 11:00p.m. and reported an hour later to Harriet and the family about the accident and her husband's condition.

Although the Captain's injuries had been dressed before leaving Braddock, they were again thoroughly dressed at the hospital. At midnight the Captain was resting quietly under the influence of an opiate.

The night of the accident few in Braddock slept as they awaited news from Pittsburgh. Early on Friday morning Mary Bowman and John Lewis Jones rode to Pittsburgh and returned in the afternoon with optimistic news. Mary Bucknell Lloyd attended her invalid daughter as they awaited each report from Pittsburgh. The horror of the accident; Harrilla's incineration; and Quinn's, Nee's, and O'Connell's serious injuries set imaginations and fears to a peak so that all were sleepless, sobbing, talking fitfully, or staring into the void.

D. D. Gage had heard the news in Pittsburgh and arrived at the home on Kirkpatrick Street on Friday morning around ten o'clock to find the newly married Mimi and her husband, William Yost, at the house. Cora was distraught; her mother was upstairs under sedation. Will and the Lewis and Bowman cousins arrived to comfort the family and assist Mary Bucknell Lloyd in dealing with well-wishers who flocked to the house for the latest news. The morning newspapers were full of the story, and crowds mobbed Kirkpatrick Street in both directions, to the west all the way back to the Carnegie Library. Rumors abounded.

On Friday three newspapers stated that Captain Jones was suffering intensely but was still conscious, and Drs. McClelland and Willard were quoted saying that they expected his recovery. More than one hundred years later, Kenneth Warren, the only scholar who has had access to the Frick papers, recalled that Frick, too, understood that Jones would live (Warren, personal communication). On Friday morning the *Pittsburgh Post* reported: "Dr. McClelland . . . gave it as his opinion last night that Captain Jones will recover."

Similarly, from the *Youngstown Weekly Telegram* on October 2: "At midnight the Captain was resting under the influence of an opiate. The attending physicians are apprehensive but hopeful."

The late edition of the *Commercial Gazette* gave a more thorough account and was more optimistic.

> Capt. Jones was brought to the Homeopathic Hospital and placed in a private room. Drs. J. H. McClelland and D. H. Willard and the resident physician of the hospital proceeded to make an examination and treat the injuries. All the hair had been burned from the head, one side of his face was burnt and the eyebrows were gone, but the eyes were unharmed. It was stated by Capt. Jones's brother that when he pulled him from the cinder he first remarked that his eyes were all right and then asked if anybody else was injured. One hand and the arm were badly burned and the other was in better condition. The body had endured rather well, only being burned in spots. After Capt. Jones's injuries had been addressed and his entire person swabbed in cotton, Dr. McClelland gave his opinion. He said: 'There is no immediate danger. I do not mean that Capt. Jones's condition is not grave, but there are no indications of collapse. He is a big strong man, and if no inflammation sets in, will recover, but he is going to have a very serious time." (27 September 1889)

D. D. and Cora walked down to the river to escape from the home that had been so full of music and laughter but was now shrouded in a pall. Before she and D. D. took the train into Pittsburgh, Cora picked at lunch, her first bite since the accident. At the hospital the doctors were optimistic and told her that her father sent her his love, asked her to look after her mother, and wanted her to do what she could to stop her brother from heading west. Dr. McClelland said that such a vigorous man would recover, though they would probably have to amputate a leg and arm as soon as his condition stabilized. Knowing that Cora's mother awaited news, the two returned by train to Braddock's Field. D. D. Gage spent the night at the boarding house of Charlie Schwab's mother-in-law near the entrance of ET.

The next day, Frick wrote Orrin Potter of Illinois Steel, who had cabled his concern: "Very sorry to say it is too true. Captain Jones was dangerously burned yesterday evening but not fatally. He is resting easily and we think he will pull through all right" (Warren 1996, 59). He wrote a similar letter to Jay Morse of Union Steel in Chicago.

The Saturday morning *Pittsburgh Commercial Gazette* reported "The physicians said last evening that while Cap. Jones had been restless all day, there was not cause for alarm and, on the whole, they were very well pleased with his condition."

Carnegie is reported to have been stunned by news of the explosion. He immediately ordered a special train to bring his personal physician, Dr. J. J. Carmondy, from vacation in California to attend the Captain (Whipple n.d., 21).

When Cora and her Uncle John visited the Homeopathy Hospital on Saturday, Dr. McClelland, whom Cora liked so much, was no longer there. A new team of doctors presided, and the mood had changed from the earlier optimism. She thought that if D. D. had been with her perhaps the news would have been better.

According to the *Commercial Gazette*, on Saturday evening apparently only Henry Clay Frick and Carnegie, aside from the immediate family, were allowed to visit the wounded man in a private room. The newspaper report to the contrary, Cora remembers that she encountered not only Mr. Frick and Mr. Carnegie but also Mimi's husband in tears as they left the private room; they conveyed to her and the family their deepest consolation and departed. Wasn't it kind, she thought at the time, for Mr. Carnegie to come to visit her father and for him to send for his private doctor? Cora would cogitate over this scenario for the rest of her life. Prevented from seeing her father, Cora assumed the doctors wanted him to continue to sleep peacefully, and returned home with her uncle.

The evening papers carried more news: Quinn would die, but the Captain would recover. The body of the article, clearly written before McClelland was replaced, reported "Dr. McClelland gave his opinion. He said: 'There is no immediate danger.'"

While servants were cleaning up after a late dinner on Saturday night, Harriet's sister, Eileen Lewis, and the Captain's older sister by four years, Mary Elizabeth Bowman, said good-bye and left for their homes. Minutes later, Harriet from upstairs heard knocking at the front door and cried out through the upper story talking-tube down to the servant's quarters for someone to answer the door. A messenger from the wire service awaited as Cora in her nightgown opened the front door; immediately she knew her father was dead.

The Captain had succumbed at about 10:30 p.m. on Saturday, September 29, 1889. "He was a hero who died with his boots on, a noble end he had anticipated years earlier when he said, 'Thank God when I die, I will die like a man at my post of duty, or at whatever helm it is" (Krass 2002, 269).

The shock to the family and close friends was overwhelming. Cora and D. D. Gage had seen Captain Bill, three newspapers had carried accounts from interviews with the doctors attending him, and his brother John Lewis Jones had been with him on the journey to Pittsburgh and his admittance to the hospital. His death, especially so soon, had not been expected. Jones had been alert to the situation, voicing concerns about other workers' injuries, his anxiety about his wife's reaction to the accident, and his assurance that his eyes were not harmed though

Carnegie ordered his physician to replace Dr. McClelland immediately

he was in pain from burns on arms and legs. His torso and his vital organs had not been burned. Moreover, while his hair had been burned, he had no known head injuries. McClelland and Willard, the presiding doctors quoted in the press, did not mention anything about Jones being unconscious. Even if he had some infection, it would not have been expected to take such a toll so soon. On October 2, four days after he died, newspapers were reporting that when he had entered the hospital "He was suffering intensely, but he was still conscious" (*Youngstown Weekly Telegram*, 1889). In spite of this, books written some years later stated that he was rendered unconscious in the fall and died from a blow to the head; this is a falsehood that seems to have been passed from one secondary source to another, without verification in primary records (Warren 1996, 59). His family, in addition to the contemporary newspaper accounts, witnessed Jones alive, conscious, and talking following the accident. John Lewis Jones reported this to both the newspapers and to the rest of the family, as did Cora, who visited her father in the hospital. Casson's book on steel, published in 1907, is the source of this error:

> [Jones] sprang forcibly backward and fell into a pit, striking his head upon the iron edge of a car. One of his workmen, a Hungarian, fell beside him and was instantly killed. The next day Jones died in the hospital, having never regained consciousness. His burns were severe, but probably would not have caused his death, as he was a man of amazing vitality. Mr. Gayley, from whom this account of Captain Jones' death has been obtained, stood at his side when the treacherous furnace broke, and narrowly escaped. (1907, 33)

Jones was injured Thursday evening and died Saturday evening, two days later. Nearly two decades after the accident, time had blurred the particulars.

On Sunday, September 30, 1889, the grief expressed in Braddock over their Czar's death was visible everywhere. The entrances to the Edgar Thomson Works, all the churches, and the Carnegie Library had black crepe paper framing the doors and black muslin over windows (*Commercial Gazette*, 1889, September 30).

Captain Jones's funeral was worthy of his appellation, the Czar of Braddock. Two thousand workers at ET met at Lytle's Opera House Sunday evening to debate closing the works as fitting tribute to their leader. But it was decided that Jones himself would have felt holding the works idle would cause financial stress for the men. Instead they voted to accompany the casket to the cemetery. Captain Jones's Grand Army of the Republic Post No. 181 marshaled an honor guard to transport his body from Pittsburgh to Braddock. The Masons, Odd Fellows, and Royal Legion designated troops to attend the march. When the body arrived at Braddock aboard the train, more than ten thousand citizens of Braddock accompanied it to the cemetery on the street henceforth named Jones.

Among those attending were Henry Clay Frick and Charles Schwab (Holbrook 1939, 214).

Section 34: The Theft

The death of Bill Jones, the head not only of his family, but also of the Edgar Thomson Steel Works and to a great degree the city of Braddock, was a tragedy that left all concerned shocked and grieving. But, instead of leaving the Jones family to grieve, members of the Carnegie Brothers Company paid them a visit, not to offer consolation, but for business reasons: they were concerned about Jones's patents.

As recorded in Joseph Frazier Wall's seminal biography of Andrew Carnegie, "Two days after Jones's funeral, [Dod] Lauder hurried over to Jones's home and got from his widow a bill of sale for all of Jones's patents, for which Carnegie Brothers paid Mrs. Jones the sum of $35,000" (1970, 532-3). Uncle Dan, in a letter to Wall, corrected the mistake:

> The story starts out very much the same [as you present it] in that a representative of the Carnegie Company called on Mrs. William R. Jones at her home in Braddock two days after the funeral, or at least, a very short period thereafter. However, the family story has this representative as Henry Clay Frick and not Henry Phipps. My mother was 18 [sic] years old at the time and was present when Mr. Frick called, ostensibly to offer condolence to the widow. My mother told us (my father, brother, and myself back in the 20s while her memory was quite clear) that after some casual discussion of the recent events and an expression of sympathy, Mr. Frick turned as he was leaving the house to say: "By the way, Mrs. Jones, do not do anything about the patents until you have seen the Company's attorney, Mr. John [sic] Yost." My mother (who passed away in 1947) remembered her mother saying: "What a strange man is Mr. Frick, he came here to offer condolences, but he really came to prepare me for a business transaction."

The year before his death, my father wrote that two days after the funeral, on Friday, October 5, both Frick and William Yost arrived at the Jones home. Cora Gage had told her sons repeatedly from the time they were very young that she remembered thinking to herself how well her friend's husband had succeeded. Yost was the Jones family attorney and had looked into Mary Bucknell Lloyd's claims on property in Chattanooga.

When Yost did call, as Frick had promised, perhaps in the company of George Lauder or Harry Phipps, Harriet was sequestered in her bedroom, where she now permanently resided. Yost attempted to convince her that $35,000 for the patents to all of Jones's inventions was ample remuneration. As Yost finalized the arrangement, the physically and emotionally suffering Harriet, who knew little about business or her husband's technology, asked Yost, the family lawyer, if this was a fair offer.

"Yes, I think the company is being very generous. As you may, or may not know, patents can be very troublesome because of the necessity of preventing infringement upon them and possible lawsuits for infringements on other patents held by competing patentees." After a bit, she signed.

All versions of this event are in agreement that by October 24, less than a month after Jones's death, Carnegie controlled all of Bill Jones's patents. Soon Cora's mother received by post a document with blue ribbons and red-orange seal from the Department of the Interior. It certified that she, Harriet Jones, sold, assigned, transferred, and set over to Carnegie Brothers for $35,000, the patent rights of inventions for use in the United States, Great Britain, France, Belgium, Germany, and Austria.

By November 1889 the grieving Jones family resumed daily routines. Harriet's mind was embittered towards all except her son, Will, who reported to Harriet that Cora had been seeing D. D. During the days that D. D. and the Captain had worked relieving the suffering in Johnstown, they had become closer. They had in common a taste for poetry and history, and a deep love and concern for Cora. Their proximity during the flood rescue had the sum effect of smoothing differences between the two. D. D.'s wit and feisty sense of justice won the support of the Captain, who confided that he, too, had weathered Harriet's spells: "Love flames a year; ashes, for thirty." Jones had made Daniel promise to be patient.

Harriet's state of mind seriously deteriorated. Cora related how, from the moment of Captain Bill's death, Harriet linked D. D. Gage to the actor John Wilkes Booth. Although D. D. had been nowhere near ET at the time, Harriet was convinced he was somehow involved in her husband's death. D. D. understood her confusion and the difficult situation in the Jones house, and he accepted the fact that his presence would cause the Captain's widow greater grief. He and Cora continued to meet in private.

If Jones's Youngstown negotiations with Butler's associates were leaked to Frick and Carnegie, the two knew that the loss of Bill Jones would mean the collapse of the whole industry. Several years later Schwab asserted this fact to his biographer that Carnegie never would allow this to happen (Krass 2002, 208). Should Jones leave without his patents this would be another story entirely, as cited in the recent biography by David Nasaw, historian and professor at the City University of New York,:

> The death of Jones had a profound—though short-lived—effect on the senior partners. Harry Phipps, who like Carnegie had his fortune tied up in Carnegie Company stock, was increasingly worried that their investment might not be safe. He proposed that he and Carnegie either sell their interests in the Pittsburgh firms or consolidate them into a new trust . . . Unfortunately for Phipps, who wanted to cash out his investments, the value of his and Carnegie's stock had grown so large that there were few capitalists anywhere who could afford to buy them out. (2006, 374-75)

The effect was "short lived" because the Firm acquired Jones' patents. Had Jones died months later in Youngstown, the effect would have meant the collapse of Carnegie's industry.

Although there seems to have been an assumption among early historians that Carnegie continued to succeed due to his savvy business skills (Krass2002, 269), nearly all of Carnegie's recent biographers imply less than savory practices. Krass compares the purchase of Jones's patents at such bargain basement prices with the events after Kloman's death years earlier. But the Captain's concern then had been "what would happen to Kloman's patents." The fact was that Kloman, who had clashed with the Carnegies and set up the rival plant at Homestead, owned patents to apparatuses that the Carnegies would be interested in obtaining on the market. At that time, Jones wrote the following:

> Please pardon me in approaching you on so delicate a subject: you no doubt know of the death of Mr. Kloman. I would merely suggest that on the settlement of Mr Kloman's estate, his patent for the rolling eye bars may be thrown on the market. The developments that will certainly follow the steel business will make this patent very valuable. My object in writing you is for you to keep an eye on this subject. (1880, December 21)

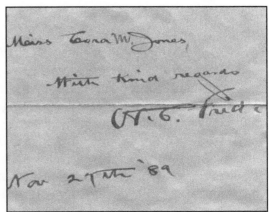

Henry Clay Frick's consolation note, written two months after Jones' death.

Jones's suggestion was prudent business, alerting Carnegie to act during the settlement of a rival's estate; it was not an exhortation to behave in a fraudulent manner.

More importantly, at the time of the explosion that injured Jones, Carnegie, as we have seen, knew the potential <u>value</u> of the mixer and direct process. His use of the concept "homogeneity," the term Wall judged subterfuge but in fact evidenced Carnegie's understanding: that the Cradle of Civilization homogenized by blending two or more batches of liquid iron. Carnegie likely knew that Jones was on the verge of leaving for a new position in Youngstown. Relevant to this matter is that patents were very much on Carnegie's mind in the fall of 1889. That year, the new American secretary of state, James G. Blaine, who was a close friend of Carnegie, had organized a pan-American conference, to which Carnegie was named one of the American delegates. When the meeting opened in October, Carnegie was on the committee on patents and trademarks, which met over the four-month period prior to making its report in March 1890 (Nasaw 2006, 378-79).

Wall is even more emphatic about Carnegie's near-obsession with patents. Carnegie, he writes, ". . . gave far more attention to acquisition and protecting patent rights than he ever gave to promoting tariff legislation" (1970, 642). Jones's insistence for filing patents independently and refusing partnership positioned the Captain holding the reins. A letter to J. G. A. Leishman in 1895 regarding Captain Jones's Bessemer mixer patent, which the company had acquired at the time of Jones's death, also indicates the importance of patents to Carnegie:

> Yours received in regard to our Mixer Patent. I feel very strongly about the

action of our friends the Illinois and Pennsylvania Steel Companies. No one pretends that a mixer was ever used successfully except ours [sic].

These companies saw the results and had already realized that a mixer was necessary to the direct process. They deliberately appropriated our invention without arranging with us for a liscence[sic]. (ibid., 642-43)

That Carnegie was fully aware of the value of the Jones Hot Metal Mixer is further indicated in the rest of this letter to Leishman, who had become president of Carnegie Steel when Frick resigned in 1895:

We can prove that the invention was worth to the Illinois Steel Co at least $150,000 per year, probably $200,000, and will be worth the same to the Pennsylvania and the Sparrow Point works. Stated truthfully, it was nothing but a pure theft of our property by men who were in close relations with us, and with whom we were cooperating.... As if to add to the injustice done us, they now endeavor to rake up some old trumpery claims that the mixer was known before Captain Jones invented it.... Our patent is recognized everywhere throughout Europe, and we can obtain from parties using it, testimony proving its value.... I think that if you will see Mr. Potter of Chicago and Mr. Morris of Philadelphia, they will repudiate the action of their officers. (1895, August 1)

Wall has stated it correctly, but without fully showing the level of deception and fraud involved in Carnegie's dealings: "Over the thirty years that Carnegie was engaged in the iron and steel business the many patents that he acquired through purchase from his inventive partners and employees such as Kloman and Jones, or leased on a royalty basis from Bessemer and Thomas, had netted him millions of dollars and were a major factor in his acquiring dominance in the field" (1970, 644).

Once he had secured these rights, fairly or unfairly, literally by hook or by crook, he used them ruthlessly against his competitors. He bought low and sold high, and "prosecute[d] vigorously any infringement of patent rights, no matter how costly and lengthy such suits might prove to be". Carnegie later wrote to his cousin Dod Lauder during the period of litigation: "Anything to win from the robbers of our Mixer Patent" (1897, January 8).

Section 35: Cora and D. D.

Around Christmas of that dreadful year, Cora, with the help of W. W. McCleary, slipped out of the house and was whisked off in the landau to see D. D. perform at the Opera House in Oakland, the downtown section of Pittsburgh, eight miles away. Just before the curtain parted, Cora slipped into the darkened theatre and found her seat in the third row. D. D. had two solos, his voice rising against the background chorus. He sang "Beautiful Dreamer," the same Stephen Foster melody Cora played on the piano on the first and only time he was invited to her home. D. D. received applause, for he had quite a following in Pittsburgh. Before escaping into the folds of the curtains, he took his bow a step in front of the chorus, his eyes surveying the loggia to find Cora, who was about to exit.

At the stage door of the theatre, Cora cut through the crowd. D. D. embraced her to the anguish of others hovering for his attention. They escaped the mob and took a taxi to Schenley Park. While in the horse-drawn cab, Cora explained that after the evening's meeting, she could no longer see him. For two months she had deliberated over her dilemma: the man she loved or her duty. Cora chose, in the manner of many daughters of that period, to give up her own life to care for her mother. Harriet was now verging on madness, and Cora's grandmother, whose wit and moral strength that had supported Cora, was failing. Her brother was trying his best to get from his mother his share of the inheritance so he could depart for the West, but with Harriet's increasing mental imbalance, even Will could not get his way. Cora asked D. D. to wait. She would have to find out if the handsome performer had patience, a lot of it.

Cora at age 23

Cora and D. D. parted in tears. Cora caught the eight o'clock train back to Braddock and relieved Mimi Corey Yost, who had spent five hours smothering Harriet with attention. Since her father's death, every joy and pleasure that Cora had taken for granted had turned to obligation. The Belle of Braddock was no longer a damsel without a care. She now had the responsibility of managing the household and its finances. It was not long before she realized that the $35,000 her mother had received for the patents was far less than her father's annual salary. Captain Jones had given so much to charity that Cora believed that the family would probably have to sell the house on Kirkpatrick Street. The estate would not last for long after meeting the needs of two ailing women and a profligate brother.

Will had all of his father's forcefulness but unfortunately possessed a hyper-vigilant disposition, a propensity to distractions, and quick tangential pursuits that disrupted a good brain. His good looks convinced his mother of his promise, and his social position in Pittsburgh ensured him of success. He was not dishonest but lazy, and this angered his father because Will got by playing the role of buffoon. Cora, living an Edwardian lifestyle, was limited by her gender, but from early on she embodied her father's hopes.

D. D.'s love was true. For seven years he sang in and around Pittsburgh, but never for engagements that kept him away from Pittsburgh for long. Cora's grandmother died in November 1891; now responsibility for her mother was entirely Cora's.

Section 36: Carnegie Company

After the death of Bill Jones, the family was succored by many. Yost and Gayley hovered over Harriet for the remainder of her life. The former, whom the Captain had always described, prophetically, as lean and hungry, maintained legal matters for the family, and the latter became increasingly involved in the family's affairs. Only joining ET in the mid-1880s, his name appears as a witness on Harriet's will. Gayley had been present at the explosion but had not been injured. According to my mother, Cora knew that Harriet depended upon Yost's wife and Cora's closest friend, naïve Mimi, to report on Cora's conversations and actions. John and Margaret Potter also spent considerable time with the family, concerned about Cora's struggle with her mother and brother.

Potter was contemptuous of Yost, who, like Gayley, had progressed up the corporate ladder of the firm, and he warned Cora to be wary. Even so, Cora relied upon Mimi Yost and her husband during the years after Jones's death. Mimi, a bit feckless, sincerely wanted to help Cora; she was unaware, until years later, that her husband and Harriet were using her. D. D. met with Mimi many times in an attempt to kindle Cora's love for him, and she helped D. D. send messages to Cora who, resigned to her fate, never answered the singer.

With the Captain's death, the company reassigned Charlie Schwab from Homestead Works to the position of superintendent at ET in Braddock. Under Schwab, ET continued to thrive, for Charlie's personal charm sustained much of the good working environment that the Captain had established. Potter, however, believed that Schwab was a glib, opportunistic showman. The voluble Schwab often claimed ownership of many of Jones's inventions, particularly innovations in management style. Within a week of his transferring from Homestead to ET, Schwab bragged to workers there that he, as the draftsman, had designed and invented the rolling mill. Behind his avowed admiration for Captain Jones, Schwab hungered for celebrity at the expense of the Captain and hinted that the Captain's glorious death was fortunate in a way, for he had been over the hill, no longer able to master a growing global industry (Whipple n.d., 24). As the years passed, Schwab showed himself to be an apt leader, and his overt respect for Jones returned, but his earlier perfidy haunted Cora for the rest of her life (D. Gage to A. Carnegie, November 9, 1906).

At the time of his death, Jones had been chief engineer for Homestead. He acknowledged the future promise of the open hearth, but with that future came the increasing power of the Amalgamated union. In 1887 with the eight-hour day, workers had averaged $46.35 per shift, with three turns per day. With rail prices dropping, Carnegie argued that steelworkers at Chicago averaged $43.60 for the twelve-hour turn. Carnegie duped his workers to compete by extending their shifts to twelve hours and adopting the sliding scale for salary based on the daily cost of rails. By 1890, those workers only averaged $35.30 a shift (Fitch 1989, 117). Laborers realized that Captain Bill had been right, and tempers were fiery as the renewal approached. Frick's hard strategy brought the simmering contention to boiling violence, and at the end of the 1890 contract at ET, the skilled and unskilled workers moved to strike. Schwab and Frick quickly brought in the sheriff and, with no union in place, a strike never got off the ground. But it should have been a warning of what was to come at Homestead in 1892, where there were two strong unions and cooperation between the skilled and unskilled workers.

Carnegie had hoped to get the Amalgamated Union out of Homestead during the late spring contract negotiations in 1889. His offer was that, to get their jobs back after May 31, workers would have to sign an agreement similar to that which he had enforced at ET in 1888. But the Homestead workers rejected Carnegie's offer—and the Amalgamated and Knights of Labor stood together. William Abbott, then chairman and general superintendent, closed the plant and locked out the workers. When scabs approached the factory ten days later, they were met by a huge gathering of Homestead workers and their families, who blocked their way. Abbott came to a quick settlement with the union, which included a sliding scale wage and a contract for three-years, but Carnegie soon blamed him for failing to break the union, and John Potter was brought in as superintendent.

Potter may have inherited an impossible situation at Homestead. The showdown which Carnegie sought in 1892 may well have been beyond even the ability of a Charlie Schwab, with his prodigious people skills, to handle. Potter lacked Schwab's showmanship and quick wits to foil worker objections. Cora always said that Charming Charlie could get away with murder.

Carnegie wanted Henry Clay Frick in charge when the 1892 contract came due. In fact Frick spent more and more time at Homestead backing up Potter in his dealings with the union while at the same time taking orders from Carnegie via telegraph from Scotland. From the union's point of view, to beat Carnegie meant victory over the steel magnates that would send a message across the country.

During the spring of 1892, John Potter with his wife spent many Sundays visiting the Jones home. Frick had been advising Harriet to sell the Jones family shares in the Frick Coke Company. William Yost urged her to take Frick's offer, as the price was fair. But Potter argued that she should keep the shares, at least until the economy improved. Not expecting to live long, Harriet bitterly responded that she could see no reason to allow Cora to have the Captain's hard-earned money, only to have Cora run off with that trashy actor. If D. D. realized Cora had no money, perhaps she would soon learn that love is but a shallow thing. But for the time being, Harriet did nothing.

Unable to afford all five of the servants, Cora released three. Her mother's demands taxed her now, as she did her part in managing the large house. In those lonely evenings, Cora would read books from her father's library; she began to absorb the Captain's inspiration and often quoted his ideas. Her father's rough ways might have resulted from a lack of formal education, but now that he was dead, she came to understand that few schooled intellects could match his self-trained mind. She learned of his vision by reading his notes and came to understand how extensive his generosity had been: he had given more than $10,000 a year in charity. Often strangers would come up to her on Main Street to tell her that her father was responsible for their house: when the breadwinner was crippled or killed at ET, Captain Jones would appear on the doorstep with the mortgage to the house redeemed, a present for the grieving widow.

In this period, Cora grew up; she began to become her father's daughter.

Section 37: Carnegie and Frick Unite

Cora believed that Captain Bill's labor policy was vindicated when John Potter relayed to her how worried and unable to solve problems management was at Homestead. In late May 1892, Potter had missed the usual Sunday visit but sent a note telling her that things were grave. Carnegie had left for Europe. Potter believed that the labor negotiations ought to acknowledge some of the union's legitimate concerns, a position which disturbed Frick. It soon became apparent that Frick and Carnegie, together, had decided this was the year to end the Amalgamated's presence at Homestead, and they were prepared to do whatever was necessary to achieve that. In the previous five years, technology had greatly changed work in the mills, so that according to Schwab, an American farm boy could be trained in only six weeks to be a skilled melter. Far fewer men were necessary to do the same job. Moreover, the population of available workers in Pittsburgh had swelled under the continued influx of Eastern European immigrants needing work (Wall 1970, 540).

When Homestead was shut down at the end of June 1892, the mill had only a single order for steel, a contract for a considerable volume of armor plate with the United States Navy. Carnegie had written to Potter to roll a lot of plate in advance, anticipating a possible lengthy shut down. Once this order was filled, the works could become idle and wait out the union. Because only eight hundred men belonged to the Amalgamated, there was some belief among management that they could avoid serious trouble; they believed the other three thousand workers would not be willing to lose very much work to support the union. Their position was that if the Navy order was filled in advance, union workers would be cut out, and anyone off the streets could be trained to fill their shoes.

Carnegie drafted a notice, which was never posted, describing the new status of Homestead:

> These Works having been consolidated with the Edgar Thomson and Duquesne and other mills, there has been forced upon this firm whether its Works are to be run "Union" or "Non-Union." As the vast majority of our employees are Non-Union, the Firm has decided that the minority must give place to the majority. These works therefore will be necessarily Non-Union after the expiration of the present agreement.

> This does not imply that the men will make lower wages. On the contrary, most of the men at Edgar Thomson and Duquesne Works, both Non-Union, have made and are making higher wages than those at Homestead which has hitherto been Union . . . A scale will be arranged which will compare favorably with that at the other works named: that is to say, the Firm intends that the men of Homestead shall make as much as the men at either Duquesne or Edgar Thomson. Owing to the great change and improvements made in the Converting Works, Beam Mill, Open Hearth Furnaces, etc. . . . the products of the works will be greatly increased, so that at the rates per ton paid at Braddock and Duquesne, the monthly earnings of the men may be greater than hitherto.

While the number of men required will, of course, be reduced, the extensions at Duquesne and Edgar Thomson as well as at Homestead will, it is hoped, enable the firm to give profitable employment to such of its desirable employees as may temporarily be displaced. . . .

This action is not taken in any spirit of hostility to labor organization, but every man will see that the firm cannot run Union and Non-Union. It must be one or the other. (Bridge 1991, 204-5)

According to Potter, Frick was worried that posting such a declaration would galvanize the public in support of the Amalgamated and thereby influence the upcoming presidential election in which Democrats appeared likely to take control of Congress. Anti-business sentiments were on the rise. Frick didn't want to add a confrontation at Homestead to the scandal of the Johnstown flood. Frick also believed that other Carnegie Steel facilities where there was a strong union presence without the problems of Homestead, such as the Union Mills, should be dealt with at a later time. His approach was more pragmatic than Carnegie's, and in one thing he resembled Captain Bill: he considered himself equal to Carnegie and would disagree with the majority owner and trust his own judgment.

Frick sent Phipps and Lauder to England where they conveyed to Carnegie how badly his notice would play for a public that favored workers' rights to unionize. Carnegie's strategy would make it look as though the company was instigating a fight. Carnegie rephrased the notice, ambiguously demanding a standard among the three steel plants but failing to allude to a forced choice between union and non-union. Potter formulated the contract; meanwhile Frick was negotiating with the Pinkerton Agency for three hundred hired guns to protect scabs hired for the coming lockout in July.

Homestead refused Frick's new contract of 1892, in which workers were required to accept three provisions: a rate based on profits of $22.00 dollars as the bottom scale, a 15 percent cut in tonnage rate, and no change in date for negotiating future contracts. In 1889, the bottom wage on the scale had been $25.00 a ton and workers averaged about $27.00. The significant reduction in pay in the new contract forced the union to do exactly what Carnegie and Frick wanted: reject the offer and thus initiate the inevitable strike.

On a Sunday in June 1892, John Potter visited Harriet Jones at her home. John asked Cora to walk with him down to the banks of the Monongahela. As they strolled, Potter bared his soul as if his companion had been Captain Jones, not his daughter. Potter said that the union presented Frick and himself with hard choices. He, Potter, wanted to use reason, but Frick wanted confrontation, as he had with coal miners at his own company. William Roberts, representing the negotiating committee, told Potter they wanted to settle without a strike (Wall 1970, 552). Nevertheless, Frick drafted a letter to Roberts in Potter's name, establishing a deadline of June 24:

Referring to my visit to the works this morning, I now hand you herewith Homestead Steel Works wage scales for the open hearth plants, and No. 32 and 119-inch mills, which you will please present immediately to the joint committee, with the request that its decision be given thereon not later than June 24th.

> These scales had had most careful consideration with a desire to act toward our employees in the most liberal manner. You can say to the committee that these scales are in all respects the most liberal that can be offered. We do not care whether a man belongs to a union or not, nor do we wish to interfere. He may belong to as many unions or organizations as he chooses, but we think our employees at Homestead Steel Works would fare much better working under the system in vogue at Edgar Thomson and Duquesne. (Bemis 1894, 373-74)

Only the day before, Roberts had asked Potter if he thought the offer was fair. The answer, if any, is lost to history.

Carnegie, meanwhile, was away from the scene in Scotland—not at his castle, but at a location where only Frick could contact him. He directed Frick by cable: "Do not [sic] seem favorable to a settlement at Homestead. If those [terms] be correct, this is your chance to reorganize the whole affair, and someone over Potter should exact good reasons for employing every man" (Wall 1970, 553).

By the deadline of June 24, the two sides had not budged. Frick declared a lockout, and the Pinkerton detectives moved in. Cora learned that as Potter was hedging with Richards, suggesting that bottom wages of $22.00 might be raised to $23.00 and likewise tonnage rates might go as high as18 percent, Frick forthwith refused any negotiations with union representatives and would negotiate only with individual workers interested in returning to Homestead (ibid., 555). The strategy was to remain firm with offers that the union could not accept. "The union hanged John Potter and Frick in effigy. Margaret nearly went back home to Philadelphia," Potter remembered many years later in Los Angeles; "people on his street stoned [Potter's] windows" (Demarest 1992, 104). On the night of July 5, the tugs pulled two barges with three hundred Pinkerton men from the Ohio River below Pittsburgh into the Monongahela in the direction of Homestead. From Pittsburgh someone spotted the tugs pulling the barges about midnight and wired McLuckie, Homestead's mayor and an officer in the Amalgamated. Nearly the whole town met the barges, which encountered some trouble when one tug, the *Tide*, malfunctioned, and the *Little Bill*, with John Potter as strategos, maneuvered both barges to the dock of Homestead (Wall 1970, 557). The poorly-armed townspeople launched a fiery raft downstream, attempting to set Potter and the barges on fire. Failing with the raft, they rolled a blazing railroad car off the wharf, which fell short of the nearest barge. John Potter and the Pinkertons were unable to exit onto the wharves because of sustained gunfire.

The newspapers carried daily reports in support of the strikers. In 1877, the residents of Pittsburgh had battled with the Pennsylvania Railroad. After the Johnstown Flood, the South Fork Fishing and Hunting Club had become the symbol of plutocracy. Now Potter shared with Frick the public's scorn. Some individuals called out for Carnegie to save the day, crowing his eleventh commandment, believing him ignorant of what was happening. But interviewed in Scotland, Carnegie said, "I have nothing whatever to say. I have given up all active control of the business" (Demarest 1992, 104).

On the morning of July 6, rumors quickly swept through Braddock about someone's head being blown off by cannon ball. At first Cora went to the office at ET, where she heard that hundreds from both sides were dead or wounded. Among the dead was John Morris, who had worked at ET. Running home, she told her mother of the events. When the evening *Pittsburgh Gazette* came out, reports indicated that far fewer had been injured in the gun battle than rumors had indicated.

Despite the violence, Frick stood firm on the lockout and refused to negotiate. The sheriff wired the governor for help. Governor Pattison, a Democrat, told local authorities that they must exhaust all means in settling the problem before he would order troops to quell the riot.

Residents of Braddock could see smoke along the river, and rumors abounded. The smoke was from random, unattended fires, while the Pinkertons, released from the barges, had to run a gauntlet from the pier through town (Demarest 1992, 86). As the detectives moved into town, they were beaten and pelted along the way by the workers and their wives, who in broken English uttered Finks, instead of Pinks, for Pinkertons. Finks eventually became the slang word for a double-crosser. The beaten mercenaries were corralled in the opera house before the sheriff could get them back to Pittsburgh, where he put them on a train heading east.

The victory over the hired guns lasted only a couple of days before the governor finally sent eight thousand troops to occupy the town to allow the reopening of the works with scab labor. Thirteen had been killed in the violence, with six more dying of blood poisoning and another seventeen wounded. The press criticized those deemed responsible for the murders and rebellion—the workers and their families. The violence was turning the press against labor. The mill owners and business community spoke out against the governor's delay in sending troops. Homestead residents accused Carnegie Steel of hiring gunmen to tyrannize workers. John Potter, in particular, was the focus of much wrath, a position he had been put in by others.

Two weeks after the showdown, an anarchist named Alexander Berkman irrevocably destroyed any chance of a fair deal for labor. Berkman at that time was the lover of Emma Goldman, the infamous international anarchist and theorist. Berkman had nothing to do with any union or anyone at Homestead, but on July 23, while Frick and Leishman were meeting in the company's main office, Berkman crept in and shot Frick twice in the neck (Nasaw 2006, 435). His pistol accidentally fired a third round, and he lunged with a knife, stabbing Frick before Leishman could wrestle the assassin to the ground. Hearing the shot, others soon came to help subdue Berkman. After wrestling him out of the office and to the jail, assistants appealed to Frick to go to the hospital, but Frick waved off them off and continued to work until 5:00 p.m., when he left for home (ibid., 163-180).

Almost simultaneously, Frick became a hero. That very week, Frick's wife had given birth to a son, who died soon thereafter. Now publicity of Frick's stoic response to attempted murder fanned a weak flame of admiration into a blazing veneration for the man who was Carnegie's agent and partner in crushing the union and hiring scabs.

In 1892 alone, there were twenty-three incidences in which Federal troops or state militia interceded on the part of capital to quell labor unrest across the United States. In the public's eye, the community and pro-union followers were connected with Berkman's murder attempt. That association, massaged by the press, reduced the Amalgamated Association to silence. Unionization of iron and steel workers was dormant until 1923. Ironically, the battle cost pro-capital Benjamin Harrison the presidency: in the November presidential election, Democrat Grover Cleveland, who backed labor, defeated Harrison, who supported protective tariffs for iron and steel.

Cora saw very little of John Potter for a long while after the massacre. There were congressional hearings in November to ascertain culpability for the great strike. Potter became the scapegoat for the mess engineered by Carnegie from Great Britain, and that November he was removed as the superintendent of Homestead Works and kicked upstairs as chief mechanical engineer for the company, a fancy title with no authority or meaningful duties. Potter resigned from Carnegie Steel before the end of the year, and Charles Schwab left ET to succeed him at Homestead, a job Schwab had held before.

John Potter went on to work in Ohio and Illinois before he and Margaret disappeared from history around the turn of the century, working in Latin America.

Section 38: Last Chapter in Braddock

On a spring afternoon in 1895, D. D. proposed to Cora while they were sailing on the Allegheny. He had proposed many times in the past, but this time she accepted. They agreed they would marry only after her mother's death, although D. D. was having serious health problems and had consulted a Pittsburgh doctor, who told him he had only six months to live. This news made D. D. angry; he was determined to heal himself. The pair made a plan, which included going to Europe right after their marriage for D. D. to obtain medical treatment for a chronic stomach ailment. Then they would settle in southern California, where D. D. had relatives.

Harriet endured, impotent and nearly helpless, until November 7, 1896. She was buried next to the Captain in the cemetery off Jones Street in Braddock, and the following day D. D. and Cora were finally married. Not a word about their wedding plans was said to Mimi or to her husband, for by the time of Harriet's death both Cora and D. D. knew how Yost had manipulated his well-meaning wife to spy on the Jones family. The ceremony was small and without frills. As a wedding present, Carnegie sent Cora a clock embedded within a lapis lazuli sphere, mounted in gold upon a marble stand.

Three days after Harriet's passing, Yost read Cora the will and disposed of what was left of the Captain's estate.

Be It Remembered

That I, Mrs. Harriet Jones of Braddock Township in the County of Allegheny and State of Pennsylvania, do make and publish to my Last Will and Testament,

I give, devise and bequeath all my property, real, personal, and mixed, to my son Wm. M. C. Jones and my daughter Cora Jones to share alike, their heirs and assigns forever.

And I do hereby constitute appoint my said son William and my said daughter Cora, the Executrix of this my last will and testament.

Witness my hand and seal 18 day of December A. D. 1890.

H. J. Harriet Jones

Signed, sealed, published and declared the above named Mrs. Harriet Jones and for her last will and testament in the presence of us who have heretofore subscribed our names at her requisition of the said testatrix and of each other.

W. Yost

James Gayley

Cora and Will each received more than $44,000. Will took his bequest and left for Nevada, against the advice of concerned mentors like W. W. McCleary who cautioned that winter was setting in with devastating early snows.

The newlyweds set out for Europe, where doctors of health science offered not only medicines but also taught the patient to recognize and understand signs that would enable him or her to "cure thyself." At a spa in Germany along the Rhine, D. D. with Cora spent several months recuperating. After six months of treatment and rigorously following a liquid diet, he was somewhat recovered, and they traveled on to Paris to further study homoeopathy.

When experiencing a flare-up of his symptoms and weight loss, D. D. was to drink nothing but the juices of certain fruits and vegetables. He learned from French and German doctors about caloric intake, vitamins, and minerals, and he recovered twenty-five pounds, returning to his normal weight. D. D.'s approach to health was to become his religion; in spite of the fact that in 1895, doctors had given him six months to live, as a result of his determination and discipline he lived another forty-six years.

My grandfather, D. D., had a repertoire of poetry and songs, which he sang with the Serenaders in Pittsburgh during the years he spent waiting for Cora. In Europe he learned German and enough Italian to entertain in the Viennese homes of Captain Jones's friends. Cora was elated to be back in Europe, where she could speak French again. For weeks at a time, my grandfather's newfound vigor exhausted her as they toured Bavaria and hiked in the Alps. In 1888, on their way to Austria, Captain Bill and Cora had been hosted by a family in the small village of Garmisch-Partenkirchen. The family owned a lumber mill built on a trace, supplied by run-off from the Alps.

My Uncle Dan while completing his post-graduate study in Germany visited in the 1930s, and again later, several times once married to my Aunt Margaret. During my stop-out year from Berkeley in 1959, I, too, spent several days at the home of the war survivors, three widowed sisters and their illegitimate nephew, who fawned over his dog Fritz.

From Bavaria to Vienna, Cora and D. D. traveled by coach. The Wittgensteins once again opened their home to the Americans. Karl and his family now owned a luxury apartment with a Baroque façade in the Adelspalais. During the previous decade Cora and Leopoldine Wittgenstein had exchanged letters, which of late had dwindled to Christmas cards, so the two were overjoyed to rekindle their friendship. D. D. sang a number of songs by Stephen Foster and lyrics from Gilbert and Sullivan. Accompanied by Cora at the piano, he also sang songs at Leopoldine's request. They would have no way of knowing that attending their performance at that lovely family gathering was nine-year old Ludwig, the future author of the *Tractatus Logico-Philosophicus*. Among his famous quotes is "Ut-

A third-generation visitor, the author, in 1959, visits members of the same German family who hosted Capt. Bill and Cora in 1888.

tering a word is like striking a note on the keyboard of the imagination," a fitting observation for perhaps the greatest philosopher of the last century, who only published during his lifetime one article, one review, and the seventy-five page *Tractatus*.

Ten years later, Karl would remember how D. D.'s singing had charmed the Wittgenstein clan: "It is only with the greatest pleasure that my family and myself remember your visit; we still talk very often of you and your esteemed wife, and we should enjoy very much another visit and hope to have as great a pleasure in hearing you sing again" (1908, March 28).

Cora and D. D. encountered criticism of the American government going to war against Spain following the sinking of the *USS Maine*. Due to this hostility, living in Europe eventually became trying, and the two felt compelled to return to the United States.

Portrait of former California Governor Henry T. Gage.

(Public Domain)

Returning briefly to Pittsburgh, Cora and D. D. prepared to travel to California. They learned that John Lewis Jones had died in July and had been buried in Braddock near the Captain. They packed the dining room table, the six Belgium chairs the Captain purchased on their last trip to Europe that had arrived after his death, several Persian rugs, an onyx end table, the Captain's desk, an étagère, a Louis XIV secretary, oil and water-color paintings by John Hammer, cast iron bas relief of Apollo and of Artemis, vases, silverware, and the Captain's library, which included a set of the *Encyclopedia Britannica*. The train left Pittsburgh for St. Louis and then crossed the western United States.

They settled east of Los Angeles in Riverside, known for its spas, similar to those in Germany. Cora and D. D. purchased ten acres of rich farmland separated from the city by an arroyo. D. D.'s study of diet and nutrition led him to a career in agriculture. They lived comfortably on their new homestead, on which they planted orange trees.

Thanks to Mimi Yost's correspondence, Cora and D. D. kept apprised of the steel industry and news about Pittsburgh. They had read in the newspapers of the battle between Andrew Carnegie and Henry Frick: Carnegie had secured the votes among the partners to eject Frick from the company. As stipulated by the Iron Clad Agreement, Carnegie was going to pay him only book value for his shares, which included those in the H. C. Frick Coke Company, which Frick had built. Frick sued Carnegie, bringing to the public eye for the first time the huge profits earned by an industry that the Republican Party had carefully protected by high tariffs. The struggle augured the end of Carnegie's active involvement in the industry when Charlie Schwab worked out an agreement with J. P. Morgan to buy the Carnegie Company and form United States Steel.

By 1902, D. D. also ventured into real estate as a buyer and seller. He speculated on properties in the Los Angeles Basin and farther north along the coast near Morro Bay and Paso Robles, where he developed an almond grove. In Riverside he purchased a home and properties with rental cottages. Gutsy and always on the alert for new and improved varieties of citrus fruits, D. D. had become a horticulturalist of considerable talent. At the Riverside orange grove, he incorporated the Golden Glen Orange Company, Inc. Eventually the California Citrus Growers selected D. D. to represent the industry in negotiations in the East. D. D. introduced Cora to friends and relatives, for there were many Gages who had lived in California for years, and the family was deeply involved in California politics. He also gave occasional musical performances and lessons in singing.

One evening at their home on Crindge Street, D. D. and Cora entertained at dinner former governor Henry T. Gage and his wife. The ex-governor, an attorney, had lost his bid for re-election in 1902 when the state voted Democratic. As the main course was being served, he brought up Cora's famous father and asked if Cora and D. D. were aware of the U.S. Steel lawsuit against Cambria Steel in Johnstown over the Jones Hot Metal Mixer patent.

One morning, not long after their dinner together, the former governor sent D. D. the following press clipping from an unidentified newspaper:

Carnegie Steel Wins Old Suit

The suit of the Carnegie Steel Co. Against the Cambria Steel Co. for alleged infringement of a patent right which hung fire in the United States District Court for more than 15 years ended last week when Judge Joseph Buffington handed down a decision awarding the prosecuting corporation damages in excess of $600,000.

The long drawn-out case had to do with a patented mixing machine invented by the late Capt. William R. Jones, who at the time he devised it, was superintendent of the Edgar Thomson works of the Carnegie Steel Co. He assigned all patent rights over to that concern.

The suit against the Cambria Steel Co. followed the exploitation of the mixer in the Carnegie plants. For a while it retained some show of life and was in a fair way of witnessing some sort of settlement. Then it dragged. Since then, year in and year out, activity in the case has been perfunctory and desultory.

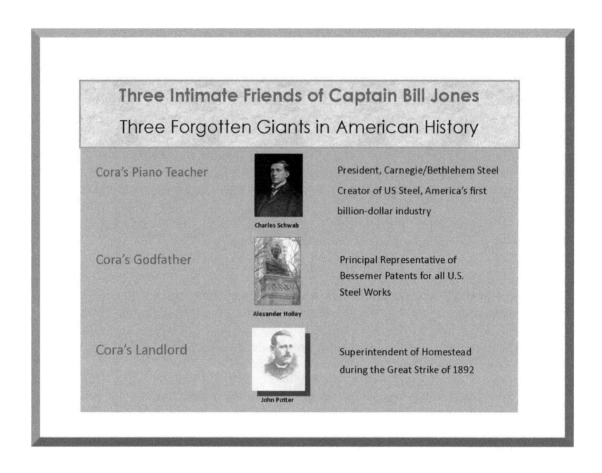

Protégés of Captain Bill Jones: Charles Schwab, Alexander Holley, and John Potter, went on to become giants in Amerian history.

Chapter 6 Sections

CHAPTER 6

GAGES AND CARNEGIE

Section 39: Cora and D. D. Approach Carnegie

When Cora and D. D. learned of the hundreds of thousands of dollars involved in the Jones mixer lawsuit and were told that every steel company was required to purchase user rights for it, D. D. was eager to confront Carnegie and considered suing him, but wasn't quite sure how to go about it. He sought counsel from his cousin the ex-governor, who had originally brought the lawsuit to the Gages' attention.

Henry T. Gage responded. Although he did not know Carnegie personally, he appreciated the Carnegie Library donated to the city of San Jose during his administration; he therefore assumed Carnegie to be an honorable man. Knowing that D. D. was soon to be in the East representing the orange cooperative, Governor Gage cautioned him about venturing into litigation with East Coast lawyers. He encouraged D. D. to speak directly with Carnegie about "the case before him and [you will] learn from his own lips his refusal (which I think improbable) of making promptly and generously the compensation to your wife to which in equity and justice, if not in strict law, she is entitled." The ex-governor continued in his letter:

> A man of such unselfish characteristics who values his fortune as nothing against his personal honor and friendship surely will not, when the matter is directly called to his attention, fail to perform an act of justice in settling without litigation the rightful claims of the family of Captain Jones, who, as I have been informed, was his most trusted employee and assistant in founding the great company which was the basis of Mr. Carnegie's fortune, and through whose inventive genius the corporation and its officers, and Mr. Carnegie himself, have reaped such great profits and from which they still continue to be the beneficiaries. . . . Mr. Carnegie will view this matter from an equitable and moral standpoint and will never permit it to be said that a dollar of his own great fortune or that of his great company shall ever bear, directly or indirectly, the taint of fraud through such a wrong done to the memory of his old friend and assistant Captain Jones. (1905, April 25)

A line in this letter, "Beyond all doubt, Mr. Carnegie is wholly unacquainted with the facts connected with the injustice done the family of Captain Jones," enraged Cora, even when she reread it many years later. During the Homestead Strike, Carnegie had managed every detail of the company's reaction to the strikers from his hideaway in Scotland, where he could claim that he was "unacquainted with the facts." Frick and Potter were mostly fulfilling his orders, and then Carnegie scapegoated John Potter for the bloodshed and mayhem. Former governor Gage held the same view of Carnegie as did the general public, which by 1905 had been molded by all the positive press surrounding Carnegie's philanthropy after the turn of the century. Homestead had faded from public memory.

Following his cousin's advice, D. D. wrote the following letter.

Mr. Andrew Carnegie,

Ardgay, Sutherlandshire,

Scotland.

Dear Sir:

As a son-in-law of the late Capt. William R. Jones and acting in my wife's interest, I beg to request your consideration of the following subject matter and enclosure. With a view to brevity I enclose a letter from Hon. Henry T. Gage to whom I have stated the case both before coming east and since having further investigated the matter during a sojourn of some weeks in which time I have endeavored to gain all consequential data and see as many as possible of those immediately concerned or, conversant with the subject matter both regarding Capt. Jones's connection with the Carnegie Steel Company and Cambria Iron Works as well as a biographical sketch of his life.

I regret not having been able to state the case to you personally owing to my not having completed my investigation until some days subsequent to your sailing for I feel that with the clear knowledge of the means employed by one of your officials who gained the audience (ostensibly to proffer sympathy), and finally the signature of Mrs. Jones to a paper the worth or import of which she could not then of all times comprehend, it would be far from your sentiment and common practice of justice and equity.

That you should be thus placed by the act of an agent as an opponent of the very just and equitable claim which his estate may well prefer, and in view of numerous expressions of esteem in which you hold Capt. Jones, as evidenced in your correspondence to him, the integrity of which I have no wish to mar, is not compatible in my estimation with your sense of fairness, and will not permit you to longer remain a party to the very palpable wrong done his family.

These patent rights have earned in various revenues, millions, yet by this official's chicanery the Carnegie Steel Company possessed itself of them but two days after the death of Capt. Jones for the munificent sum of Thirty five thousand dollars as fitting recompense to his estate for the resultant, existing product of his genius and capability as invented and applied by him during his lifetime: at a moment when overwhelmed with grief, an invalid for ten years previous, at this time and until her death, incompetent, Mrs. Jones was cajoled by this unprincipled master of business and finance into signing a release of all interest in those patents to which Capt. Jones gave all his genius, his life's blood.

I would very much appreciate an expression of your sentiment with regard to this matter and further trust I may have the honor and pleasure of fully stating the case personally at a convenient future date, which I trust you may deem it a kindness to suggest.

Awaiting with interest your pleasure, I am,
Yours very respectfully,
D. D. Gage
Crafton Pennsylvania (1905, May 12)

But, Carnegie proved the ex-governor naive by delegating his cousin George "Dod" Lauder to respond to D. D.'s letter. Evaluations of Lauder's role in Carnegie's affairs agree. Wall called him "a spy for Carnegie at the management level." Charlie Schwab thought him a huge bird, "who used to sit in my office and tell me he was 'lending dignity' to my administrations . . . He knew its [Jones Hot Metal Mixer] full impact . . . it meant [a] revolution in the business" (Whipple n.d.).

Lauder responded to D.D. with the following letter:
Dear Sir,

In the matter of the Jones Mixer patent, the facts are Capt. Jones asked me as a personal favor to use my influence to have the Carnegie Co. buy his interest, the Co. having already one-half interest and a shop right, having been at all the expense and risk of the preliminary experiments [This assertion of half interest in the two patents is the earliest documentation, some sixteen years after Bill Jones's curious and unexpected death, uttered by a man who further asserted that the value to the firm was "somewhat mythical."]. The price Thirty-five Thousand Dollars, was his own valuation, and I believe that it was only by my pressing it that the officers of the Co. agreed to take it.

As to Mrs. Jones being in any way wronged by signing the final papers, such an assertion is a great mistake. She only signed the formal transfer, which was in all points the terms arranged by the Captain before his death. Mr. Frick was President at the time and saw to the carrying out of the sale. I should add that the patent itself was deemed to be of little value by all at that time, as some prior patents had been unearthed that seemed to anticipate it, and as a matter of fact, it took years of litigation and the expenditure of hundreds of thousands to establish its validity.

The money made from the patent is somewhat mythical. The last I heard from the officers of the Steel Co. was that they had not yet recovered a cent from the Cambria Iron Co.—such is law's delay. As all our competitors used the mixer, the advantage to the Company in money is problematical.

I wish to add that personally all I did about the sale of the patent was at the

Captain's request, and I considered that I was doing him a personal favor. I was not an officer of the Co. at the time.

Very truly,

Geo. Lauder (1905, August 31)

James Howard Bridge dismisses the idea of Lauder as an individual independent of Andrew Carnegie: "Lauder was only Carnegie's echo" (1991, 317). In this case, it stretches the credulity of anyone who has researched Jones that he ever would have approached someone like Lauder in the Carnegie Brothers hierarchy, with minimal knowledge of the steel business, concerning his greatest invention or about anything to do with money. Although he was a full partner in the company at the time of Jones's death, Lauder rarely acted without being accompanied by a senior partner, usually Harry Phipps. The statement in the letter must be a fabrication; it is completely unbelievable.

In an 1895 deposition for the complainant in the Cambria vs. Carnegie lawsuit, Carnegie had testified about the Jones mixer that, "without this invention, I believe that we should have abandoned the mode of running direct from the blast furnace. Above all things, the manufacturer has to regard the uniformity of product, the quality of rails, and this uniformity cannot be obtained without the Jones invention, as far as I know." (*Cambria*, 1899 U.S. App., at 1899, 646).

In his deposition, Carnegie goes on to state, as if it were fact, that Jones was not interested in "owning anything of a commercial nature"—as if he could speak for Jones. Carnegie says, under oath, that "in the case of this patent, he wanted $35,000 for a special purpose, and asked the firm to give it to him, and we credited him on the books, paying 6 percent interest, subject to his call, and he was notified of this not four hours before he was killed in our service." Yet, four hours before the accident at Furnace C, Bill Jones was discussing the Braddock Methodist Church with Henry Clay Frick, a fact that Frick corroborates. And he died days later in a hospital bed, not killed in the accident. There is no record to support Carnegie's testimony. Bill Jones applied for his patent on the Jones Hot Metal Mixer in late 1888; the actual certificate was not received until 1889. It was only after his death, in 1889, that it was signed over to Carnegie by the aggrieved and invalid widow Harriet.

Only after this transfer could Carnegie Brothers, and its successor, Carnegie Steel, charge and litigate for millions of dollars from their competitors, monies that would and should have gone to Bill Jones or his heirs.

Lauder's letter stung D. D. and Cora. When D. D. read it, Cora exploded, calling Lauder a liar. "He is Andy's cousin! My father had utter contempt for that lackey! Lauder did nothing but sit around spying on others' work." Former governor Gage's assumption that the philanthropist was "a man of the highest and most honorable principles," who would not "fail to perform an act of justice in settling without litigation the rightful claims of the family of Captain Jones" was utterly incorrect.

Cora was particularly insulted by Lauder's claim that the firm owned half interest in the mixer and the process. This was the first she had ever heard of such a prior agreement.

Captain Jones went to great trouble to patent his inventions. The patents were a major component in what Uncle Dan referred to as his Plan and my mother called his Scheme. It is highly unlikely he would have agreed for the company to take over all the patents when he was negotiating in Youngstown to build a new company. According to Wall:

> [Jones] had more patents to his credit than any other single individual in the history of steelmaking . . . . In Jones's desk [when he died] there were patent rights for a dozen other major inventions for the making, rolling, and cutting of steel, dating from 1877 to 1889. There were also hundreds of small improvements in the design, construction, and operation of the machinery that Jones had considered too trivial to patent. . . . Jones had generously made available his patented inventions to all of Carnegie's plants, exacting only a small royalty fee on their use . . . The full value of these inventions, which now belonged to his estate, could not be accurately appraised, but [Carnegie's men] Lauder and Phipps, checking over Jones's papers the day after his death, realized how important it was for the company to take possession of these patents . . .The amount that the company ultimately realized from these patent rights can never be calculated . . . (1970, 532)

The two patents for the Jones Hot Metal Mixer and the Direct Process would have a permanent and revolutionary impact on steel making. Jones's two inventions constituted an autocatalytic process that standardized practices in plants throughout the world (Diamond 1997, 258-9). Carnegie knew this full well, as his testimony under oath in 1895 proves, as does his sending Jones to consult with the two major continental steel works, Krupp in Germany and Wittgenstein in Austria. Knowing only a few of the components of this sequence of events, D. D. bypassed Lauder by writing again to Carnegie:

> My Dear Sir:-
>
> Your letter of Sept. 6th recd. I feel that the subject in hand should be viewed from a moral standpoint regardless of its legal aspect—Capt. Jones gave the very best there was in him for sixteen years to his company, his loyalty, honor, genius, and life went out in his services to your company and in view of subsequent events the just emoluments of his life's work were not reaped by him and I now champion the cause of the Captains daughter only. From my investigations I have learned that it was Capt. Jones loyalty to his Company that made him refuse better offers from outside firms for many of his patents but I have no wish to bother you with my investigations. I ask your kind consideration of my previous letter of Aug. 30. Fully realizing your position as apart from any of the negotiations of the Captain's affairs Mrs. Gage feels that she would have been much more justly dealt with by you than at the hands of your agents.
>
> Very Sincerely Yours,
> Daniel Gage,

D. D. and the ex-governor Henry Gage then devised another strategy. D. D.'s son, Bill, had contracted blood poisoning in his right leg in 1904, when he was only three, a deadly injury before the availability of antibiotics. D. D.'s regimen, which had saved his own life, also saved the life of his son. However, Bill's leg had grown worse, requiring trips East for medical treatment. Incidentally, John Butler, Captain Bill's good friend and would-be part-ner, had arranged on one trip for the boy to see a famous orthopedist in Youngstown. Now, in conjunction with another of these trips, the family planned a visit to New York so that D. D. could hand-deliver his abbreviated biography of Captain Jones to Carnegie. D. D. would explain that he planned to expand the biography after consultation and interviewing for-mer associates. Both the former governor and D. D. hoped that the strategy would appeal to the philanthropist's conscience, as the governor had suggested, and, in a way, it did.

D. D. thought it best to simply show up with the family at Carnegie's doorstep to present Cora's claims. Carnegie would have to turn away Captain Jones's family or hear them out. And so, during the medical trip in 1906, the family traveled by train to New York City and in a horse-drawn hansom cab visited Carnegie's 91st Street residence. A butler greeted the Gages and welcomed them in, but Carnegie's secretary intervened and main-tained that since they had no appointment, Mr. Carnegie was unavailable.

On their way to the hotel, Cora was angry, piqued by D. D.'s in-your-face strategy, though he only chuckled and asked her to be patient. After they were settled in their hotel room, a bellhop alerted them that they had a message. It was an invitation to dinner the next evening at the Carnegie home.

According to my uncle, after dinner, Carnegie cradled his seven-year-old brother on his lap, like Dickens's Tiny Tim to write in pencil the famous story of Captain Jones's response to his boss's escape from the summer heat at ET:

> "I was about to take my annual holiday and went out to say good bye to the Captain and his staff. I told them I thought often about them sweltering in the heat [and] hard at work when I was at play....I wilt here and suffer but half an hour upon the bow of the ship, breasting the Atlantic waves, no matter what ails me, I get perfect relief, and the Captain exclaimed, 'Oh, Lord, think of the relief we all get."

Carnegie had shared many version of this story with friends such as Kaiser Wilhelm II and David Lloyd George, Britain's Prime Minister. Incidentally, the Prime Minister repeated this same story many years later during a visit to Pittsburgh, (The Gazette Times, 1923, Octo-ber 25, "Lloyd George Appeals for United Action by America and Britain to Prevent Wars." C 2-4).

Louise Carnegie, Andrew's wife, ever gracious, cleverly "shifted the conversation when Carnegie was center-staging too much, and chatted about things and experiences, but not necessarily ones of interest to the visitors" (Gage to Wall, n. d.).

In anticipation of the evening, D. D. had brushed up on Robert Burns, Carnegie's favorite poet. Carnegie complemented his recital with quotes and quips about the Scot's poems, and grew rhapsodic recalling the good old days with Captain Bill, ET's hero. At the end of dinner, Carnegie asked, "And Mr. Gage, do you have the manuscript of this biography of the Captain?" D. D. answered that he did not, "as I assumed this was a social meeting I did not bring it. When I return to California I will send it to you" (D. Gage, Jr. to Wall, 1972, 11 March).

When the family returned to California between 1899 and 1901, D. D. sent Carnegie a twelve-page draft of the manuscript, which now resides in the Andrew Carnegie Archives in the Library of Congress. That Christmas, Cora received an envelope from The Trust Company of Hoboken, New Jersey, with a card and a check for $1,000. The former governor pronounced: "you could hardly call this a strike, but at least it shows the signs of a nibble." For the remaining thirteen years of his life, Carnegie sent a Christmas gift of $1,000. Further legal pursuit entailed expenses that the family could not sustain.

About the time that Bill, my father, and his brother, Dan, were to finish elementary school, D. D. and Cora threw a large party for friends and business associates from Los Angeles. To everyone's surprise, Cora's brother, Will Jones, appeared uninvited with a woman from Nevada. Cora, glad to see him for the first time in a decade, showed the pair around and introduced them to guests. Will and his lady friend lived in Gold Hill, Nevada, where Will had exhausted his inheritance trying to parlay it into a gold strike that resulted in nothing. He looked haggard, not showing his previous exuberance and energy but rather a demeanor that conveyed "Just let me live in peace." Will tried to spend time with the Gage boys to become acquainted with his nephews and to tell them about their grandfather, but his companion interrupted often to drag him to talk to guests.

Since Will, too, had heard of the lawsuit over the Jones Hot Metal Mixer, he pulled Cora aside and asked her what amount the Jones family had originally received from Carnegie for the patents. After their conversation and a few drinks, he repeated to his nephews and to the guests, the redundant pun: "What a steal!"

Some years later, Cora told the author's mother, her daughter-in-law, that Will and his girlfriend from Gold Hill had spent a good part of the evening trying to convince the guests to invest in their deserted mine left over from a half-century before. Will Jones's pitch only embarrassed the party's hosts and provided the family with a good story that evoked many after-dinner laughs.

Section 40: D. D.'s Travail

The family appreciated the yearly check for $1000, Carnegie's nibble, but the theft still needed to be resolved. D. D. had no way of knowing even the approximate value of the Jones mixer, so he did what he could to acquire needed information about the Captain's invention to support the family's case against Carnegie. Who could they trust? They considered Charlie Schwab too Machiavellian to be relied upon; Cora cautioned D. D. that Charlie had long ago deserted the Captain to achieve success on the corporate ladder. John Potter, an inventor himself, surely understood the mixer's immense value. He had spent so much time with the family right after the Captain's death, but he had disappeared in 1893 soon after the congressional hearing and before the lawsuit against Cambria's abridging of patent rights.

So D. D. corresponded with the Captain's European friends. He wrote Karl Wittgenstein, the Austrian iron and steel authority, whom he and Cora had visited. Of all those associated with the Captain, it was Wittgenstein my grandmother and grandfather could trust to provide professional testimony of the mixer's value to the steel industry, but he could shed no light on the critical issue of its ownership or its transfer from the Jones family to Carnegie Steel.

> I am entirely of the opinion that Captain Jones was the foremost steel-man of his time, and that on account of his great modesty he certainly has not received the due recognition from his contemporaries.
>
> I have always had for Capt. Jones the greatest feeling of admiration and gratefulness, and it is with the greatest pleasure that I use every opportunity of expressing myself to this respect.
>
> With reference to the Jones-Mixer itself, I must say that it is destined for large works as they consist in American, England, and Germany. Great works, which have many furnaces, need a mixer for the object of being able to gather all the quantity of liquid raw iron in a large vessel from which the steelworks can then draw their needs, as they want it, and to such large works Capt. Jones has rendered a very great service through his invention of the mixer.
>
> But Capt. Jones' chief merit is that by his intrepid farseeing and energetic work he has shown new ways to the iron industry of America as well as of all other countries. (Wittgenstein to Gage, 1908, March 28)

For the next two years, D. D. Gage wrote other friends and continued research to fill out the biography. In March 1908, he sent Carnegie a draft of the opening chapters. As D. D. had collected recollections from a variety of professional and personal sources, he began to uncover stories that would incriminate Carnegie and his associates. At first Carnegie appeared encouraging with the drafts he received. But little could Carnegie afford another book like James Howard Bridge's *The Inside History of the Carnegie Steel Company: A Romance of Millions*. For his part, D. D. needed a patent attorney. He needed some time to

> *The man who had received so much wealth from Jones's inventions would not even assist his family with a loan.*

question Carnegie Steel officials about Jones's desk and the papers it had contained. He needed someone to cross-examine those who had come to the Jones house in 1889 and dealt with a widow who was isolated, uninformed about the value of her husband's patents, mentally fragile, and who they knew would not live long.

During the months of November and December 1908, D. D. visited New York as representative of the Citrus Cooperative. He met with Carnegie several times to exchange notes. On the evening of November 27, D. D. and Carnegie discussed the book's progress. Carnegie invited him to be a guest at the banquet of the Carnegie Veterans Association. D. D.'s prior commitments conflicted with the event, but he said he would try to rearrange his calendar. The Carnegie Veterans Association dinner at Carnegie's home had been held for the first time in 1902 and now was an annual event. The membership of this group did not include everyone who had worked for Carnegie; it was composed of only those who had sided with Carnegie against Frick when Frick sued Carnegie for the full worth of his partnership (Bridge 1991, 357).

Carnegie proposed that D. D. give him what he had written and D. D.'s accumulated correspondence so that Carnegie could hire a ghostwriter to compose a well-written biography, the implication being that D. D.'s ineffectiveness as a writer was the only reason to do this. But D. D. feared Carnegie's motive, so he politely refused.

Four days later D. D. wrote Carnegie, to accept his invitation to attend the annual dinner with the Carnegie Veterans Association:

#238 E. 61St St.

My Dear Mr. Carnegie:-

Having made arrangements to stay over for a few days, I accept with pleasure your kind invitation to attend the Carnegie Veterans Banquet.

Very Truly Yours,

Daniel D. Gage (1908, December 12)

To his great surprise, D. D. received an immediate reply from Carnegie's testy secretary, yet another delegation of the responsibility to deal with Jones's son-in-law. It was the same pattern that Carnegie had displayed throughout his career—making it look like he was not in control when things went badly.

New York 12/3 '08

Daniel D. Gage, Esq.,

 238 Est 61st St., New York

Dear Sir,

Yours of December 2nd received. There is some misunderstanding. Mr. Carnegie says he has no power to invite anyone to the Veterans' Banquet. What he did say was that if you will come here between six thirty and seven tomorrow night he will introduce you to some of the best friends that Captain Jones ever had.

Respectfully yours,

P. [John A. Poynton] Secretary

Stung again, my grandfather D. D. immediately wrote a response, regretting his presumption and canceling the meeting at six o'clock. This ended the direct encounters between the Gages and Andrew Carnegie about Captain Jones for some time. The restitution of the lost fortune was never forthrightly discussed. D. D. went his way and continued to work on the biography, but it was an indirect and ultimately ineffective means of dealing with a financial and legal issue of great portent. In addition to an attorney, D. D. needed an eye witness to events after Bill Jones was taken to the Homeopathy Hospital and to the meetings with Harriet Jones after her husband's death.

As the Gages continued to struggle with finances, they decided to move from Riverside to Pasadena where their two adolescent sons entered high school. One day when D. D. was leaving an appointment in downtown Los Angeles, he nearly had a collision on the sidewalk with Margaret and John Potter. Potter, D. D. learned, had corresponded with Schwab and Frick about various steel projects up until 1900. He then had worked for Guggenheim as a metallurgical engineer in Latin America for a number of years before returning to the United States. He had done well financially, and the family of four settled in Los Angeles, where Potter had built an eighteen-room home in not far from the downtown. The Potters had two sons, about ten years older than the Gage boys.

A week later during dinner at the Potter home, Cora told how she had fired up ET's first blast furnace, the Cora. When the conversation turned to their time in Pittsburgh and the Captain's many colleagues, John became animated. This agitation was not at all like the younger man she remembered from Braddock. Potter was eager to show them an invitation to the annual banquet of the Carnegie Veterans Association in New York, the same celebration to which Carnegie had invited and then uninvited D. D. in 1908. Potter said that every year since resettling in Los Angeles, he had received an invitation but never responded; it infuriated him that they would think he would attend after the treatment he had received.

D. D. said that Carnegie had reneged on his earlier invitation only when D. D. had chosen not to give him the manuscript for a ghostwriter to finish. Potter became agitated about all the negative events of the past, to the point that Margaret insisted that it was time for all to call it a night. While Cora, D. D., and their sons descended the stairs to the street, Potter shouted that the Gage boys should know that their grandfather was the only man Carnegie ever apologized to in the presence of others. "And, mark my words, behind all the smiles, he hated the Captain for that. That so-called 'pacifist' killed the Captain!"

Had John had too much to drink? That was a pretty strong assertion, one which the family would never forget. Although the Potters and the Gages often spent time together, the subject of the Captain's death was rarely mentioned because when it came up John would become so angry, his wife worried that he would have a stroke.

At another dinner months later, Cora shared with John how much poor weather, the real estate market, and her son's medical condition had eaten into the family's savings. They badly needed money. Medical bills and the lack of profits for three years from their oranges had driven them to desperation. The ex-governor Henry Gage had recommended a Philadelphia lawyer to D. D., who informed him, completely in error, that there was a seventeen-year statute of limitations on patents, meaning Jones's patent would have run out by 1906. Cora was planning to write Carnegie to request a loan with interest, so they could pay off their debts. Potter believed that if they were to detail their present plight, even Carnegie might understand.

Cora wrote the following letter to Andy, asking for a loan of $6,000 with interest.

> Dear Mr. Carnegie:
>
> I called on you last Wednesday and your secretary informed me that you were leaving for Washington and requested me to write you, stating my business and asking for an appointment. I am the daughter of Capt. Jones. I came east on account of our older son William, thinking something might be done for him. He has met with three serious accidents, having broken the right leg and later fracturing the hip of the same leg, leaving him at present lame. William has been a great expense to us and will be for some time to come. I am going to be perfectly frank with you regarding our financial condition and the progress we have made since going to California. We have stuck to our mark and I feel proud of the showing we have made in spite of the great odds against us, and yet at the time we are financially involved.
>
> In order to dispose of our orange groves after three disastrous frosts, we were obliged to trade out and assume or pay cash difference on other properties. Mr. Gage's real estate business has been substantial. We have been able, through strict economy, to carry our obligations but owing to the present terrible financial condition aggravated by the horrible war there is no chance of disposing of any property or of renewing loans under the existing financial stringency.
>
> We need some assistance to tide us over this crisis. Would you advance us the

amount to take care of our much pressing needs, the same to be secured and the amount to be returned to you as soon as we can dispose of some of our holdings. It is quite possible that $6000 would be sufficient. I do hope we will not lose anything, for which we have worked so hard. If you decide to help us it will be help extended when most urgently needed, as everything is at a complete standstill excepting taxes and interest, and no chance of moving anything at present. I wish to again express my appreciation and gratitude to you for your kind remembrance at Christmas and also for your contribution to my Father's biography that is fully appreciated by both Mr. Gage and me. We regret very much that we were unable to get reliable information in the first instance and trust that you will pardon us for the mistake we made.

> Very Sincerely Yours
>
> Cora M. Gage (1914, December 14)

The next day, Carnegie answered her.

> Dear Mrs. Gage:
>
> I am deeply moved by your letter of fourteenth December, never suspecting that your affairs were in such condition.
>
> I had to resolve long ago never to have anything to do with business affairs. Several who had been my partners became involved after leaving the Steel Company and more than one was pensioned after failure.
>
> This is the most trying time I have ever known. One mail delivery brought forty-five requests for financial aid; one day recently we had over a hundred. I must confess myself unable to deal with them.
>
> You show so great a remaining value that I am sure your creditor will see you thru. It would be wrong in them not to do so in these times. Wise and good creditors never fail to make due allowance and forbear pressing for reductions. It is really not right for mortgage holders to demand these at present. They finally conclude to forge such reductions if satisfied they cannot be made by the mortgage. I advise you to bring this to their notice.
>
> Sincerely yours.
>
> Andrew Carnegie (1914, December 15)

The family read this letter over and over, resigning themselves to the fact that the man who had received so much of his wealth from Bill Jones's inventions, labor, and management would not even assist his family with a loan. This was a bitter irony, for Captain Jones had benevolently helped many workers disabled on the job at Carnegie factories as well as the widows and dependents of men injured or killed on the job. It is unlikely that Carnegie ever knew of Jones's charity or the degree of his concern for those he managed. The same could not be said of Andrew Carnegie, no matter how much charity he tried to publicize in his later years.

Dismayed at Carnegie, Cora and D. D. decided to move the family so they could make profitable a 365-acre ranch where they planted five thousand almond trees. Paso Robles, like Riverside, had world-famous spas that provided D. D. with relief when his condition flared up. The Gage brothers, now in high school, met and became close friends with Dorothy and Patrick Hamilton and their cousin John Steinbeck. My father maintained a lifelong friendship with Steinbeck, who eventually would read D. D.'s manuscript about Bill Jones.

A letter from author, John Steinbeck who maintained a lifelong friendship with the author's father, Bill Gage. Steinbeck read D. D.'s manuscript about Bill Jones.

After 1913, America was being drawn into World War I. Able-bodied men in the Salinas Valley were being drafted, including the Gage tenant and most workers on the property. More damaging financially was that with the war, barley and beans became much in demand, while there was no market for D. D.'s almonds. Cora stayed in touch with Margaret and John Potter, who often invited the Gages when in town to dinner at their home on Lakeview Street.

One evening D. D. reported the extent of their losses—oranges damaged by drought and frost and almonds without a market during the war. From 1900 to 1908, D. D. had increased the family estate by a net value of 123 percent. But between 1910 and 1914, the years of droughts, depression, and war, the family had lost 50 percent of those gains. John implored Cora to once more write to Carnegie. The Gages agreed, and when they returned to Paso Robles, Cora wrote Andy again, explaining how poorly the family was enduring financially. Nearly all their property was heavily mortgaged. They had sold the Riverside orange groves and buildings since the previous letter to Carnegie (C. Gage to Taylor, 1917, December 17).

Over the years my mother stewed about Carnegie's treatment of her mother- and father-in-law. I remember the last time she said to me as she derided Carnegie: "A black heart for the man who gave out so much gold." How humiliating it was for Cora. How hypocritical and dishonest it was of Carnegie.

Section 41: Living with the Potters

After two years, the fickle Salinas Valley, which John Steinbeck has documented in *East of Eden*, crushed the Gages. D. D. found a reliable couple to manage the Paso Robles ranch, and the family returned to Los Angeles where the boys completed their last year of high school.

For more than half a decade, D. D. and Cora had been in touch with John and Margaret Potter, whose finances also had dwindled. Now that the Potter's two offspring, John A. and Robert Forsyth, had left for careers and homes of their own, the big house in downtown Los Angeles was too much for the couple. The Potters renovated it into two apartments, one on the ground floor that they lived in and one on the second floor that they invited the Gages to rent.

The Gages and the Potters continued their friendship, having dinner either upstairs in the Gage apartment or downstairs at the Potters. John increasingly exhibited nearly uncontrollable rage alternating with depression.

Living in an apartment for the first time in their lives proved trying for the Gage family. Two teenagers, who had recently been tackling mules and horses on a large ranch, now had to cautiously tiptoe around the house so as not to disturb the Potters. Still, the boys would wrestle one another before their mother rushed in, scolding them for being inconsiderate. Although suffering from depression and becoming a bitter recluse, John Potter never complained about Bill or Dan.

That spring of 1919, Bill, as a graduating high school senior, landed a job in the advertising department at the *Los Angeles Evening Herald*, where he continued to work summer months while he and Dan attended Stanford University. One day he dashed home with that day's newspaper in hand with the news that Andrew Carnegie had died. Many years later, Bill and Dan read of Carnegie's last moments in Burton J. Hendrick's *The Life of Andrew Carnegie*, which describes him gazing up at the portrait of Captain Jones and reminiscing:

> "How much did you say I had given away, Poynton?" he would ask.

> "$324,657,399," the secretary replied, his gift for figures being precise.

> "Good Heaven!" Carnegie would answer with a chuckle, "where did I ever get all that money?"

> "How fortunate I was in my 'boys'!" he frequently remarked, recalling Pittsburgh companions. His devotion to one of the noble company was shown in a touching way. Carnegie's sleeping room in the Fifth Avenue house was extremely simple, almost the only wall decoration being a painting of "Bill" Jones, the masterful autocrat of the Edgar Thomson Works, the man who, under Carnegie's captainship, had made America the world's greatest producer of steel. (1932, 383)

Cora did not receive a Carnegie Christmas check in 1919, but from his death until hers in 1946, she received a pension of $150.00 annually. Adding the $35,000 for the patents, the thirteen years of Christmas checks, and her pension for the rest of her life, the family ultimately received a paltry $55,000 or so, nearly a third of which resulted from D. D.'s persistent follow-up and his dogged assembly of a biography on Captain Jones that in last draft amounted to fifty thousand words.

Dan and Bill received sound educations, attending Stanford University in 1920 and Harvard in 1925. At Stanford, the two teamed up again with John Steinbeck, who initiated the Gage brothers into the more raucous aspects of college life, though Dan often opted to bear down on the books. Steinbeck and my father worked on the Stanford paper, but the former had a habit of dropping out of school to travel, later to return and resume classes.

During the 1925 Christmas break of their first year in the MBA program at Harvard, the boys returned home. My father remembered visiting Margaret and John Potter, who brought up the days when Captain Bill was at ET. Bill and Dan mentioned that they had visited the Frick Museum in New York City. Potter then showed them the invitation to the 23rd Christmas Dinner of the Carnegie Veterans Association to be held in just a few days. Swearing, he crumpled it up and threw it in the fireplace. On the following Friday evening, the night of the Carnegie veterans dinner, Potter brooded over Carnegie and Frick, both long dead. He ascended the stairs and asked to see the Captain's daughter. Dad looked at D. D., both surprised at Potter's usage, then ushered John in to Cora for a private talk. Within a few moments, Potter left the house without saying a word to those in the living room. He walked some blocks from his house to the corner of Carnegie Street, and in an empty lot, shot himself in the head. When Mrs. Potter answered the door downstairs, my family heard a wail that all present would recall for the remainder of their lives with painful incredulity. D. D. and my father went to the morgue to identify the body to spare Margaret any additional grief.

Section 42: Schwab is the Biographer

In 1917 Charlie Schwab, then chairman of Bethlehem Steel, published *Succeed with What You Have*, in which he included copious information about Captain Bill Jones. He had learned from Carnegie of D. D.'s earlier manuscript and eventually wrote to Cora asking to visit her in Los Angeles to obtain the latest draft of it. In 1926, Schwab visited them at the Potter home. D. D. gave Charlie the manuscript; he was tiring of the project and did not think he would live long enough to see it published. Schwab, to cement his word that he would see the project through, promised Cora that on his return East he, as chair of the Carnegie Veterans Association, would build a mausoleum to Captain Jones at the Braddock Cemetery. In this Charlie kept his word. The mausoleum was completed in 1930 (Dickson 1938, 193).

My father, Bill, and his wife, Alice, my mother, were living with Cora and D. D. at the time of Charlie Schwab's visit. They had married that year in the Stanford Chapel and were living in the upstairs apartment. John had only recently committed suicide. "After the visit Charlie descended to the downstairs and walked out the door to his chauffer holding open the rear door of his black Packard. Mrs. Gage followed him out and called to him: 'Charlie, Charlie! Tell me the truth; do you think we got a fair deal in the sale of the patents?' But Schwab quickly ducked his head and entered the rear seat of his car and sped off" (Gage, Kith and Kin). During Schwab's entire visit with Cora and D. D., no one had mentioned John Potter. On his way out, Charlie unknowingly walked by the front door of Margaret, widow of the hapless John, whom Schwab succeeded as superintendent after the famous strike of Bloody Homestead.

Even David Lloyd George, the British prime minister, became part of the legend of Captain Jones. Schwab, during his 1926 visit, had given Cora a tattered clipping from the *Gazette Times* of Lloyd George's speech in Pittsburgh promoting the League of Nations:

> Thirty years ago I heard of [Jones] from Mr. Carnegie, from Mr. Frick and from Mr. Schwab. Mr. Schwab, whom I had the pleasure of meeting in London this year, spent the whole of the evening in telling me stories about "Bill" Jones. And they were so good that I said to him it is a great pity that the life of that great character is not published, because there is a good deal of inspiration in many of those stories, and I am glad to be able to assure you that Mr. Schwab told me in New York that he was actually engaged in writing the life of "Bill" Jones himself. (1923, October 25)

But Schwab was also thinking about his own autobiography and in the mid-1930s negotiated with Stephen Whipple, a staff writer for the *New York World Telegraph*, to write one. Although Whipple promised Schwab that nothing would appear in print until after Schwab's death, some intimate stories of which only Schwab and Whipple had knowledge were leaked in the press, and Schwab fired Whipple, who then returned to Schwab all notes along with D. D. Gage's biography of Captain Jones. In 1935, Sydney B. Whipple found the biography among Schwab's papers. He stated: "it is some 50,000 words. We have the entire unpublished life of Bill, contains perhaps, 50,000 words of material. Schwab wants all the credit given him as 'the first great influence'" (n.d., ts14). It was known to be among Schwab's papers at Bethlehem, but eventually that archive was divided between the Canal Museum in New Jersey and the Hagley Museum in Delaware. Neither archive has D. D.'s biography today.

No biographies of either Schwab or Bill Jones were published at that time. D. D. had kept a single carbon copy of the Jones manuscript with the hope that he could return to it or that perhaps one of his sons might finish it. By the early 1930s, the family was aware that their old friend John Steinbeck was making a name for himself as an author. Perhaps John might want to revise or recast D. D.'s manuscript as a novel about the travail of a middle class family. They weren't thinking about it now as a means to expose Carnegie, but to tell the story of the Captain's remarkable life and death. In 1936, Bill sent Steinbeck a proposal to center a novel on the life of Captain Jones and included the carbon copy of the biography, the only copy still in the family's possession. Steinbeck turned down the project in part because he and Bill had very different theories about Captain Jones's potential to influence subsequent labor/management relations. Both my father and uncle believed that if Captain Bill had lived and moved to Youngstown, he might have contributed at least as much as he had at ET, the future of American capitalism might not have turned out so negatively for labor, and America's wealth might have been distributed more equally, resulting in a stronger middle class. Steinbeck, in his response to my father, wrote that he saw individuals like Jones or Schwab as unknowingly part of an economic structure that was developing precisely due to the opposing forces of labor and wealth. He thought one would have to tell Jones's story within the context of the entire movement, an undertaking he wasn't interested in. My father lost interest in a biography after his divorce from my mother in 1939.

Through the years, as biographies on Carnegie and Schwab and Holbrook's volume on the steel industry appeared, the brothers Gage exchanged letters with the authors to correct errors and to express appreciation for the authors' affirmation of the Captain's pivotal role in the history of the American steel industry. Once, re-reading Steinbeck's letter, Mother summed up why she believed neither her brother-in-law nor her former husband had ever reconstituted D. D.'s biography: "Remember the Captain's economic philosophy smacked of socialism. The boys always felt they deserved something they didn't get, but ran around with the country club set. 'Attacking Carnegie is attacking money,' I can hear them say."

221

***Fugue** [fyoog] a musical composition in which one or two themes are repeated or imitated by successively entering voices and contrapuntally developed in a continuous interweaving of the voice parts*

CHAPTER 7

FUGUE

223

Fugue

The Jones Hot Metal Mixer entails two patented components: the apparatus or material vessel, and the concept, the Jones direct method for handling molten iron headed for steel conversion. In 1905 my grandparents did not know the value of the mixer to the Carnegie Company, but clearly Carnegie did (Cambria Iron Co. v. Carnegie Steel Co. 1899. 644). Consequently, what Carnegie, through Lauder, conveyed to my grandparents, "The money made from the patent is somewhat mythical . . . As all our competitors used the mixer, the advantage to the Company in money is problematical," is demonstrably not true (1905, August 31).

Peter Krass, drawing from Schwab's remarks in the Whipple notes, underscores the Firm's duplicity:

"The Bridge book stirred to life more skeletons in the closet. Captain Jones's son-in-law, D. D. Gage, concluded his family was owed millions more than the paltry sum of $35,000 that was paid them for the patents in the days immediately after the Captain's death, and he wrote Carnegie for restitution. When there was no response to his first letter, he wrote a second demanding the injustice be corrected. Carnegie either refused to accept any responsibility in the matter or couldn't bear to dredge up more memories, so he asked Dod [Carnegie's cousin] to deal with Gage. Dod did so in a perfunctory manner, claiming Jones was lucky to have gotten even $35,000 — a stark contradiction to what Dod had told Schwab, who recalled, "Jones was not very much impressed with his mixer. He seemed to think it was just part of the day's work. But 'Dod' Lauder, who used to sit in my office and tell me he was 'lending dignity' to my administration was the one most enthusiastic. He knew the full impact and although it was costly —well, it meant revolution in the business" (Krass 2002, 452-3),

As Bill Gaughan asked me in 1994, "Tom, how many of those nineteenth century inventions are still in use? Not the Bessemer, not the open hearth, but everyone still talks about the mixer. Who else created something that's still being used today in steel? It's still worth money."

In the Carnegie lawsuit against Cambria in 1895, the original verdict by the U.S. District Court of Western Pennsylvania held that Carnegie Steel alone had a right to use the Jones Hot Metal Mixer and others had to purchase the rights to use it. Cambria appealed and the Circuit Court of Appeals overturned the verdict. The case was then heard by the U.S. Supreme Court and not resolved until 1901. But the case, as we have seen, revealed to the world the windfall profits that owners of steel companies were amassing on the backs of their workers.

At the time of the lawsuit against Cambria, other steel companies were using the Jones Hot Metal Mixer but had not paid royalties. Carnegie was attempting to get all of the money due him for ownership of the patent. The firm had been negotiating the rights to this invention for some time, as is clearly evident when Frick, at the board meeting of Carnegie Steel Company held at Carnegie Building in Pittsburgh on September 13, 1898, reported:

"Had a call this morning from Mr. McCortney, President of the Bellaire Steel Company, who wants to build a Mixer; desired to know on what terms he could arrange. Told him we would not be able to let him know before about the first of November. This was satisfactory to him."

The following year, a decade after Jones's death, Carnegie wrote his cousin Dod Lauder:

My Dear Dod:

All right we can wait for fall for mixer & for the windfall that's sure to come provided somebody doesn't bestow it upon others.

I am dead opposed to settling now with anyone except to assure any intending building that our Royalty will be reasonable not exceeding 50 cents per ton—and that we would not enjoin other building.

That's all the length Ide go

We shall get the verdict sure
Y
AC (1899, January 31)

Finally, the United States Supreme Court refused to consider the lower court's findings, settling the matter in Carnegie's favor. Carnegie Steel (which by 1901 had been purchased by and folded into the new company, U.S. Steel) is the sole owner of Patent 404414 on the mixer and the Jones direct process, which provides the most efficient delivery of iron to Bessemer, open hearth, or any other method of steel conversion (Ginter 1912). The following *Pittsburgh Post-Gazette* clipping came from D. D.'s file.

Washington, D.C., Nov. 8.—Under a decision of the United States Supreme Court today the Cambria Iron Company of Johnstown, Pa., must pay to the Carnegie Steel Company of Pittsburgh $568,305.93, with interest from May 1, 1912, making a total of about $700,000, for infringement of the Jones patent for the direct process of making Bessemer steel. . . .

Capt. Jones, who for years was superintendent of the Edgar Thomson Steel Works at Braddock, and who was killed in an explosion there, was the inventor of the direct process mentioned in the suit. The process makes a material reduction in the cost of production by avoiding the necessity of casting the rough iron into pigs and re-heating it in the converters. In this suit the Cambria company is charged with infringing this patent from November 1, 1895 to October 31, 1898, and in that period it is charged that 520,188,55 tons of metal was converted into steel by this process.

The low court held that this process effected a savings of $1.0925 a ton and it was upon this basis that a verdict of $568,305.93 was given, with interest from the date of the master's report. ("Verdict to Cost Cambria Iron $700,000," 1912, November 8)

We have seen that Carnegie prosecuted vigorously any infringement of patent rights on the mixer, a policy that Joseph Frazier Wall sees as justified (1970, 644). But Wall makes a major mistake: he assumes that Carnegie came by these patents honestly. In the case of the Jones patents, he did not. Peter Krass later made the pertinent observation: "Control of such patents made a critical difference in an industry where a penny a ton gained in effi-

Savings Per Ton: Steelmaking Costs 1890-1898

Date	Billet Cost	% of Total Cost	Coke	Actual Cost
1890	30.32	1/100th	1.32	0.30
1891	25.32	1/100th	1.7	0.25
1892	23.63	1/100th	1.45	0.24
1893	20.44	1/100th	1.35	0.20
1894	16.58	1/100th	1.00	0.17
1895	18.48	1/50	1.30	0.37
1896	18.83	1/50	1.75	0.38
1897	15.08	1/50	1.50	0.31
1898	15.31	1/50	1.45	0.31

(Derived from Kenneth Warren's Triumphant Capitalism, Table 20: Price Trends 1890-1898).

(Pittsburgh, PA: U of Pittsburgh, 1996)

ciency could translate to millions of dollars" (2002, 178).

Stewart Holbrook reported that the Supreme Court's decision on the mixer caused the price of U. S. Steel common stock "to skyrocket" since only U. S. Steel possessed the rights to the Jones Hot Metal Mixer and Jones Direct Process. Subsequently, the price of a ton of rails shot from $23.75 to $28.00 with no effect whatsoever on wages, in fact a little later, wages "were slashed unmercifully" (Holbrook 1939, 261).

After Jones's death, the mixer and process saved the Carnegie Company ten cents per ton through 1895, fifty cents per ton through 1899, and $1.10 through 1912 for every ton of iron converted into steel. Take the year 1899; using fifty cents savings for Carnegie (a cost to be added to rail prices of competitors without patent rights), comparable prices for fuel and transportation fees appear below (Warren 1996, 165, 173).

The savings to Carnegie amounted to two-fifths the cost of ore, or one-fourth the cost of transportation fees, or one-third the cost of fuel (ibid.). Carnegie charged competi-

The Jones Mixer Savings in Steel Production

Jones Mixer savings per ton	$0.50
Mining a ton of ore with 57% iron averaged	$1.25
Cumulative delivery fees for ore ton to Lake Erie*	$1.95
Cost of coke needed to fuel iron per ton of steel	$1.55
1898 price for one-ton steel rail	$17.62

(Derived from Kenneth Warren's Triumphant Capitalism, Table 20: Price Trends 1890-1898).

(Pittsburgh, PA: U of Pittsburgh, 1996)

tors in the United States, England, Germany, France, Belgium, and Austria a similar fee for rights to use Jones's patents for each ton of iron converted to steel for any product (rails, bridge girders, structural steel and soon armor plate, ordinance, and weapons for a world war). For Carnegie, it was a financial goldmine. He realized enormous income, in the millions of dollars each year from all the dozens of steel mills in the world, from patent royalties in addition to savings from not having to pay them.

In 1890 a ton of billet steel cost $30.32. That year the mixer saved Carnegie $.10 or 1/100 of price= $.30 for every billet ton produced. Below in the fourth column is the cost of coke to produce that billet through 1894. The fifth column is the Firm's savings with the mixer, which Lauder and Carnegie would have known. The mixer's savings for years 1895 to 1899 averaged $0.50.

In 1901, the total steel for the United States was 13,474,000 tons (ibid., 174). At $1.10 fee per ton of steel, fees for that patent right amounted to $14,821,400, not including fees for use of the Jones Hot Metal Mixer in Germany, England, France, Belgium, and Austria. Considering $14,821,400 for only the year 1901, the Jones mixer's value to U.S. Steel was far more than Joseph Frazier Wall's extraordinarily low estimate of it being equal in value to the purchase price of the Duquesne Steel Works or one million dollars. The Jones Hot Metal Mixer patent was easily worth one hundred times that.

In 1898 the *New York Times* quoted from the *Iron Trade Review*, as follows:

> The decision in the United States court on the Jones mixer patent is one of far-reaching importance to the steel manufacturers of the country. The common use of the direct process by the Bessemer Steel Works and the economic advantage resulting from the interposition of a hot metal reservoir between the blast furnace and the converter have made it an almost indispensable adjunct of steel making in this day of cheap steel and close competition. If the decision just given shall be sustained in the court of last resort it can be ap-

preciated that enormous tribute will come to the Pittsburg company in royalties and penalties and that by so much will its competitors be handicapped in the race for cheapest production.

In essence, the owner of the Jones Hot Metal Mixer patent had a tremendous advantage in the steel industry (Department of the Interior, Liber N. 40: 479).

Lauder's letters and Carnegie's testimony raise a more general issue: how autonomous is an employee who claims ownership of inventions developed during work? The Supreme Court differentiated between trifling devices and major innovations that were created by geniuses like Edison, Bell, and Jones:

> The process of development in manufactures creates a constant demand for new appliances, which the skill of the ordinary head-workmen and engineers is generally adequate to devise, and which, indeed, are the natural and proper outgrowth of such development. Each step forward prepares the way for the next, and each is usually taken by spontaneous trials in a hundred different places. To grant a single party a monopoly of every slight advance made, except where the exercise of invention somewhat above the ordinary mechanical or engineering skill is distinctly shown, is unjust in principle and injurious in its consequences. It was never the object of [the patent] laws to grant a monopoly for every trifling device, every shadow of a shade of an idea, which would naturally and spontaneously occur to any skilled mechanic or operator in the ordinary progress of manufactures. Such an indiscriminate creation of exclusive privileges tends rather to obstruct than to stimulate invention. (Usselman1984, 1059)

So, in this case, the patent belonged to the inventor, who had a monopoly thereof because this invention is above ordinary mechanical or engineering skill. No one during Bill Jones's life or in the 120 years since has considered the Jones Hot Metal Mixer anything but an ingenious and indispensable invention. The patent from the government lists Jones, and only Jones, as the sole owner. Under oath Carnegie states "The great merit of the Jones invention is that it was a commercial success as well as a successful invention. That is the reason that most works wished to adopt it" (The Cambria Iron Company vs. The Carnegie Steel Company, 653). If Jones, taking his patents, had become a competitor in Youngstown, where transportation fees for ore would be considerably less than for ore carried to Pittsburgh, the additional savings from having the mixer would have damaged Carnegie absolutely and relatively in the steel marketplace. Because he knew its value, Carnegie had to find a way, any way, to bring it into his possession. How far would Carnegie have gone, knowing that he was losing his most valuable employee and all his patented inventions?

Turning to the absence of correspondence between Jones and Carnegie after 1885, it is pertinent to digress into the matter of document creation and retention prior to digitization. At ET, among managers and board representatives, the annual letterbox provided copies of correspondences, written dialogues between two parties. There appears to be only one letterbox extant of Captain Bill Jones and that is for the year 1877. This was retrieved by Bill Gaughan, who salvaged it when the superintendent's office at ET was renovated sometime after the 1970s; it is now in the William Gaughan collection at Pittsburgh's Hillman Archive. There must be letterboxes at Clayton in Pittsburgh, though to my knowledge only Kenneth Warren has been granted access to Frick's archives.

Composing a letter required the official or his secretary to write in longhand the discourse for the intended audience. A carbon sheet registered an impression of the original, like that John Steinbeck received from my father, the 50,000 word, proto-palimpsest of this book. Jones employed a hard-drinking secretary named Getty (Whipple n.d.). In the few handwritten letters available, Getty's penmanship is distinct, as he is the scrivener who copied out the many letters of resignation Jones stuffed into his pockets to present to Carnegie. Nearly all of the letters available from Jones and Carnegie have been copied at some time by typewriter. Onion skin paper with impressed graphite lingers as a record of communication.

Jones and Carnegie teamed to out-produce all other steel mills in the world; is it likely that for the last forty-eight months of their joint labor—from late September 1885 to the Captain's death in 1889—there was no correspondence? I tallied correspondence I was able to locate between the two men. There were twenty-seven letters between 1875 and 1877, thirty-eight between 1878 and 1881, and twenty-one between 1882 and 1885. In March of 1877 alone, there were eight letters exchanged and in November of 1880, there are six. On the same day in November 1882, Jones wrote two lengthy letters to Carnegie and on December 18, 1883, he wrote three! How can there have been no correspondence in the final four years of Jones's life? During that time, Carnegie was ill and his brother, Tom, and his mother died. Carnegie's articles, likely inspired by Jones's views, were published in the *Forum*; the Haymarket Riot over the eight-hour day and Carnegie's push for a sliding salary scale took place; the Jones Hot Metal Mixer was invented and patented; and Jones was promoted to chief engineer for the Carnegie, Phipps, & Co. Given that the quantity and detailed nature of Carnegie's correspondence to men like Frick when important matters were at stake has been well documented (Warren, 1973, p. 148), it is unreasonable to believe that there was no correspondence with Bill Jones for such an extended period. As I have noted above, over the years Jones wrote many notes to Carnegie regarding mill functions. There must have been notes about when the mixer would be installed and about its potential to save money and about the royalties the company would pay for its use. Carnegie was able to quote the cost to install the mixer at $48,000 quite accurately seven years later.

Why would there be a four-year gap? Either Carnegie or someone else must have removed the letters typed from carbons, and, for the years 1878-1888, the letterboxes, leaving no report of events after September 1885. Perhaps the correspondence that must have been there was deleted around the time of the Cambria lawsuit in 1895. The removal of Jones's letters would hide something, but what?

Immediately following Jones's accident on Thursday evening, two doctors in Braddock attended the badly burned Captain. Later that night at Pittsburgh Homeopathy Hospital, another pair treated him in the presence of his brother John Lewis. He was conscious, and recovery was expected, and this was reported in the local newspapers and by Jones's brother, sister, and daughter to the rest of the family and noted by Henry Clay Frick in correspondence. Nowhere in the press interview with this team of doctors is there any reference to a head wound or lack of consciousness. However, writings after the turn of the century, beginning with Gayley's account in Casson's *The Romance of Steel* assert that the Captain never regained consciousness after being thrown from the platform high up in front of the furnace (Casson 1907, 32). Gayley, who had become ET's superintendent of furnaces in 1885 and was present at the explosion, is the likely source of this version of events, and even reputable scholars like Wall and Warren have perpetuated this error of blurring if Jones was conscious. What might have led to the glaring discrepancy between the records at the time of the accident and the reports, that is, the summaries, the interpretations, and inferences to be passed on from one writer to another, years later, continuing to the present?

Jones had been on the verge of leaving Carnegie for Youngstown, taking with him the rights to his more than fifty inventions, including that of the Jones Hot Metal Mixer. As Peter Krass called to my attention in a telephone conversation, Carnegie in late summer was looking for British buyers to get him and Phipps out of the steel business. This might have been sufficient motive to commit a crime. The lack of extant correspondences between the inventor of the Jones Hot Metal Mixer and Carnegie, in addition to Lauder's misrepresentations to my grandparents, raise the question: could Carnegie, in some manner, be connected to the death of Captain Bill? It certainly implicates him in the defrauding of Harriet Jones.

That Andrew Carnegie would stop at nothing to achieve his fortune and maintain his absolute control over his company is well-documented, as is the fact that he was most ruthless and unforgiving in his dealings with those who worked for him and with him. Carnegie was skilled in relegating and/or humiliating those who clashed with him. Jones's comrade at Fredericksburg and Chancellorsville, Henry Curry, is a case in point. Curry returned to Pittsburgh after the Civil War to devote his life to Carnegie iron and steel. Carnegie offered a partnership to Curry, who accepted in 1884. Curry then amassed the sixth greatest number of shares after Carnegie, Phipps, Frick, Lauder, and Schwab, respectively. He died in 1899 with $5,000,000 in stock in the Carnegie Steel Company, $771,183 of stock in Frick's coal company, and an account of $81,486 (Warren 1996, 255-6).

Such a fortune can turn a loyal partner into a sycophant. However, Curry's courage returned to him on his deathbed when he supported Frick against Carnegie, when the latter attempted to eject Frick. Of those on the board, only Curry, Lovejoy, and Phipps did not sign the agreement to force Frick to sell his shares in the company at book value without interest. During Carnegie's final visit to the dying partner, he asked why Curry voted against him.

"Mr. Frick is my friend," Curry uttered.

"And am I not also your friend?" asked Carnegie.

"Yes, but Mr. Frick has never humiliated me," said Curry to Carnegie with nearly his last breath (Bridge1991).

My uncle Dan wrote to Joseph Frazier Wall that Bill Jones told his family that one of the reasons he never accepted Carnegie's offers of partnership was "I do not trust the man." Contrasting Carnegie and Frick, Jones told his daughter, "I don't particularly like Frick, or do I admire him, but you know where you stand. With Carnegie it is a different matter, he is a side-stepper" (1972, March 2).

Perhaps the best contemporary judge of Carnegie's probity was Henry Frick, who had a checkered relationship with "the Scot" during their twelve years together at the Carnegie companies and H. C. Frick Coke Company. Frick's duration was only two years shy of the years that Jones endured with Carnegie. When Carnegie tried to cheat Frick, as he had Kloman, Shinn, Scott, Miller, and others, Frick wrote to him: "For years I have been convinced that there is not an honest bone in your body. Now I know that you are a god damned thief. We will have a judge and jury of Allegheny County decide what you are to pay me" (Standiford 2005). Frick, who had the means to challenge Carnegie in the courts, won this suit, which lends authority to his accusation. The loss destroyed Carnegie's company, and he soon sold out for more than four hundred million dollars, making him the world's richest man at the time.   For a century, Carnegie has been criticized by his biographers for misrepresentation and twisting facts. At the end of the twentieth century, James Howard Bridge wrote:

> *Carnegie has been criticized by his biographers for twisting facts.*

> . . . and of them all [faulty sources of information about the history of 'things Carnegian'] I found Andrew Carnegie's own narrative the least trustworthy. Knowing how excellent is his verbal memory, it puzzled me to find him mistaking his own birth-year; claiming to have been the first in America to operate the Bessemer process of steel-making; to have originated iron railway bridges; to have been the founder of the business that bears his name; to have been ever on the alert to adopt new processes and mechanical improvements; to have maintained without a break the friendliest of relations with his partners; to have been the principal factor in the gigantic growth of the business; to have fervently tried to carry his high ideals concerning labor into his own works. Instead of this I everywhere found proof of the contrary; and when, finally, I was notified that I must agree to submit my manuscript to the usual Carnegie revision before I could count on any assistance of the present officers of the company, my disillusionment was complete. (1991)

At the opening of the twenty-first century, Peter Krass wrote of Carnegie's inaccuracies as reformulations of fact: "While seemingly a trivial revision, [Carnegie's side of a story] was not, because it was part of a more duplicitous pattern of revisionism that emerged once Andy began to attain prestige. He felt it necessary to refine, aggrandize, and sanitize much of his life, some of it to prove painful to others" (2002, 42).

Ultimately, Carnegie's honesty and legacy must be judged by the record, for example, his statement under oath in 1895 when he asserted that Captain Bill "made many improvements in our works. I think he did not trouble himself much about taking out patents." Contrast this assertion with the reality that between May 15, 1888, and June 4, 1889, Jones had filed six letter patents with the U.S. Department of the Interior. In the 1895 deposition Carnegie conveniently ignored the fact that two of those patents, whose worth, documented at more than fourteen million dollars in the single year of 1901, were evidence of Jones "troubling himself" to take out patents.

We have reviewed Carnegie's misstatements regarding Jones's declining offers to be a partner as late as the day when he was wounded in the explosion, September 26. It is unlikely, that Carnegie—who had other business that day—would have delegated to Frick the offer of a partnership and the negotiations for royalties on a patent Jones owned. Carnegie, undeterred by the contradictions in his deposition, goes on to say: "In the case of this patent, [Jones] wanted $35,000 for a special purpose, and asked the firm to give it to him, and we credited him on the books, paying 6% interest, subject to his call, and he was notified of this, not four hours before he was killed in our service" (Cambria Iron Co. v. Carnegie Steel Co. (1899). US Circuit Ct. of Appeals, p. 650). The verb "killed" begs for a missing agent. Carnegie, under oath, did not say "he *died* in our service."

Is this wording a slip of the tongue? Which antecedent for the occasion of this meeting did Carnegie have in mind: September 26, the day of the explosion, with Jones left conscious and concerned for the other men and his family and glad to have his eye sight? Or September 28 when Captain Jones was under the care of new physicians, with only the immediate family and Carnegie with his chosen associates allowed access to the patient?

And what was the "special purpose" for which Carnegie states that Jones needed the money that same evening? There is no answer provided by the four members of my family who discussed these events with the Captain's daughter. We know from McCleary that on September 26 Jones was asking Frick for money to offset cost overrides for a church (1933, March 9). Would this agnostic gladly give up his patents to pay off the debt of someone else's church, particularly when the debt was only $11,000? Jones surely knew the worth of his patent.

Carnegie's likely agents in carrying out the defrauding of Harriet Jones and later distorting what occurred were James Gayley and William Yost, who witnessed Harriet's last will and testament in 1890. Wall sized Gayley up as one of the board members who "knew how to drive his subordinates to get the most out of them, stayed in the good graces of Carnegie . . . and did nothing to rock the boat (1970, 667). In 1899 Carnegie gave him the five shares necessary to become a board member and stand with Carnegie against Frick in the bitter ousting of Frick from Carnegie Steel.

William Yost was in an untenable position. He had long been the family lawyer and had come to Braddock with Jones and others deserting the Cambria works. But he had now become the corporate lawyer for Carnegie Company. The major conflict of interest in which he found himself should have prevented him from dealing with Harriet Jones, because his own financial interest was tied to Carnegie Brothers. Bill Jones had so much else on his mind that September: his suffering wife's downward spiral of health and mind; his anticipating the move to Youngstown; his bitterness over the Johnstown Flood, resulting from

Handwritten excerpt from letter to the author from Carnegie biographer, Joseph Wall

the pleasure lake above Johnstown — Pittsburgh's wealthy had neglected to repair, the members' use of the press to blame the Hunkies, as if like the Bard's "to busy giddy minds/ With foreign quarrels." Replacing Yost likely ranked low on his to-do list.

Though I have no proof, I believe that Yost had drawn up at least one other will, perhaps more, for Captain Bill during the 1880s, which was destroyed after the accident. It is not credible that Bill Jones would possess so many patents, as well as a dwelling, the town mansion only dwarfed by the new Braddock Library, and fail to update his will in view of how diligently he had designed his Plan.

Yet, his Plan could never have anticipated for the terrible accident and its consequences. Mimi Yost's letters to Cora in Europe, for obvious reasons, had never mentioned the Jones Hot Metal Mixer or that Carnegie had been battling with Johnstown over royalty fees for the Captain's invention. The legal issues had begun in 1895, and the lawsuit had been going on for many years by the time former California governor Henry Gage brought it to D. D. and Cora's attention. In 1903, Bridge in *The Inside History of the Carnegie Steel Company* had reported how the Jones mixer and his many other innovations had saved the company "millions of dollars every year" (80, 105). The thought of Captain Jones's coveted invention helping to make Carnegie the richest man in the world made members of the family furious: Carnegie had committed fraud against them, and they wanted to prove it.

According to Bill Gaughan "it takes a ton of steel to make a Cadillac." At $1.10 per ton of iron converted to steel, Captain Jones would have earned from 1/60th to 1/100 the cost of every ton of steel produced at ET from 1890 to 1898 and his family would have lived very comfortably just from the royalties on the Cadillacs made in the last century—excluding rail, nail, boxcars, bridges, ships, guns, tanks, fifty-five-gallon drums, and the structural steel in the world's skylines.

Instead, due to the "deal" that Yost offered to the ailing, sedated, and grieving Harriet Jones, she received a single lump sum of $35,000 for the patents. Carnegie could have offered Harriet Jones shares of Carnegie stock, which the Captain had passed up many times. Perhaps 885 shares, as were given to Thomas Morrison, Carnegie's cousin, who presided over Duquesne. Perhaps 147 shares, which were awarded to D. G. Kerr, of whose service to the company I have been unable to find any record other than that he, with two others, dodged in the right direction when a furnace exploded.

Was Carnegie, directly or indirectly, responsible for Captain Jones's death? All the evidence leads me to answer in the affirmative. How might it have happened? With control over access to Jones's hospital room, it would have been easy to lay a pillow over the face of the sedated patient for just thirty seconds or so, then remove it, and respectfully leave the room. I have come to believe that it is just such a scenario that came to pass. I have always thought it extremely strange that Carnegie kept Jones's picture in the bedroom where he died. Was it that guilt plagued his soul?

In 1995, I shared this possibility with my Pittsburgh friends, but they wanted nothing to do with it. But I did not have the pieces of the puzzle I do now: that Jones had been negotiating with Youngstown, about which Carnegie may have been privy. In 1995 I ventured the theory that a crime had been committed to Kenneth Warren—Frick's and Schwab's biographer — the one researcher who has had access to the Frick Archive. He recalled that the correspondence among Frick, Schwab, Carnegie and Leishman might suggest some nefarious secret among them. Leishman had joined Carnegie Steel as vice-chairman in 1887, but Carnegie, according to Wall, treated him mercilessly until he was forced out. But things changed. Leishman ultimately became U.S. Ambassador to Italy and later, Germany, and he repeatedly asked the three for money in a tone suggesting earlier success, as if he "held some important leverage over Carnegie Steel" (Warren, 1995, summer in interview at Hexham, Northumberland, UK.).

Historians and authors unrelated to the family have registered interest in discrepancies among the sources and alarm about possible injustice. Several have raised with me the issue of the fate of the many patents. In 1995 at that dinner at Pittsburgh's Poli's Restaurant at Squirrel Hill, Bill Gaughan and David Demarest wondered how Carnegie secured the Cradle of Civilization along with many of the other patents. I spent fall semester 1998 traveling with my wife, Anita, on my last sabbatical in India. During that period a B.B.C. reporter, interested in the concurrent production of a video docudrama on Carnegie, left a message on voice mail at my office at Humboldt State University. Some months later when I returned I called Ms. Rachael Grant, who had learned of my work on Captain Jones. Her questions dealt with why and how the many patents were so quickly transferred from Jones's family to the Carnegie firm. Since the television project had been wrapped and was to be aired in Britain soon, I thought it injudicious, given the extent of my research at that point, to share with her much of what appears here.

As I incrementally uncovered what I record in this book, previous skeptics began to reconsider. The most authoritative biographer, Joseph Frazier Wall, wrote that he too was "mystified as you . . . why there was almost no correspondence between Capt. Bill & AC in the Carnegie papers. Carnegie was very meticulous in keeping his correspondence . . .," (Wall to Thomas Gage, 1995). After publishing my article "Hands-On, All Over (Tom Gage 1998), the editor of *Pittsburgh History*, after rummaging through Carnegie's papers and discovering the gap in correspondences, telephoned me, breathlessly, expressing that the hairs on his neck curled, and he thought I might be right about Jones not dying of natural causes.

The inconsistent accounts that I found regarding Captain Bill's activities on the day of the accident, regarding Jones's state of consciousness following the accident, and regarding how the Captain's patents were secured are effects. These effects indicate a cause. I believe that cause to be a cover-up. Jones meticulously patented dozens of inventions in his and only his name. Jones did not trust, never had trusted, Carnegie and refused to make any deal with him other than for his annual salary. Jones was going to Youngstown to start up a new plant with a new partner. Jones spent the afternoon with Frick to obtain funding to pay for a church building. These "tracks" do not square with either Carnegie's testimony of 1895 or Lauder's letter of 1906 that Jones was settling on a buy-out for the Jones Hot Metal Mixer "for a special purpose." For what would Jones need money? He gave more of it away than any man in Braddock at the time of his death and that includes Carnegie. ("Grief in Braddock: The Entire Town Mourns the Death of Capt. W. R. Jones," 9/30/89.)

A plethora of musty old documents celebrate many aspects of Jones's achievements. The Captain was "the greatest steelmaker of all time, either in America or in foreign parts" (Holbrook 1939, 209) and "the man who, Henry Bessemer said, knew more about steel than any other man in America." I also discovered how important Jones was in fostering philanthropy, which may have inspired Carnegie, whose charity began while under Jones's influence (Stevenson, n.d. n.p.). Holbrook compared the fame of Jones and Carnegie, as reported by those still alive in the 1930s: "But inside the steel business, where men knew the hows and whys of things, the boys talked of Andy Carnegie hardly at all as a steelmaster. They talked endlessly and admiringly of this dynamo of a Captain Bill Jones. The likes of him had never been seen" (1939, 211). And finally, according to the local Braddock register:

> Here must have been a remarkable man. After a lapse of almost 30 years his aging employees still glow with pleasure at the mention of his name, and the most calm and philosophic of them flush with resentment at the suggestion that he could have had a fault. The whole world, in fact, seems leagued together to give this man a title of nobility which it will forever defend. Frankly admitted on all sides is the fact that Jones had a fiery temper. Beyond that, the most cynical, the most philosophic of his men utterly refused to say one word that is not complimentary to the dead lion, and the conscientious historian can do nothing but record eulogy on eulogy. (1917, 107)

A memorial photograph of the Carnegie Veterans Association, 1912, with portrait of Captain Bill Jones (front row) more than 20 years after his death.

(Rivers of Steel NHA Museum, Homestead PA)

(Annandale Archives, Boyers PA)

AFTERWORD

THE JOURNEY

On June 12th, 1994, I boarded a United Airlines flight for Pittsburgh in quest of answers at the Annandale Archives, a large storage facility located in a former limestone mine, near Boyers, Pennsylvania, where the US Patent and Trademark Office stores original records. Arriving at an airport abuzz with newscasts of the infamous murder trial of O.J. Simpson, I drove a rental car toward the city of Butler, likely named after the man who planned to hijack the Captain from Carnegie. Deep into the Appalachian Mountains, I drove in a moonless night, following the directions that the superintendent of the Annandale Archives had given me over the phone. There, I spent the night before heading for the Annandale Archives of U.S.X., banked deep in some mine some miles further north in the town of Boyers.

Early the next morning, I left the motel for Boyers. My crazy shorthand notes for directions instructed me as I drove: I was to arrive and park next to an outhouse-like structure where I'd find a telephone with which to call in. Over every mile, I had been listening to the radio hearing that the wife of a charismatic football hero and Hollywood celebrity had been murdered and that O. J. Simpson looked guilty. Baffled, I drove on for what seemed like miles with no signs of life except an occasional cow before spotting a lone MiniMart, where I parked to get directions. It was a very hot day.

The woman proprietor of this all-service outpost hailed me before I could even pose my questions, as if she intuitively knew my destination.

"You've went too far. Didn't yah see that road back there, bout thousand yards. Well, that where yah shoulda turned left. Don't feel bad, they all do. Just head west for two miles. Won't see nothin' until the cars. No signs, just park and head in."

Thanking her for her experienced wisdom, I drove back to turn and continue past deserted land save for the occasional dwelling or abandoned RV, growing a refrigerator or wash tub. And there, as I made the turn, were the cars: three-layered tiers of parking lots stepping up a mountain--no signs, as my oracle proprietor had assured. I only found empty parking spaces at the top.

I walked down the steaming asphalt paths, provided with railings down to the entrance of the mine, with complementing silver sheathing rock faces meeting at a vast portcullis, a huge closed garage door and the entrance of opaque glass reinforced with chicken wire. Before I was within thirty feet, that door opened and out came an official to greet me in a reverse baseball cap with a holster packing a gun.

"You need help?"

"Is this the Annandale Archives? I have an appointment with Superintendent Mennett."

Settling back and seemingly relaxed, he replied "Oh, you haven't gone far enough. It's in the other side of this same mountain. In Boyers."

I retreated, panting, after the hike back in that heat. I drove back down and headed on. I switched radio stations back and forth from the Simpson saga to the opening of a national golf tournament just west in Ohio. Maybe six miles farther, my car slowed into Boyers and the outhouse was the first thing I saw on the skirts of the hamlet. I telephoned from there and waited a couple of minutes before a pickup surfaced

A shuttle bus drives through the gates of the Annandale Archives to the parking area. (Annandale Archives, Boyers PA)

from the mine; the driver waved for me to follow him into the mountain or cave.

Into the gloom I followed his red tail lights, at times progressing too far away causing me to speed in the narrow channel, until too many minutes later when we entered a cavernous hall with only a light ahead of us illuminating a door of a broad cylinder block facade, with darkness to the far right where shapes of pickups, cars, and small vans appeared parked. We entered into a blaze of neon color, with men and women sitting at desks or striding down long corridors full of boxes stacked to the rough rock ceiling, irregularly reaching to dirt and rock.

At the offices housed within the Annandale Archives, employees sit at desks with boxes stacked to the rough rock ceiling of the mountain fortress. (Annandale Archives, Boyers PA)

In the next six days, I learned there that this hollowed mountain had been the source of shale needed in blast furnaces for over a century, that later in the 1950s, the executives of U.S.X. had squirreled away supplies for themselves and their families to endure the plutonium winter after our nuclear war with the U.S.S.R. Then there came a period when Congress

241

> *I had a clear sense that the archives in Butler County and Washington, DC had been picked over.*

provided tax write-offs for building bomb shelters until Anthony Ostroff, poet and friend at U.C. Berkeley, hived more than a million letters to Congress from citizens who favored peace initiatives rather than war preparations leading to the Vietnam War. His record of these correspondences continued until the period following the Kennedy assassination to outlaw guns. "Here are the types of things that we often find," the superintendent said, handing me olive green tins of preserved foods like the war rationed supplies used when I was a child in Oakland during World War II.

In that mountain's stable temperature of 56 degrees Fahrenheit, I read and wrote and copied documents that are still filed in boxes at my home, all while outside temperatures reached over a hundred degrees and the U.S. Open persisted while O.J. and his friend cruised the Los Angeles freeways followed by fleets of police cars.

In my search, I peeled through the documents in the 54 boxes forklifted to my dining table-sized desk in the Archives. I often patiently waited while women at the duplication machines finished their tasks. I, great-grandson of the company legend, may have been the only scholar allowed these privileges, I learned, when Joseph Frazier Wall informed me in a note that he never was granted access to the Archives office.

"Superintendent Mennett, let's me ask you a question," and I shared with him my curious tale of wandering the wrong roads of his Appalachia. "Where had I first mistakenly gone before coming here?"

"Oh, that's the other side of the mine," he replied. "In fact, from here, you could once actually reach that guard at the door. That side of the mountain houses Social Security records for all the citizens of the United States."

In the modern office deep in an Appalachian mountain, I raked through unmarked boxes looking for answers to learn more about the man so often the subject of stories told me by four family members who generationally bridged the events of this story, three of whom had read his disappeared biography written by my grandfather.

Summers passed as I poured over those reams of documents. In addition, I finally addressed notes, records, and letters left me from those who'd passed away. In addition, I drilled deeper into texts provided me by Humboldt State University's Interlibrary Loan Office, documents that complemented what I knew from the oral history of my family.

I had found fewer than one hundred letters by, or from, or about, Jones between 1875 and 1889 in addition to what I gleaned from Bill Gaughan, Jones's 1877 letterbox.

Surely, Carnegie and Jones corresponded during these feverish years when America, led by ET, surged ahead of all other nations in steel production. Surely, during the strike of 1887, they wrote one another about Carnegie's sabotaging of Jones's 8-hour day. Surely, the two discoursed on the potential of the Jones Mixer and the process, which still today operates between furnaces and torpedo cars carrying glowing iron to conversion furnaces. Surely, Jones would have registered his anguish to Carnegie and Henry Clay Frick after returning to Pittsburgh with the 300 Edgar Thomson workers that he drafted for relief efforts after the Johnstown Flood—a flood killing nearly three thousand people because of the Robber Barons' pleasure lake. Surely, Jones must have voiced his dismay with the owners who built the South Fork Fishing and Hunting Club directly responsible for the South Fork dam that caused the flood, until 9/11/01, one of America's greatest disasters caused by human hand.

I had a clear sense that the archives in Butler County and Washington, DC had been picked over. Carnegie, that model of propriety among those zealous believers of the survival of the fittest, had seen it fit that his trail was cleared of nasty affairs. This was the man, who fled to Scotland, when Frick faced the Homestead Strike three years later, though according to both Demarest and Gaughan the two were in continual contact via Morris code. There had been a cover-up, but of what: industrial sabotage? Perhaps murder? Definitely swindle.

I believe they were, so as to erase, at the very least, any evidence that would refute Carnegie's contention during the suit against Cambria that Jones agreed to sell the patent four hours before his death; perhaps, also, to erase the animosity between the two that Grandmother remembered vividly.

And from working so closely with these letters and testimony, I feel the presence of one ever looking over my shoulder as Jones, the cavalier, the social activist, who in many endeavors dealt with major crises of his time, including management and labor, the extent of individual property rights, all of which persist today, a century later. The Janus Carnegie, too, reveals himself through these documents as a public Carnegie, claiming to be a socialist, whose philanthropy erases a private, vengeful and petty Carnegie, who elevated his five-foot two inch stature by dragging down and humiliating others except my great-grandfather, whom he might have ultimately felled.

When Carnegie died, some thirty years after Bill Jones, the only adornment in his bedchamber was a portrait of the Captain, on which Carnegie could gaze from his bed. (Hendrick 1932, 383).

BIBLIOGRAPHY

Prelude

Barr, A. P., ed. *Zadig's Method: The Major Prose of Thomas Henry Huxley.* Athens, GA: University of Georgia Press, 1997.

Wall, Joseph Frazier. *Andrew Carnegie.* New York: Oxford, 1970.

Preface

Bell, Thomas. *Out of this Furnace: a Novel of Immigrant Labor in America.* Pittsburgh: University of Pittsburgh Press, 1941/1976.

Cambor, Kathleen. *In Sunlight, in a Beautiful Garden.* New York: Farrar, Straus & Giroux, 2001.

Davenport, Marcia. *The Valley of Decision: a Novel of Steel.* Pittsburgh: University of Pittsburgh Press, 1942/1989.

Gage, Tom. "Steinbeck Knew Dad Better than I Did." In *East of Eden: New and Recent Essays,* edited by Henry Veggian. Amsterdam: Ropodi, 2012.

Gazette Times (Pittsburgh, PA). Late edition. "Lloyd George Appeals for United Action by America and Britain to Prevent Wars." October 25, 1923.

Krass, Peter. *Carnegie.* New York: Wiley, 2002.

Whipple, Sidney B. Notes. Charles Schwab Papers. Hagley Museum and Library, Wilmington, DE.

Introduction

Casson, Herbert N. *The Romance of Steel: the Story of a Thousand Millionaires.* New York: A.S. Barnes, 1907.

Gage, William R. "To My Kith and Kin." In the author's possession.

Gage, Daniel D. To Joseph Frazier Wall, March 11, 1972. Copy in the author's possession.

Holbrook, Stewart H. To Daniel Gage, October 11, 1939. In the author's possession.

[Jones, William R.] To Andrew Carnegie, November 9, 1880. In the author's passion.

McHugh, Jeanne. *Alexander Holley and the Makers of Steel.* Baltimore: Johns Hopkins University Press, 1980.

Shakespeare, William. *The Complete Works of William Shakespeare.* Edited by Geoffrey Cumberlege. Oxford, UK: Oxford University Press, 1955.

Wall, Joseph Frazier. To Professor Tom Gage, October 5, 1995. In the author's possession.

Chapter 1

Biographical Sketch of Jones. Andrew Carnegie Papers. Library of Congress, 45722.

Bridge, James H. *The Inside History of Carnegie Steel Company: a Romance of Millions.* Pittsburgh: University of Pittsburgh Press, 1991.

Cambria (PA) Tribune. "The Copperhead Organ of Facts." April 22, 1863.

Cambria (PA) Tribune. "The Copperheads and Foreign Intervention." April 1, 1863.

Cambria (PA) Tribune. W. R. Jones, letter to the editor. April 3, 1863.

Cambria (PA) Tribune. "Union Leagues." April 1, 1863.

Casson, Herbert N. *The Romance of Steel: a Story of a Thousand Millionaires.* New York: A. S. Barnes, 1907. Also available at file:///Users/tomgage/Desktop/Full%20text%20 of%20%22The%20romance%20of%20steel%3B%20the%20story%20of%20a%20 thousand%20millionaires%22.webarchive.

Contemporary Biography of Pennsylvania. "Jones, Capt. Bill." http://books.google. com/books?id=r7IbAQAAMAAJ&pg=PA199&pg=PA199&dq=Contemporary+Biogra-phy+of+Pennsylvania&source=bl&ots=Ja6VUZgi70&sig=iNGY7Hs9FqODSyvZxrrxFmKT-KNA&hl=en&sa=X&ei=NklmT6HKciliALB39iiDw&ved=OCDYQ6AEwAw#v=onepage&q=-Contemporary%20Biography%20of%20Pennsylvania&f=false.

Duram, J. and E. Duram, eds. *Hartsock, Soldier of the Cross: Civil War Diary and Correspon-dence of Reverend Andrew Jackson Hartsock.* Manhattan, KS: American Military Institute, 1979. The humorless Hartsock entered the following in his diary on May 16: "Somebody tried to blow Gen. Humphreys up last night. A gun barrel was filled with powder and put in the ground, covered with stones, and then put off. It made a great noise, but no one was hurt.

Faust, Drew G. *The Republic of Suffering: Death and the American Civil War.* New York: Thorndike, 2008.

Gallagher, G. W. *Chancellorsville: The Battle and Its Aftermath.* Chapel Hill: University of North Carolina Press, 1996.

Gayley, Alice J. "76th Regiment, Pennsylvania Volunteers." ://www.pa-roots. com/~pacw/76thorg.html. September 26, 2002

Gray, Wood. *The Hidden Civil War: the Story of the Copperheads.* New York: Viking, 1942.

Green, Wilson. "Morale, Maneuver, and Mud: The Army of the Potomac, December 16, 1862-January 26, 1863." In *The Fredericksburg Campaign*, edited by G. W. Gallagher. Chap-el Hill: University of North Carolina Press, 1995.

Hamilton, Bentley E. *The Union League: Its Origin and Achievement in the Civil War.* Illinois State Historical Society, 1921.

Hennessy, J. J. "We Shall Make Richmond Howl: the Army of the Potomac on the Eve of Chancellorsville." In *Chancellorsville: the Battle and its Aftermath,* edited by G. W. Gallagher. Chapel Hill: University of North Carolina Press, 1996.

Humphreys, Henry H. *Major General Andrew Atkinson Humphreys at Fredericksburg.* Chicago: R. R. McCabe. 1886. You would think the discussion as to who got closest to the wall dealt with touch football; was it Humphreys's two brigades that attacked at 5:00 p.m. or those with Crouch in the earlier advance with the Second Corps? Accompanying his father in that charge, Henry Humphreys sustained a debate for half a century that his father's brigades came closest, nearly reaching the wall. Both Humphreys's son, a year older than Jones, and those from among Confederate officers who remembered what they saw looking down at the slaughter identified Humphreys's brigades and verified that Jones and his comrades under Allabach came closest to the wall.

Ingham, John N. *Making Iron and Steel: Independent Mills in Pittsburgh, 1820-1920*. Columbus: Ohio State University, 1991.

Jones Burned the Government Works at Harpers Ferry. In Biographical Sketch of Jones. Andrew Carnegie Papers. Library of Congress, 45722.

Johnstown (PA) Democrat. Editorial. April 18, 1863.

Johnstown (PA) Democrat. *"From the 12th Regiment Penna Reserves: Our Army Correspondence."* March 31, 1863.

Johnstown (PA) Democrat. February 23, 1864.

Johnstown (PA) Democrat. "Our Army Correspondence." April 15, 1863.

Johnstown (PA) Democrat. "Our Army Correspondence." April 29, 1863.

Johnstown (PA) Democrat. "Reign of Terror in Ohio." May 13, 1863.

Johnstown (PA) Democrat. "Revolution in the North." April 29, 1863.

Johnstown (PA) Democrat. Late edition. "Union League Conspiracy—Their Founders: In Johnstown: Cyrus Elder, lawyer; Robert W. Hunt, Morrell's chemist; George McLane, boss of laborers; Samual Do Boggs, clerk; Ino A. Bowman, publisher of Abolitionist organ [the Cambria Tribune] and US assessor of taxes; E. Schafer, no one in particular; Douglas, coal-weigher; James A. Lane, iron-weigher; Albert Gregg, miller." April 22, 1863.

Johnstown (PA) Democrat. "Union League." April 8, 1863. "Witness Wendell Phillips [famous abolitionist] who says—I am proud to say I have successfully devoted nineteen years of my life to the destruction of the Union."

Johnstown (PA) Democrat. "Union Leagues—Their Objects—Their Founders." April 15, 1863.

Johnstown (PA) Democrat. Morning edition. "Desertion." April 8, 1863.

Jonesboro (IL) Gazette. Editorial. April 4, 1863.

Krick, Robert K. "The Smoothbore Volley that Doomed the Confederacy." In *The Fredericksburg Campaign*, edited by G. W. Gallagher. Chapel Hill: University of North Carolina Press, 1995.

Knowles, Anne Kelly. "Labor, Race, and Technology in the Confederate Iron Industry." *Tech-*

nology and Culture 42, no.1 (2001): 1-28.

Lippard, George. *The Quaker City.* Edited by David S. Reynolds. Amherst, MA: University of Massachusetts Press, 1995.

Livermore, T. L. *Numbers & Losses in the Civil War in America: 1861-65.* Bloomington, IN: Indiana University Press, 1957.

Manakee, H. R. *Maryland in the Civil War.* Baltimore: Maryland Historical Society, 1959.

McKenna, C. F. "The Hoe-Down, Co. E of 155th Regimental Association." In Under the Maltese Cross, Antietam to Appomattox: The Loyal Uprising in Western Pennsylvania, 1861-1865. Library of Congress, 121 (1013487), 1987.

Menand, *Louis. The Metaphysical Club: a Story of Ideas in America. New York: Farrar, 2001.*

Rable, George. "It is Well that War is So Terrible: The Carnage at Fredericksburg." In *The Fredericksburg Campaign,* edited by G. W. Gallagher. Chapel Hill: University of Carolina Press, 1995.

Raftsman's Journal (Clearfield, PA). Editorial. May 20, 1863.

Reardon, Carol. "The Forlorn Hope." In *The Fredericksburg Campaign,* edited by G. W. Gallagher. Chapel Hill: University of Carolina Press, 1995.

Robertson, J. J., Jr. "Medical Treatment at Chancellorsville." In *Chancellorsville: The Battle and Its Aftermath,"* edited by G. W. Gallagher. Chapel Hill: University of North Carolina Press, 1996.

Schweikart, Larry. *"William R. Jones."* In *Encyclopedia of American Business History and Biography: Iron and Steel in the Nineteenth Century,* edited by Paul F. Paskoff. New York: Bruccoli, 1989.

Stackpole, Edward. *Chancellorsville.* 2nd ed. Harrisburg, PA: Stackpole, 1988.

Swetnam, George. "The Magnificent Welshman." *Pittsburgh (PA) Press.* August 29, 1965.

Under the Maltese Cross, (1861-1865) Antietam to Appomattox: The Loyal Uprising in Western Pennsylvania, 1861-1865. Library of Congress, 109 (1013487), 1987.

Wellman, M. W. *Harper's Ferry: Prize of War.* Charlotte, NC: McNally, 1960.

Whitman, Walt. From "A March in the Ranks Hard-Prest, and the Road Unknown." http://www.assumption.edu/users/lknoles/Packet/Whitman2.html.

Chapter 2

Bridge, James H. *The Inside History of Carnegie Steel Company: a Romance of Millions.* Pittsburgh: University of Pittsburgh Press, 1991.

Brown, Sharon A. *Historic Resource Study. Cambria Iron Company: America's Industrial Heritage Project: Pennsylvania.* Washington, D. C.: U.S. Department of Interior, 1989.

Casson, Herbert N. *The Romance of Steel: the Story of a Thousand Millionaires.* New York:

A. S. Barnes, 1907.

deKruif, Paul. *Seven Iron Men.* New York: Harcourt, 1929.

Duram, J. and E. Duram, eds. *Hartsock, Soldier of the Cross: Civil War Diary and Correspondence of Reverend Andrew Jackson Hartsock.* Manhattan, KS: American Military Institute, 1979.

Fitch, John A. *The Steel Workers.* Pittsburgh: University of Pittsburgh Press, 1989.

Gage, Daniel D. "The Watchmaking Industry, Yesterday, Today, and Tomorrow." *Oregon Business Review,* XX, no. 4 *(*April 1961): 1.

Gage, Tom. "Braddock's Defeat—The Role of Lt. Col. Thomas Gage." *Bulletin [of the] Braddock's Field Historical Society,* 2 (May/June 1998): 4-5. Coincidentally, this was the site where, the century before, Gen. Thomas Gage, a remote relative, with George Washington led the British troops to safety after the death of Gen. Braddock during the French and Indian wars.

Greenough, Horatio. *Form & Function: Remarks on Art, Design & Architecture.* Berkeley: University of California Press, 1947.

Harris, Joseph S. "The Beneficial Fund of the Lehigh Coal and Navigation Company." *Transactions of the American Institute of Mining Engineers* 12 (1883-84): 599-600.

Holbrook, Stewart H. *Iron Brew: a Century of American Ore and Steel.* New York: Macmillan, 1939.

Hunt, Robert. "Cambria Steel Workers' Reunion." *The Iron Age* 88, no. 1(October 3, 1911): 742.

Johnson, Tom L. *My Story.* New York: B. W. Huebsch, 1911.

Jones, W. R. To Andrew Carnegie, March 28, 1877. 1877-8 Letterbox, owned by W. J. Gaughan. Hillman Library, Pittsburgh.

Jones, Captain W. R. "On the Manufacture of Bessemer Steel and Steel Rails in the United States." *Journal of the Institute of Iron and Steel.* London: Ballantine, Hanson. 1881. Jones explicitly enumerates diversity as a requisite. Also, one who writes history treads upon shaky ground when introducing contemporary concepts like multiculturalism into an earlier period. I do this deliberately because two documents among the limited number of texts written by Jones specifically enumerate ethnic populations in his design. See also Jones, "On the Manufacture of Bessemer Steel and Steel Rails in the United States," *Journal of the Iron and Steel Institute*, 1880, 270. Also see W. R. Jones "to David McCandless" in Bridge, *Inside History of Carnegie Steel Company*.

Jones, W. R. "Discussion of Beneficial Fund of Lehigh Coal and Navigation Co." *Transactions [of the] American Institute of Mining Engineers,* 1883-4, 599.

Krass, Peter. *Carnegie.* New York: Wiley. 2002. Referring to Morrell's contemporary: "When he started his career in iron manufacturing, there had been mutual respect and goodwill between capital and labor, an unspoken agreement that wages would fluctuate depending on market conditions" p.213.

McCullough, David. *Johnstown Flood.* New York: Simon & Schuster, 1887.

McHugh, Jeanne. *Alexander Holley and the Makers of Steel.* Baltimore: Johns Hopkins University Press, 1980.

Menand, *Louis. The Metaphysical Club: a Story of Ideas in America.* New York: Farrar, 2001. See pages 52-7 for an epistemological contrast with his transcendentalist father, Oliver Wendell Holmes, Sr.

Royal Blue Book of Pittsburgh International Eisteddfod. Pittsburgh: Press of American Printing Co., 1913.

Schweikart, Larry. "*William R. Jones.*" In *Encyclopedia of American Business History and Biography: Iron and Steel in the Nineteenth Century,* edited by Paul F. Paskoff. New York: Bruccoli, 1989.

Shakespeare, William. *The Complete Works of William Shakespeare.* Edited by Geoffrey Cumberlege. Oxford, UK: Oxford University Press, 1955.

Townsend, E. Y. *Cambria Iron and Steel Works: Rules and Regulations* [poster]. Johnstown, PA: Cambria Iron Company, April 6, 1974.

Unwritten History of Braddock's Field. Prepared by the History Committee for the Celebration of the Golden Jubilee of Braddock and the One-hundred Seventy-fifth Anniversary of the First White Settlement West of the Alleghenies. Braddock, PA: History Committee for Celebration of Golden Jubilee, 1917.

Wall, Joseph Frazier. *Andrew Carnegie.* New York: Oxford, 1970.

Whitman, Walt. *Leaves of Grass and Democratic Vistas.* New York: Everyman, 1921.

Chapter 3

"Arbitration in Labor Contests." *Atlanta Georgia Constitution,* April 2, 1886.

Bridge, James H. *The Inside History of Carnegie Steel Company: A Romance of Millions.* Pittsburgh: University of Pittsburgh Press, 1991. Some of Bridge's assessments may be due to the fact that at the time he wrote the book, he was in the employ of Henry Frick, who was engaged in a bitter legal battle with Carnegie. Exactly at the time of Jones's death, Bridge left Andrew Carnegie deeply embittered. I suspect that Frick brought him back from California to New York City because he valued Bridge's dislike for Carnegie.

Bridge, James. *Millionaires and Grub Street: Comrades and Contacts in the Last Half Century.* Freeport, NY: Books for Libraries, 1931.

Carnegie, Andrew. To William R. Jones, November 9, 1880. Annandale Archives, Boyers, PA.

Carnegie, Andrew. To Cap't W. R. Jones, April 1, 1887. Andrew Carnegie Papers. Book no. 1887-1888]. Library of Congress.

Carnegie, Andrew. *The Andrew Carnegie Reader.* Edited by J. F. Wall. Pittsburgh: University of Pittsburgh Press, 1992.

Casson, Herbert N. *The Romance of Steel: a Story of a Thousand Millionaires.* New York: A. S. Barnes, 1907.

Cowan, Frank. *Short Stories from Studies of Life in Southwestern Pennsylvania.* Pittsburgh: Stevenson & Foster, 1878.

David, Henry. *The History of the Haymarket Affair: a Study in the American Social-revolutionary and Labor Movements.* New York: Russell & Russell, 1958.

Fischer, David H. *Paul Revere's Ride.* New York: Oxford, 1994.

Fitch, John A. *The Steel Workers.* Pittsburgh: University of Pittsburgh Press, 1989. The topic is well-covered, though difficult to follow. Fitch reports that at one point the furnace workers went on strike for the eight-hour day when the converter staff favored two shifts.

Gage, Daniel D. "The Banana Industry: the United Fruit Company in Central America." *Oregon Business Review,* March 1960, 1-7. This banana would lead my Uncle to research this field.

Gage, Daniel D. To Joseph Frazier Wall, March 11, 1972. Copy in the author's possession.

Gaughan, William J. Personal interview, June 5, 1994. Discussion of two photos that Gaughan contributed to the collection bearing his name at the Hillman Library.

"The Genesis and Early Years of the Edgar Thomson Steel Company as Disclosed by Hither to Unknown Facts Gleaned from Certain Private Papers of Andrew Carnegie. Annandale Archives, Boyers, PA.

Goodale, Stephen L. *Chronology of Iron and Steel.* Edited by J. Ramsey Speer. Cleveland, OH: Penton, 1931.

Hessen, Robert. *Steel Titan: the Life of Charles M. Schwab.* New York: Oxford, 1975.

Holbrook, Stewart H. *Iron Brew: a Century of American Ore and Steel.* New York: Macmillan, 1939.

Holbrook, Stewart H. To Daniel D. Gage. October 11, 1939. In the author's possession.

Holley, A. L. and L. Smith. *The Works of the Edgar Thomson Steel Company.* London: Engineering, 1878.

Holley, Alexander. "The Siemens Direct Process." [Rept. By A. L. Holley for A. C.] November 20, 1882. Annandale Archives, Boyers, PA.

Jones, W. R. 1877-8 Letterbox, items 50 & 58, owned by W. J. Gaughan. Hillman Library, Pittsburgh.

Jones, William R. To Andrew Carnegie, January n.d., 1877. 1877-8 Letterbox, owned by W. J. Gaughan. Hillman Library, Pittsburgh.

Jones, William R. To Andrew Carnegie, February 22, 1877. Andrew Carnegie Papers. Library of Congress.

Jones, William R. To Andrew Carnegie, March 31, 1877. 1877-8 Letterbox, owned by W. J. Gaughan. Hillman Library, Pittsburgh.

Jones, William R. To Andrew Carnegie, December 11, 1877. 1877-8 Letterbox, owned by W. J. Gaughan. Hillman Library, Pittsburgh.

Jones, William R. To Andrew Carnegie, March 24, 1878. 1877-8 Letterbox, owned by W. J. Gaughan. Hillman Library, Pittsburgh.

Jones, William R. To Andrew Carnegie, May 4, 1878. 1877-8 Letterbox, owned by W. J. Gaughan. Hillman Library, Pittsburgh.

Jones, William R. To Andrew Carnegie, May 6, 1878. 1877-8 Letterbox, owned by W. J. Gaughan. Hillman Library, Pittsburgh.

Jones, W. R. To Andrew Carnegie, December 5, 1879. Annandale Archives, Boyers, PA.

Jones, W. R. To Andrew Carnegie, April 2, 1880. Annandale Archives, Boyers, PA.

Jones, Wm. R. To Andrew Carnegie, October 29, 1880. Annandale Archives, Boyers, PA.

Jones, William R. To Andrew Carnegie, November 5, 1880. Annandale Archives, Boyers, PA.

Jones, W. R. To Andrew Carnegie, November 11, 1880. Annandale Archives, Boyers, PA.

Jones, William R. To Andrew Carnegie, December 19, 1880. Annandale Archives, Boyers, PA.

Jones, William R. To Andrew Carnegie, February 28, 1882. Annandale Archives, Boyers, PA.

Jones, W. R. To Andrew Carnegie, December 18, 1883. Selected Papers. Annandale Archives, Boyers, PA.

Kleinberg, S. J. *The Shadow of the Mills: Working-Class Families in Pittsburgh, 1870-1907.* Pittsburgh: University of Pittsburgh Press, 1989.

Krass, Peter. *Carnegie.* New York: Wiley, 2002.

Lendon, E. "Review of *Triumphant Democracy* by Andrew Carnegie. *Boston Globe,* May 12, 1886.

McHugh, Jeanne. *Alexander Holley and the Makers of Steel.* Baltimore: Johns Hopkins University Press, 1980. Holley's biographer, McHugh, substantiates Uncle Dan's point by describing how Holley and Jones during one of those evening conversations addressed inventions, like the rail mill feed tables, jointly developed by the two of them.

Meese, Hugh P. "Edgar Thomson Steel Works." *The Unwritten History of Braddock's Field. http://pghbridges.com/articles/places/edgarthomsonworks_un.htm.*

Montgomery, David. *The Fall of the House of Labor.* Cambridge, UK: Cambridge University

Press, 1987.

Parsons, Lucy. *Famous Speeches of the Eight Chicago Anarchists: Mass Violence in America.* New York: Arno & New York Times, 1969.

Royal Blue Book of Pittsburgh International Eisteddfod. Pittsburgh: Press of American Printing Co., 1913.

Shakespeare, William. *The Complete Works of William Shakespeare.* Edited by Geoffrey Cumberlege. Oxford, UK: Oxford University Press, 1955.

Shinn v. Carnegie. 3OQ. [Settled out of court] Annandale Archives, Boyers, PA.

St. David's Society of Pittsburgh. *"Transcribed minutes,"* 1885, 1887, 1888, 1888. Annandale Archives, Boyers, PA.

Teeter, C. C. To Captain Jones, March 3, 1877 Letterbox, owned by W. J. Gaughan. Hillman Library, Pittsburgh.

Unwritten History of Braddock's Field. Prepared by the History Committee for the Celebration of the Golden Jubilee of Braddock and the One-hundred Seventy-fifth Anniversary of the First White Settlement West of the Alleghenies. Braddock, PA: History Committee for Celebration of Golden Jubilee, 1917.

Wall, Joseph Frazier. *Andrew Carnegie.* New York: Oxford, 1970. Joseph Frazier Wall alluded to the more than fifty drafts in blueprints found in Bill Jones's office drawer at his death, which he did not file.

Wall, Joseph Frazier. To Professor Tom Gage, January 30, 1995. In the author's possession.

Warren, Kenneth. *Triumphant Capitalism: Henry Clay Frick and the Industrial Transformation of America.* Pittsburgh: University of Pittsburgh Press, 1996.

Whipple, Sidney B. Notes. Charles Schwab Papers. Hagley Museum and Library, Wilmington, DE. Much of what follows is directly reworked from the notes of Schwab's prospective biographer, left among the Bethlehem Archives.

Chapter 4

Bayly, C. A. *The Birth of the Modern World 1780-1914: Global Connections and Comparisons.* London: Blackwell, 2006.

Bridge, James H. *The Inside History of Carnegie Steel Company: a Romance of Millions.* Pittsburgh: University of Pittsburgh Press, 1991.

Bridge, James. *Millionaires and Grub Street: Comrades and Contacts in the Last Half Century.* Freeport, NY: Books for Libraries, 1931. Bridge wrote: "I still cherish a book that he [Jones] gave me. It is by Miss Murfree "Charles Egbert Craddock.""

Brown, Sharon A. *Historic Resource Study. Cambria Iron Company: America's Industrial Heritage Project: Pennsylvania.* Washington, D. C.: U.S. Department of Interior, 1989.

Butler, Joseph G., Jr. *Fifty Years of Iron and Steel.* Cleveland, OH: Penton, 1922.

Butler, Joseph G., Jr. *Recollections of Men and Events: An Autobiography.* New York: Putnam, 1927.

Carnegie, Andrew. "Address to the Workmen." Dedication of the Carnegie Library at the Edgar Thomson Steel Rail Works, March 30, 1889. Reprinted March 1998 by Braddock's Field Historical Society. Also see http://www.invaluable.com/auction-lot/andrew-carnegie-dedication-of-the-carnegie-librar-7262-c-a874bb69d5.

Carnegie, Andrew. To Billy Gage, 1908. In the author's possession.

Casson, Herbert N. *The Romance of Steel: the Story of a Thousand Millionaires.* New York: A. S. Barnes, 1907.

Connelly, Frank and George C. Jenks. *Official History of the Johnstown Flood.* Pittsburgh: Journalist Publishing, 1889.

Couvares, Francis G. *The Remaking of Pittsburgh: Class and Culture in an Industrializing City 1877-1919.* Albany, NY: State University of New York, 1984.

Cowan, Frank. *Short Stories from Studies of Life in Southwestern Pennsylvania.* Pittsburgh: Stevenson & Foster, 1878.

Cowan, Frank. *The Meaning of the Monument.* Pittsburgh: Wm. G. Johnston, 1887.

Fischer, David H. *Paul Revere's Ride.* New York: Oxford, 1994.

Flow Chart of Steelmaking [chart]. Pittsburgh: American Steel Institute, n.d.

Gage, Daniel, Jr. My uncle Dan used to list off the names of his mother's friends like a catechism: Lulu Unvurzat (sp), Kate Fritz, and Nannie Elder, the daughter of Cyrus Elder, who was Mr. Morrell's lawyer and active in the Union League during the war—and Mimi Corey Soule, who was still alive and living in Medford, OR when Dan taught at the University of Oregon. Elder, his wife, and his daughter often visited the Jones home at Braddock.

Gage, Tom. "Braddock's Defeat—the Role of Lt. Col. Thomas Gage." *Newsletter [of the] Braddock's Field Historical Society*, May/June 1998.

Gaughan, William G. Personal conversation, June 7, 1994. John Potter designed and patented the 32-inch universal slabbing mill.

Higley, George. "Youngstown: An Intimate History." Youngstown, OH, 1953. http://memory.loc.gov/master/pnp/habshaer/pa/pa3900/pa3995/data/pa3995data.pdf.

Holbrook, Stewart H. *Iron Brew: a Century of American Ore and Steel.* New York: Macmillan, 1939.

Johnson, Tom L. *My Story.* New York: B. W. Huebsch, 1911.

Jones, Wm R. To Andrew Carnegie, February 26, 1882. Annandale Archives, Boyers, PA.

Jones, William R. To Andrew Carnegie, February 17, 1884. Annandale Archives, Boyers, PA

Krass, Peter. *Carnegie.* New York: Wiley, 2002.

Krause, Paul. *The Battle for Homestead 1880-1892.* Pittsburgh: University of Pittsburgh Press, 1992.

Livesay, Harold C. *Andrew Carnegie and the Rise of Big Business.* Boston: Little, Brown, 1975.

McCullough, David. *The Johnstown Flood.* New York: Simon & Schuster, 1968.

McHugh, Jeanne. *Alexander Holley and the Makers of Steel.* Baltimore: Johns Hopkins University Press, 1980. See p. 324: "The development of the Thomas process was responsible for a complete turnaround in the European supply of ore suitable for the use in steelmaking."

McLaurin, J. J. *The Story of Johnstown.* Harrisburg, PA: James M. Place, 1890.

Misa, Thomas J. *A Nation of Steel: the Making of Modern America 1865-1925.* Baltimore: Johns Hopkins University Press, 1995.

Pittsburgh (PA) Commercial Gazette. October 1, 1889.

Pittsburgh (PA) Commercial Gazette. "Mourning in Braddock." October 1, 1889.

Pittsburgh (PA) Post. "Taking 300 Men to Johnstown." September 26, 1893.

Pittsburgh (PA) Press. W. R. Jones quoted in "Take Several Weeks." June 7, 1889.

Pittsburgh (PA) Press. "Adding to the Fund." June 7, 1889.

Pittsburgh (PA) Press. "Mark Capt. W. R. Jones on the Situation at Johnstown." June 7, 1889.

Royal Blue Book of Pittsburgh International Eisteddfod. Pittsburgh: Press of American Printing Co., 1913.

Shakespeare, William. *The Complete Works of William Shakespeare.* Edited by Geoffrey Cumberlege. Oxford, UK: Oxford University Press, 1955.

Shappee, Nathan D. "The Johnstown Flood and Pittsburgh's Relief, 1889." *Western Pennsylvania Historical Magazine* 2, 23 (1940).

Schorske, Carl E. *Fin-de-Siecle Vienna: Politics and Culture.* New York: Random House, 1981.

Unwritten History of Braddock's Field. Prepared by the History Committee for the Celebration of the Golden Jubilee of Braddock and the One-hundred Seventy-fifth Anniversary of the First White Settlement West of the Alleghenies. Braddock, PA: History Committee for Celebration of Golden Jubilee, 1917.

Wall, Joseph Frazier. *Andrew Carnegie.* New York: Oxford, 1970. See p. 522: Wall explains that Jones was responsible for Carnegie's paradoxical stance in the two Forum articles that supported profits and a fair deal for workers: "the ability of Captain Jones to convince him that an enlightened labor policy was good business practice, and that his two basic desires, to make money and to be a kind and good employer, were not antithetical, but rather complementary."

Warren, Kenneth. *Triumphant Capitalism: Henry Clay Frick and the Industrial Transformation of America.* Pittsburgh: University of Pittsburgh Press, 1996.

Wittgenstein, Karl. To Daniel D. Gage, March 28, 1908. In the author's possession.

Chapter 5

Ancestry.com. "Pennsylvania Biographical Sketches." 1868, 9 of 10. http://search.ancestry.com/search/db.aspx?dbid=4557.

"Confessions of a young lady laudanum-drinker." *Journal of Mental Sciences*, January 1889. [Published by the Authority of the Medico-Psychological Association of Great Britain and Ireland.]

Bemis, E. "The Homestead Strike." *Journal of Political Economy*, June 2, 1894.

Butler, Joseph G., Jr. *Fifty Years of Iron and Steel.* Cleveland, OH: Penton, 1922.

Bridge, James H. *The Inside History of Carnegie Steel Company: a Romance of Millions.* Pittsburgh: University of Pittsburgh Press, 1991.

Carnegie, Andrew. To J. G. A. Leishman, August 1, 1895. Andrew Carnegie, v. 32. Library of Congress.

Carnegie, Andrew. To George Lauder, January 8, 1897. Andrew Carnegie, v. 41. Library of Congress.

"Carnegie Steel Wins Old Suit." In the author's possession.

Casson, Herbert N. *The Romance of Steel: the Story of a Thousand Millionaires.* New York: A. S. Barnes, 1907.

Demarest, David P., Jr. *River Ran Red: Homestead 1892.* Pittsburgh: University of Pittsburgh Press, 1992.

Fitch, John A. *The Steel Workers.* Pittsburgh: University of Pittsburgh Press, 1989. Twenty-seven of the 195 fatalities in the Pittsburgh area works were furnace-related in the fiscal year 1906.

Gage, Daniel D. To Andrew Carnegie, November 9, 1908. Andrew Carnegie Papers. Library of Congress.

Gage, Daniel D., Jr. To Joseph Frazier Wall, February 4, 1972. My uncle mistakenly called him John Yost, not William.

Gage, Tom. *Hands-On, All Over.* Pittsburgh: Pittsburgh History, 1998. In my earlier essay, I conflated what Wall and the Gage brothers documented. That was a mistake, as the reader will understand in chapter 6.

Harris, Joseph S. "The Beneficial Fund of the Lehigh Coal and Navigation Company." *Transactions of the American Institute of Mining Engineers* 12 (1883-84): 599-600.

Holbrook, Stewart H. *Iron Brew: a Century of American Ore and Steel.* New York: Macmillan, 1939.

Jones, William R. To Andrew Carnegie, March 24. Selected Papers from the Edgar Thomson File. Annandale Archives, Boyers, PA.

Jones, William R. To Andrew Carnegie, January, 187-. Annandale Archives, Boyers, PA.

Jones, William R. To Andrew Carnegie, May 24, 1878. Selected Papers from the Edgar Thomson File. Annandale Archives, Boyers, PA.

Jones, Wm R. To Andrew Carnegie, December 21, 1880. Annandale Archives, Boyers, PA.

Jones, William R. To Andrew Carnegie, September 16, 1885. Selected Papers from the Edgar Thomson File. Annandale Archives, Boyers, PA.

Jones, William R. To H. W. Wood, August 8, 1889. Photocopy in the author's possession.

Jones, William R. To W. P. Shinn, January 19, 1876. Selected Papers from the Edgar Thomson File. Annandale Archives, Boyers, PA.

Kleinberg, S. J. *The Shadow of the Mills: Working-Class Families in Pittsburgh, 1870-1907.* Pittsburgh: University of Pittsburgh Press, 1989.

Krass, Peter. *Carnegie.* New York: Wiley, 2002.

McCleary, W. W. "Address to Braddock Rotary Club." 1933. Typescript. In the author's possession.

McCullough, David. *The Johnstown Flood.* New York: Simon & Schuster, 1968.

McGough, M. R. *The 1889 Flood in Johnstown Pennsylvania.* Springfield, PA: Charles C. Thomas, 2002.

McHugh, Jeanne. *Alexander Holley and the Makers of Steel.* Baltimore: Johns Hopkins University Press, 1980.

Nasaw, David. *Andrew Carnegie.* New York: Penguin, 2006.

Pittsburgh (PA) Commercial Gazette. "Quinn is Dying . . . Capt. Jones Will Recover." September 27, 1889.

Pittsburgh (PA) Commercial Gazette. Friday morning early edition. "A Flood of Molten Metal." September 27, 1889.

Pittsburgh (PA) Commercial Gazette. Friday late edition. *"An Awful Flame."* September 27, 1889.

Pittsburgh (PA) Commercial Gazette. Monday early edition. "Grief at Braddock." September 30, 1889.

Pittsburgh (PA) Post. [article title lacking] June 7, 1889.

Pittsburgh (PA) Post. Morning edition. "Fatal Furnace C." September 27, 1889.

Royal Blue Book: Prize Productions of the Pittsburgh International Eisteddfod. Pittsburgh:

American Printing Co., 1913.

Unwritten History of Braddock's Field. Prepared by the History Committee for the Celebration of the Golden Jubilee of Braddock and the One-hundred Seventy-fifth Anniversary of the First White Settlement West of the Alleghenies. Braddock, PA: History Committee for Celebration of Golden Jubilee, 1917.

Wall, Joseph Frazier. *Andrew Carnegie.* New York: Oxford, 1970.

Warren, Kenneth. *Triumphant Capitalism: Henry Clay Frick and the Industrial Transformation of America.* Pittsburgh: University of Pittsburgh Press, 1996.

Wittgenstein, Karl. To Daniel D. Gage, March 28, 1908. In the author's possession.

Wood, H. W. To William R. Jones, August 16, 1889. Photocopy in the author's possession.

Youngstown Weekly Telegram. "Buried in Molten Iron." October 2, 1889.

Chapters 6 & 7

Bridge, James H. *The Inside History of Carnegie Steel Company: a Romance of Millions.* Pittsburgh: University of Pittsburgh Press, 1991. "No former partner is eligible for membership in this association who did not take part in the attempt to depose Mr. Frick, such as Henry Curry."

The Cambria Iron Company vs. The Carnegie Steel Company: Patent No. 404414, Record, Vol. I. United States Circuit Court of Appeals. Third Circuit. March Term, 1899. National Archives-Mid Atlantic Region.

Carnegie, Andrew. To Daniel D. Gage, December 3, 1908. Andrew Carnegie Papers. Library of Congress, 30236.

Carnegie, Andrew. To Cora Gage, December 15, 1914. Andrew Carnegie Papers. Library of Congress, 42996.

Carnegie, Andrew. To George "Dod" Lauder, January 31, 1899. Lauder, 1191 A, Andrew Carnegie Letters. Library of Congress.

Casson, Herbert N. *The Romance of Steel: the Story of a Thousand Millionaires.* New York: A.S. Barnes, 1907.

Diamond, Jared. *Guns, Germs, and Steel: the Fates of Human Societies.* New York: Norton, 1997. An autocatalytic process parlays prior technological developments into geometric or exponential advances that make impossible reversion to pre-invention production.

Dickson, William B. *History of the Carnegie Veterans Association.* Montclair, NJ: Mountain Press, 1938.

Frick, Henry Clay. Minutes of Meeting of The Carnegie Steel Company, Limited. September 13, 1898, 3, letter 10617. Andrew Carnegie Letters. Library of Congress.

Gage, Cora. To Andrew Carnegie, December 14, 1914. Andrew Carnegie Papers. Library of Congress, 42980.

Gage, Cora. To Charles Taylor, December 17, 1917. Andrew Carnegie Papers. Library of Congress, 44438.

Gage, Governor Henry T. To Daniel D. Gage, April 25, 1905. Andrew Carnegie Papers. Library of Congress, 21759-61.

Gage, Daniel D. To Andrew Carnegie, May 12, 1905. Andrew Carnegie Papers. Library of Congress, 21938.

Gage, Daniel D. To Andrew Carnegie, September 23, 1905. Andrew Carnegie Papers. Library of Congress, 22562.

Gage, Daniel D. To Andrew Carnegie, December 12, 1908. Andrew Carnegie Papers. Library of Congress, 30229.

Gage, Daniel D., Jr. To Joseph Frazier Wall, March 11, 1972. In the author's possession.

Gage, Daniel D., Jr. To Joseph Frazier Wall, n.d. In the author's possession.

Gage, William R. "To My Kith and Kin." In the author's possession. My father claimed that he inspired Steinbeck to write that quirky book, The Short Reign of Pippin IV: a Fabrication about the French—Dad, working for the Marshall Plan helping to restore the French economy after the war, spent many evenings talking with Steinbeck about Gallic mannerisms.

Gazette [Pittsburgh, PA] Times. Late edition. "Lloyd George Appeals for United Action by America and Britain to Prevent Wars." October 25, 1923.

Ginter, Robert M. "Verdict to Cost Cambria Iron $700,000: Decision for Carnegie Steel is Untouched by U. S. Superior Court." Pittsburgh Post-Gazette, November 8, 1912.

Hendrick, Burton, J. The Life of Andrew Carnegie. Garden City, NJ: Doubleday, 1932.

Holbrook, Stewart H. Iron Brew: a Century of American Ore and Steel. New York: Macmillan, 1939.

Krass, Peter. Carnegie. New York: Wiley, 2002.

Lauder, George. To Daniel D. Gage, August 31, 1905. Andrew Carnegie Papers. Library of Congress, 22464. This assertion of half interest in the two patents is the earliest documentation, some sixteen years after my great-grandfather's unexpected death, written by a man who further asserted that the value to the firm was "somewhat mythical."

McCleary, W. W. "Address to Braddock Rotary Club." 1933. Typescript. In the author's possession.

Meese, Hugh P. "Edgar Thomson Steel Works." The Unwritten History of Braddock's Field. http://pghbridges.com/articles/places/edgarthomsonworks_un.htm

New York Times. [article title lacking] September 8, 1898.

Standiford, Les. Meet You in Hell: Andrew Carnegie, Henry Clay Frick, and the Bitter Partnership that Transformed America. New York: Crown, 2005

Stevenson, William M. "Carnegie and His Libraries," n.d. British Museum.

United States. Department of the Interior. Liber N 40: 479.

Usselman, Steven W. *Regulating Railroad Innovation: Business, Technology, and Politics in America, 1840-1920*. Cambridge, UK: Cambridge, 1984.

Wall, Joseph Frazier. *Andrew Carnegie.* New York: Oxford, 1970. My uncle corrected Wall—it was Frick, not Lauder.

Warren, Kenneth. Personal interview at Hexham, Northumberland, UK, summer 1995.

Warren, Kenneth. *Triumphant Capitalism: Henry Clay Frick and the Industrial Transformation of America.* Pittsburgh: University of Pittsburgh Press, 1996.

Whipple, Sidney B. Notes. Charles Schwab Papers. Hagley Museum and Library, Wilmington, DE. "Jones was not very much impressed with the mixer. He seemed to think it was just part of the day's work. But 'Dod' Lauder, who used to sit in my office and tell me he was 'lending dignity' to my administrations, and the man who . . .knew its full impact and although it was costly . . . well, it meant revolution in the business."

Wittgenstein, Karl. To Daniel D. Gage, March 28, 1908. In the author's possession.

CPSIA information can be obtained
at www.ICGtesting.com
Printed in the USA
BVHW01s1403140518
515840BV00005B/1/P